Bush League Boys

Amarillo's Joe Bauman (*standing far right*) and Bob Crues (*kneeling below Bauman*) would play together one last time, as members of the 1947 West Texas–New Mexico League All-Star team. The Amarillo manager, a bat boy, and five other Gold Sox players made that squad. In spite of such talent, Amarillo finished runner-up to the Lubbock Hubbers in the playoffs that year. (Steve Lagomarsino collection.)

Bush League Boys

The Postwar Legends of Baseball in the American Southwest

TOBY SMITH

UNIVERSITY OF NEW MEXICO PRESS • ALBUQUERQUE

© 2014 by the University of New Mexico Press
All rights reserved. Published 2014
Printed in the United States of America
19 18 17 16 15 14   1 2 3 4 5 6

Library of Congress Cataloging-in-Publication Data

   Smith, Toby, 1946–
   Bush League boys : the postwar legends of baseball in the American
Southwest / Toby Smith. — First edition.
      pages cm
   Includes bibliographical references and index.
   ISBN 978-0-8263-5521-8 (paper : alk. paper)
   ISBN 978-0-8263-5522-5 (electronic)
   1. Minor league baseball—Southwest, New—History—20th century.
I. Title.
   GV863.S615S55 2014
   796.357'640979—dc23
                  2014006336

Cover photograph courtesy Jim Waldrip
Designed by Lisa Tremaine
Composed in Plantin and Rockwell, both designed by the Monotype
Foundry Studio under the supervision of Frank Hinman Pierpont.

For Jedediah Royall and Carson Keil, who know the score

Just meet the ball like you was meeting the bathroom door.
　　　　　　　　　　　　　　　　—JOE BAUMAN, 2004

Contents

Introduction

One year during the 1950s, when I was nine or ten, baseball cards carried small, cartoon-like illustrations on their flip sides, along with brief messages. One of those cards—I don't recall the ballplayer on the front—showed a line drawing of a figure swinging a bat. In the background stood a tall, coatrack-shaped cactus and a stately, towering mountain. Beneath the drawing were words that went something like this: "Joe Bauman of the Roswell Rockets in New Mexico's Longhorn League hit seventy-two home runs in 1954."

I grew up in Connecticut, at sea level. I had never heard of the Roswell Rockets or the Longhorn League or Joe Bauman. Even so, I was struck. The *Rockets*. Could there be a baseball team with a niftier name? *New Mexico*. That cactus and that mountain made the state seem otherworldly. I still felt that way years later, when I learned there were no mountains or saguaro cacti in Roswell. *Seventy-two home runs*. I'm not sure if I knew the Major League Baseball record then was sixty—by Babe Ruth. Seventy-two to me might as well have been seven thousand.

In 2004, I was among the last journalists to interview Joe Bauman in person. As a staff writer for the *Albuquerque Journal*, I visited Bauman in Roswell, where he had lived since his historic 1954 season. Joe did not answer when I knocked at the door of his tidy, light-blue house. Joe's wife, Dorothy, tiny and gracious, saw me in. The victim of a stroke that limited his mobility, Joe spent his days sitting in a well-cushioned recliner in the front room, watching ball games on TV or waiting for people like me to stop by or call and present him with variations on a question he'd been asked many times before: How did you manage to hit so many home runs?

Halfway into our interview, I mentioned to Bauman the little illustration of him on the back of an old baseball card.

"Spare bedroom," Joe said, not in an unfriendly way but not taking his eyes off the television either. The Atlanta Braves, two incarnations removed from Bauman's old keeper, the Boston Braves, were playing a game. "Go on back there. You'll find a whole dang pile of my stuff."

Lying on a bed at the rear of the house, awaiting a guest's perusal, were several photographs and scrapbooks. There was even one of his baseball bats, which when hoisted felt like a Neanderthal war club might. There were a few baseball cards, but none of Bauman because he did not play in the major leagues. A card of Mickey Mantle, who grew up in Commerce, Oklahoma, not far from Joe's Oklahoma birthplace, was there. One card looked vaguely familiar. I turned it over. There was the little drawing that had roosted undisturbed in the storage bin of my brain all these years. The back of that card, it turns out, was in a sense the closest Bauman came to the big leagues.

I never saw Joe Bauman swing his massive cudgel in a game. I never saw Bob Crues, in some ways Bauman's opposite number back then, do so either. I never saw anyone play baseball in any of the four minor leagues that took residence in West Texas and eastern New Mexico in the 1940s and 1950s. But as I worked on this book, I often caught myself imagining. Imagining what it was like for fans of long ago who sat in splintery wooden stands in little towns and took in games on stuffy summer evenings, nights too hot to stay home. Imagining what it was like for ballplayers who slept sitting up in tottering station wagons or cast-aside school buses that chugged across the Permian Basin. Imagining what it was like wearing one of those wool uniforms, so heavy it needed two hangers to stay on a curtain rod. Imagining what it was like playing baseball in dust storms so thick and so mean you couldn't see your shoe tops.

As they remembered their time in this neglected slice of Americana—a slice that was frequently transitory yet often fulfilling—the people in this book made my imaginings become real.

Bush League Boys covers fifteen years, starting in 1946, on the heels of World War II, and ending in 1961, with the folding of the fourth and final league in the Southwest. By coincidence, the years loosely follow the career arc of the great Stan Musial, who started with a Class D outfit in up-country West Virginia.

Two of the leagues I write about—the West Texas–New Mexico and the

Southwestern—were newer versions of coalitions begun decades earlier. The other two, the Longhorn League and the Sophomore League, were created more recently: the Longhorn in 1947, the Sophomore in 1958. At times, in order to avoid repetition and confusion, I use the word "leagues" when referring to all four together.

Almost sixty different minor leagues occupied the American landscape in 1950. Many seemed to exist in a world of their own. Not counting off-season leagues and independent leagues, only nineteen minor leagues endure. Today's leagues—with signing bonuses of seven figures, stadiums even at the lower levels selling sushi and crepes, and the media digging into every little thing—are so different from the old. Scouts now frequently track players who are still young teens.

In the four leagues of the 1940s and 1950s that I follow here, older players from Nowheresville often showed up, having had but a season in semi-pro ball, as Robert Redford did in the movie *The Natural*. There was Roy Hobbs, an eager hand from an unheard-of nine named the Heber Oilers, searching for one final chance. In the novel *The Natural*, by Bernard Malamud, the team is the Oomoo Oilers, which sounds even more geographically remote. The sticks.

Many of the players in the leagues were part of the Greatest Generation. They had left World War II behind, eager to be doing something familiar, wanting to hear applause and not gunfire. Some came from the Korean War as well, anxious to get out of the cold even for a short spell, unnerved by a sun that beat like a fist or a wind that never knew a day off. All were glad to be paid, even a little bit, before it was time to begin life's calling.

I estimate that more than 90 percent of those who performed in the leagues never made it to the majors. For several who did arrive at the top echelon, the stay was brief. Jackie Sullivan's career in some ways resembles that of "Moonlight" Graham, the character in the hit movie *Field of Dreams*. In 1905, Graham found a spot in right field with the New York Giants. He held down that position for only part of one game and never came up to bat. He soon left baseball and later became a respected country doctor. In 1944, Sullivan, a bright-with-promise second baseman, received a call from the Detroit Tigers. His career also lasted one game, but unlike Graham, Sullivan had an at-bat. In that single appearance at the plate, he went hitless. Rather than leave baseball, two years later Sullivan began what turned into an admirable career as a player and manager in the leagues of the Southwest. Dressing out for five different teams, he spent ten seasons in the leagues.

At least 50 percent never made it any higher than Class C or Class D baseball, groupings that, along with Class B, have passed from sight. The leagues simply kept alive boyhood yearnings. Most of the men surely knew the odds were against them, with these small-potatoes teams that carried only sixteen players. But for those who signed on, playing ball was the last shot to go back to the game of childhood, to be a boy again, to smell the baked scrub grass, to track a fast-falling line drive, to feel the handle of a freshly taped bat, to hear the sound of a teammate's loony laugh.

The leagues constantly toughened you. A stretch of brutally hot weather in August 1950 led the Abilene Blue Sox to take to the field in shorts. Somehow, players endured two nights of dive-bombing squads of ravenous mosquitoes before finally going back to long pants. On May 17, 1954, five members of the Blue Sox were hospitalized in Albuquerque for carbon monoxide poisoning. The source? The team bus.

The leagues were then a melting pot of life, which for a writer is pure platinum. Where else could you find a pitcher who could throw with either arm? Or another pitcher who hopped about the mound on a wooden leg? Or a third pitcher who never wore socks?

Where else but on those bottom rungs of baseball's long-ago ladder could you come across a DiMaggio (Bartolo, Joe's cousin) batting? Or a Carl Hubbell (son of the esteemed New York Giant) pitching? Or still another pitcher, southpaw Dale Grove, who proudly carried the nickname "Lefty" even as he stood 281 career wins behind the revered Baseball Hall of Fame hurler.

Where else could you meet a player with the first name of Socrates or Lois or Rachel? The latter, known as Rac Slider, was not, alas, a pitcher, but a fine shortstop. Where else could you learn that a starting pitcher went seventeen innings to win a game? Or that a pitcher won both games of a doubleheader, the second game allowing but one hit? Or that a batter socked two inside-the-park home runs in the same *inning*?

Bats were indeed hot during those Cold War days. In the leagues' sixteen years of existence, through approximately thirty-five thousand games, only eleven no-hitters were recorded. By comparison, major leaguers in that same period, pitching six thousand more games, accumulated twenty-nine no-hitters.

Shutouts came seldom and scoreboard results time and again resembled football contests. It was almost midnight on a July evening in 1951 when the Pampa Oilers slipped past the Abilene Blue Sox, 24–22. Six years later, on a May night that never seemed to end, the Carlsbad Potashers edged the Midland Indians, 26–22. Not surprisingly, defense was not a priority.

A stumbling, fumbling affair between Carlsbad and Sweetwater on September 2, 1954, resulted in twenty-two errors.

This book was the idea of John Byram, the director of the University of New Mexico Press. My wife, Susan, helped me expand on John's idea by accompanying me on research trips to the eastern edge of New Mexico and along the west side of Texas. Susan listened patiently to the stories I gathered and gave her thoughts on what I turned up. She lent encouragement when I struggled to track down former ballplayers and sympathy when I discovered a man I badly wanted to talk to was no longer among us. Jim Waldrip of Roswell, an alumnus of two of the leagues and a close friend to Joe Bauman, was always a cheery phone call away. Many times Jim straightened me out on something or pulled from the past a detail I did not know. Karin Kaufman, a keen-eyed copy editor, went the distance in sentence unscrambling and fact amending. To all four I am immensely grateful.

CHAPTER ONE

Joe and Bob

"Feel this," the little man said as he tapped his left shoulder. The shoulder was cinderblock hard. "Grip this," the man went on, offering two of his fingers then forcing the visitor's hand back against his chest and holding it there. Try as the visitor might, he could not move that hand forward.

Julio Ramos is eighty-eight years old and stands all of five feet six inches. The young woman who later became his wife thought he was the team batboy until he took the pitcher's mound.

"Look, I can run good," Ramos said, his voice still coated with the sugarcane fields of his native Cuba. He stood at one end of the living room in his northeast Albuquerque home. Suddenly he sprinted across that room and through an adjoining den, past family photos, end tables, a hi-fi, and then back again, without pausing. Heavy breathing could not be heard.

Ramos, who never achieved major league status, pitched to both Joe Bauman and Bob Crues, who in a time gone by were two of the biggest stars of the minor leagues.

"I had a curveball and Joe, he can't hit it," Ramos said. "Crues, he can." He pronounced the name "Cru." For the unknowing, it's pronounced "Cruise."

"I bet I throw seventy mile per hour still," he crowed. "Crues, he got many hits from me," Ramos admitted. Crues was playing for Roswell, New Mexico, in the Longhorn League in 1949, and Ramos was pitching for Big Spring, Texas, in that same alliance. Six years after that, when Ramos pitched for three different teams, he faced Bauman, then playing for Roswell, several times.

1

A good many pitchers gave up home runs to Joe Bauman and Bob Crues. Ramos said Bauman never hit one off him. "My curveball, it drop down. I keep it outside. Down and outside, I want it. Joe, he swing like this"—Ramos imitated a weary farmer hoeing a patch of dirt. The little man smiled. "Crues, he go after any pitch."

His Eminence—the venerated Rogers Hornsby—had long advised ball-players to stand at the back of the batter's box, the better to see pitches. Bob Crues, who swung from the right side, heeded that wisdom, but not always. In the same manner, Crues became a very good bad-ball hitter. Impetuous and undisciplined at the plate, Crues hit balls outside the strike zone more often than inside it. Joe Bauman, who batted from the left, launched balls to deep right field much of the time. Patient for the most part, he laid off high-and-inside stuff but had a tendency to chase a keeling-over curve. Some of Bauman's home-run balls traveled so far they were never found. Bauman's strategy at the plate was no secret, according to the San Angelo Colts' Bob Gregg, who pitched to him several times: "Hit the ball out of the park."

Their batting inclinations aside, the two players were alike in many ways. Modest and humble, of rustic roots, Bauman and Crues grew up in shotgun houses during the Great Depression. As adults, both worked at filling stations. They served their country during World War II, and each signed contracts with separate major league teams out of Boston. When they talked, which was never a lot, they spoke in low, chicken-fried-steak drawls.

Most career minor leaguers aren't remembered. These two men are re-called less by name than for two extraordinary achievements. Numbers mean a lot in baseball, maybe more so than in any other sport. Numbers owned by this pair define and bond them. The better-known Bauman hit his seventy-two home runs in only 138 games for Roswell, in 1954. That set a professional baseball record that stayed put for forty-seven years. Of-ten overlooked, Crues in 1948 knocked in 254 RBI in 140 games for the Amarillo Gold Sox, a mark never approached at any level.

Those extraordinary feats are by themselves two good reasons to keep alive four vanished minor leagues in the Southwest. Several other power hitters came out of those leagues, but Bauman and Crues easily stand to-gether at the top.

There are guardians of the national pastime who pooh-pooh the accom-plishments of the two Sunbelters. Those bygone ballparks out West were matchbox small, purists will say, even if they never set foot in one. The pitching was weak, the air thin, the wind a big boon, the baseballs not up to spec. The nitpicking seldom ends, yet one constant remains: If it were so doggone easy to swat seventy-two homers or rap in 254 base runners, why didn't more people do it? Why didn't more people at the big-league level even come close to doing it for such a long, long time?

. . .

Joe Willis Bauman was born in Welch (population five hundred), a fly-speck on the far northeast corner of Oklahoma. That Robert Fulton Crues came into this world in Celina, Texas (population nine hundred), up near the Red River, seems appropriate for someone who may have been named after the brains behind the steamboat.

Welch, which sits in a coal-mining strip, has pretty much the same population today as it did in 1922, when Bauman saw first light. Celina, meanwhile, has grown prosperous as houses and businesses have filled much of the real estate all the way south to the Dallas–Fort Worth environs. Celina now has almost seven thousand people, and it recently gained a Sonic Drive-In. Bob Crues, born in 1918, would never recognize the place.

Bauman and Crues began playing Class D baseball before World War II. After the war, each worked his way up to A ball in the Eastern League. Bauman performed for Hartford, Connecticut, then a Boston Braves affiliate, and Crues for Scranton, Pennsylvania, a Boston Red Sox franchise.

During the war, Bauman played baseball in the U.S. Navy, and Crues played for the U.S. Army until he came down with pneumonia. The future wives of both men worked in defense plants during the 1940s. Dorothy Ramsey labored at an Oklahoma City aircraft factory. A foot and a half shorter than Joe, in high school she had worn his letter sweater. It dragged on the ground. A hard twist from the one-horse farm town of Tahoka, Texas, the daughter of a road grader, Billie Lane punched a clock at the Pantex Ordnance Works in Amarillo. It was on the assembly line that she met her husband-to-be, before the army took him, a kind and restless plugger named Bob.

While still playing baseball and afterward, Bauman and Crues pumped gas at different Texaco filling stations. Each man died in the city where he gained greatest acclaim. For Bauman, it was Roswell, New Mexico. For Crues, Amarillo, Texas. Their wives outlived them.

. . .

For as many similarities as the two ballplayers shared, there were differ-
ences. Joe and Dorothy Bauman did not have children. Bob and Billie
Crues raised four sons. Bauman creaked into his eighties but remained
reasonably healthy until the last couple of years of his life. Crues began to
have serious health problems in his forties. Bauman took care of himself;
Crues did not. Bauman had a full head of hair. Crues had no hair. After
baseball, Bauman led a fairly stable working life. Crues's employment record was marked by years of peripatetic job chasing.

Joe Bauman left Welch as a boy when his father took a job with the Rail-
way Express Agency, a successor to the old Pony Express, and moved the
family to Oklahoma City. Joe Senior knew something about baseball, for
early on he changed his natural right-handed son into a lefty—throwing a
ball, fielding a ball, and, most important, hitting a ball. The senior Bauman
taught the boy to bend his left leg in as he hit. Taught him to wrap his right
palm around the knob of the bat instead of gripping the handle. Cowtail-
ing, that's called. It lets a batter get under a pitch and apply leverage. It's
not easy to do. Bauman became a master at it.

Always big, a naturally strong kid with brick-thick fingers as long as
snakes, Bauman starred in football and basketball at Capitol Hill High
School in Oklahoma City. He considered those two sports hobbies until
baseball season came around. After graduating in 1941, he played in the sub-
terranean minors of the Deep South. He struggled badly. His long, upper-
cut swing deserted him. Returning to Oklahoma, he joined the navy, where
he taught phys ed and guarded first base. When the war ended, he was un-
sure if baseball was in his future. He liked the game well enough, but he'd
just as soon stay in Oklahoma, where the ground was flat as home plate and
the sights common as pump water.

Like Bauman, Bob Crues departed his hometown early. But not before,
as one tale has it, he unknowingly gave highway directions to a motoring
couple later believed to be Bonnie and Clyde.

Crues was an orphan, a fact he kept hidden for most of his life. His
new family moved to a ranch high in the Texas Panhandle. When he was
about six, curious as any kid, he lost part of his forefinger while probing
the sucker rod mechanism on a windmill. The severed tip was placed in
a cigar box. By the time a local doc saw the boy, it was too late to save the
finger. This eventually caused Crues, like Bauman, to hold a bat differ-
ently. Loosely, as if palming a buggy whip. In spite of the partially missing
finger, Crues started out as a pitcher. In fact, the pinched-off finger helped
him throw jitterbugging knuckleballs and curves that dropped like dead

birds. All of this in the fashion of Hall of Famer Mordecai "Three Finger" Brown. Brown, a Chicago Cubs hurler who befuddled batters at the turn of the last century, had lost the ends of two fingers, also in a farm accident.

Playing for the Class D Borger Gassers in 1940, Crues went twenty and five. The Red Sox took notice and sent him off to Scranton. During a spring exhibition game in Greenville, South Carolina, a wild pitch struck Crues's right shoulder as he sat in the dugout. Doctors treated him, but the shoulder didn't get better. The Red Sox sent him down so he could work himself back into pitching form. When that didn't take, he landed back in Borger. He tried pitching there, but now his arm hurt like the dickens. Crues thought his pro baseball dream was over until he got into the batter's box. His arm didn't pain him one bit when he swung a bat. Even so, a baseball career seemed unrealistic.

. . .

Coming to the rescue of both Bauman and Crues was a horse-faced fellow named "Suitcase Bob" Seeds. In the spring of 1946, Seeds was the player-manager of the Amarillo Gold Sox of the West Texas–New Mexico League. Because that league's teams were limited in size, player-managers were not at all uncommon. Suitcase Bob, like all those in charge of postwar ball clubs, scrambled to find available men. Seeds had heard about Joe Bauman, the lumbering, jumbo-sized Okie who had fallen on his face down in Arkansas. Seeds took a flier and gained charge of Bauman's contract. Similarly, Seeds found Bob Crues, a washed-up pitcher now putting in a day's work at a poultry-plucking plant in Oklahoma City.

As teammates for the Gold Sox, Bauman and Crues became friends, though never best buddies. This is not to say a rift existed between the two, because it did not. Much like Mickey Mantle and Roger Maris, sluggers supreme for the New York Yankees in the 1960s, Bauman and Crues respected each other. In the mold of that famed Yankee twosome, Bauman and Crues were small-town, plainspoken guys who merely wanted an opportunity to play hardball and be paid for it. When Suitcase Bob offered them a second chance, they seized it.

That spring of 1946 more than two hundred ballplayers showed up in Amarillo looking for jobs. Many had come back from the war out of shape, not having touched a bat or a ball since Pearl Harbor. Some were so old Suitcase Bob wondered if they could last an inning much less a season. Some were simply unqualified. All had boundless enthusiasm, however.

Such peacetime optimism, expressed so clearly in the 1946 movie *The Best Years of Our Lives*, could be seen all over Gold Sox Field. For instance, in early April, Percy Ching, described in the *Amarillo Daily News* as a "diminutive Chinese," scooted about the Gold Sox training camp with the hope of being a first baseman. Ching was in fact from Hawaii. He was also five feet five inches tall. Like everyone else there, he was given a shot—as a first baseman. Ultimately he did not make the cut. Harry Gilstrap, the sports editor of the *Daily News*, wrote this of Ching: "He displays class aplenty, but he is too small to be a good target for the other infielders." Ching understood. He thanked Suitcase Bob for the opportunity and confessed it wouldn't have worked anyway. Percy Ching pined for home.

In late April 1946, Joe Bauman, a rawboned, twenty-four-year-old first baseman, came aboard. At six feet five and 230 pounds, Bauman clearly presented a bigger bull's-eye at first base than Percy Ching. From the get-go Bauman's Arkansas stumble looked to be history. He had learned to foul off high pitches and even hit to the opposite field. In his hands a thirty-five-inch, thirty-four-ounce bat looked like a kiddy toy. In batting practice, he cowtailed ball after ball over the right-field fence but showed expansive oomph by slicing pitches past left fielders and to deep center. His official debut for the Gold Sox was anything but auspicious, however. On April 31, 1946, the Amarillo Gold Sox beat the Clovis Pioneers, 5–2. The following day, Harry Gilstrap wrote, "Joe Bauman, giant first baseman who was playing his first game for Amarillo, struck out."

Bauman eventually got things together, and on May 13 his single in the tenth inning let the Gold Sox top Abilene, 5–3. On May 25, 1946, the Gold Sox shut out Pampa, 10–0. Bauman in that game slammed his eleventh home run of the season.

Gilstrap began to call Bauman "Little Joe," an attempt at tongue-in-cheek humor. The joke didn't catch on. He was "Big Joe" Bauman and always would be. His size today would hardly be that of a colossus, or "Bunyanesque," as one writer gushed. Yet far too many stories to count began, "Big Joe Bauman hit . . ." Or even "Huge Joe Bauman slammed . . ."

Of that May 25 game, Harry Gilstrap wrote, "Amarillo had a new right-fielder, Bob Crues. Crues, who can also play second, beat out a bunt in the second for his only hit."

Suitcase Bob Seeds surely grinned jug ear to jug ear over how well these two recruits were doing. Seeds was a busy man that season, his last in the minor leagues. He not only put himself at age thirty-nine into several ball games—he played outfield, mostly—but also signed players and kept the grass cut at Gold Sox Field. In fact, he co-owned the Gold Sox.

What's more, he owned Bob Seeds Hardware and Sporting Goods store in Amarillo.

Seeds had begun in professional baseball in 1926, with the Class D Enid, Oklahoma, Boosters. He spent twelve seasons in the minors, wearing the uniforms of ten different teams. He reached the big leagues with Cleveland in 1930. He put in nine years in the majors, spread around five clubs. In 1936, as a New York Yankee, he was part of a World Series championship.

All that hopscotching surely was responsible for his nickname. However, some said he acquired "Suitcase" for his size-14 shoes. The amiable Seeds was one of the boys. His players liked him, and so did reporters. Harry Gilstrap, whose column regularly shone a light on the goodness of the human race, referred to Seeds reverently as "Boss Bob" and "Skipper Bob." Suitcase Bob found a kinship in Bauman and Crues. The two were country boys, as was he. Seeds was born and raised in Ringgold, Texas, where folks still cooled pies on windowsills.

In an April 2, 1946, column, Gilstrap wrote that Seeds credited the Gold Sox players' "splendid attitude" to the war and to the participation of most of them in the armed services. Gilstrap agreed with Seeds. "The boys have a new and better sense of values now. They realize how lucky they are to be in baseball, to have a chance to make a living while playing a game." Gilstrap added that Seeds was not interested in any old-timers who were on the way down, no matter how well they might hit or field, "unless they are team players." Bob Crues was on the high side of twenty-seven when he joined the Gold Sox.

A rangy six feet one inch, Crues was less a physical presence than Bauman, who was four years younger. Nonetheless, Crues could hit a baseball almost as far. To his credit, Suitcase Bob kept Crues in the lineup—and not just for his bat. Playing right field, Crues made eight putouts in one game, a league record.

The 1946 Gold Sox, with Crues batting third and Bauman cleanup, won a more than respectable ninety-three games. Often those contests were considerably one-sided. On June 8, 1946, the Gold Sox annihilated the Lamesa Lobos, 32–0. Save for Bill Evans, a tall Texan with a sling arm, Amarillo pitching that season sagged down the stretch and the Gold Sox wound up in third place. The Gold Sox lost in the postseason to Pampa, which won the playoffs. For Bauman and Crues, the season was a winning one. Big Joe stroked forty-eight home runs, and Crues, after missing the first month, collected twenty-nine. His arm couldn't hold up to pitching, but he could play a worthy center field and right.

The following year, the Joe and Bob Show brought out Act II. Bauman

slammed thirty-eight homers and Crues fifty-two. The Gold Sox finished in second place. No team that season was a match for the Lubbock
Hubbers. Lubbock sent a murderers' row to the plate and dressed out a
pitching staff that gave opposing teams fits.

Steve Lagomarsino, a young pitcher for the Gold Sox in 1947, remembered Bauman as being more aloof than Crues and Crues more rough-
and-tumble than Bauman. Lagomarsino had never been out of Los
Angeles when he arrived in Amarillo in the spring of 1947. "When I saw
tumbleweeds blowing in the streets, I felt like I was on the dark side of the
moon," he said. The Gold Sox were a rowdy bunch in '47. During a poker
game, another pitcher on the team stabbed Lagomarsino in the hand. For-
tunately, it was not his pitching hand.

. . .

Impressed with Bauman's numbers, the Boston Braves called him up in
1948 and sent him to Class A ball in Connecticut. Bauman dented no
fences there. He didn't like the East Coast, where people talked peculiarly,
where everybody lived on top of each other, and where not an oil well could
be seen. Heck with this, he told Dorothy. He returned to Oklahoma and sat
out the rest of the 1948 season.

On the basis of Crues's 1946 and 1947 statistics, the Boston Red Sox told
him to report to Little Rock in the Southern Association, where Bauman
had played earlier. Crues looked good in exhibition games, but then he suddenly disappeared. Just as Hawaii had pulled back Percy Ching, Crues had
returned to Amarillo. "Homesick," Crues told Harry Gilstrap. "A homesick ballplayer ain't good to no one." In truth, Billie Crues had told her
husband she wasn't packing up for who-the-hell-knows-where with one
toddler and a baby on the way. *You'll play in Amarillo or you'll play nowhere,*
Billie said. "Oh, yeah, Mom was tough," the Crueses' second-oldest son,
Larry, recalled. "She didn't take a whole bunch of crap from anyone."

Joe Bauman had found out that the higher minor leagues were not paying much more than Class C and D ball clubs. And Single A and Double
A teams didn't have screen money, either. That was the folding money fans
stuck in chicken wire behind home plate at minor league ballparks across
the Southwest. The cash saluted a home run or some other kind of heroic.
Bauman and Crues were used to hauling in lots and lots of screen money.

Out of the formidable shadow of Joe Bauman, Crues had in 1948 one of
the greatest six months of any minor leaguer ever. He batted .404, and his

slugging percentage was nearly off the charts at .848. His home runs came in bundles. In June he missed out on what later would be an important one when an umpire with questionable eyesight said a high, arcing Crues-struck ball had hit the fence at Blue Sox Stadium and bounced back onto the field, keeping it in play. Just about everyone at the Abilene ballpark that night, including the scoreboard operator, saw the ball thunk the scoreboard and rebound to the field, clearly a home run. Amarillo players protested, but the ump would not back down and kept Crues at third base. A certain home run went into the record books as a triple.

Crues shrugged off that call, and by late August he had taken dead aim at the professional baseball mark of sixty-nine home runs.

• • •

That record of sixty-nine had been set in 1933 by Joe Hauser, a Milwaukee native. Hauser was lovingly called "Unser Choe," or Uncle Joe, by his many fans when he played before crowds of German ancestry in Milwaukee in the thirties. Like Bauman, he was a first baseman, but of medium size. Unlike Bauman and Crues, Hauser played in the majors. Oddly, most of Hauser's sixteen years in the minor leagues came *after* his six-year tour in the big leagues, something that would never happen today.

All of a sudden newspapermen took to calling Crues "Home Run Bob" and "Round Trip Bob." When Amarillo held a Bob Crues Night that season, the Crues family needed to borrow a truck to take home all the gifts from fans. Toward the end of the season, *Look* magazine went to Texas to cover Home Run Bob's chase for seventy home runs. Everyone wanted to help him get the record. Crues, honest as bread, refused to allow pitchers to lob balls for him to tee off on or let outfielders intentionally muff flies so he might get an inside-the-park homer and snatch the record from Hauser. By season's end, though, Crues had to settle for a tie with Unser Choe. The Gold Sox didn't need Big Joe's bat that year. With Home Run Bob swinging for the scoreboard, Amarillo took the playoffs.

To go with all the home runs and the .400-plus batting average was that stunning RBI total—254. The major league record then and now was 191, done in 155 games in 1930 by Hack Wilson, a squat, rummy-eyed center fielder for the Chicago Cubs. Numerous observers thought Wilson could have had more RBI if he had eased off the booze. Years later, Chicago columnist Mike Royko wrote that Wilson should have been moved to first base from the outfield, "because he wouldn't have as far to stagger to the dugout."

Crues became the first player in professional baseball to hit sixty or more home runs and bat .400 or more in the same season. In 1954, Joe Bauman became the second. The third has not yet come along and may never.

. . .

Without anywhere to land in 1949, Joe Bauman became something of a lost figure. The Boston Braves did not give up on him, however. They offered Big Joe a new minor league contract. Bauman returned the paperwork unsigned. He scribbled upon it what has to be among the most memorable rejection notes ever: "I can make more money selling twenty-seven-inch shoelaces on a street corner in Oklahoma City than I can playing for you."

Bauman's thoughts of suiting up in the major leagues went into a stall. He couldn't go to another big league team's farm club because of baseball's reserve clause, which bound a player for life to the first club to sign him, unless he was sold, traded, or given his unconditional release. Boston refused to release Bauman from his contract. From then on, Bauman spoke of baseball in the major leagues as "slavery." He compared the majors to cotton plantations down south a century earlier.

Crues, meanwhile, worked the winter of 1948–1949 at an Elk City, Oklahoma, meat-packing plant. Always on the lookout for a larger payday to support his growing family, he signed on to play the following summer with the Elk City Elks, a fine semipro team. Crues could do that because the reserve clause did not include semiprofessional baseball. The decision was made easy because Home Run Bob knew there was little likelihood at age thirty that he could work his way into the big leagues.

The Roswell Rockets, however, came up with a better deal and offered Crues a spot. What to do now? Crues told the Elks that Bauman was available and the team ought to sign him. So that's what happened.

For the next three years, Big Joe became the Elks' bell cow. He hit seventy-eight home runs in 213 games, though few people beyond the borders of the Sooner State knew the Elks existed. Bauman and an Elks teammate, Jack Riley, opened a Texaco service station on U.S. Route 66 in Elk City. The money Big Joe pocketed pumping gas and playing semipro ball was more than anything he could have made back east. Big Joe and Dorothy had always wanted children. When that didn't happen, they considered adopting but eventually gave up on that. They came to think of Elk City as their baby, their gift from providence. They were over-the-moon happy there.

As much as Crues liked Amarillo, the Roswell job in 1949 was too good to pass up. Roswell was a new town in a new league, the Longhorn League, which had sprung up just two years earlier. What's more, Crues would have a new role: he would be the Rockets' player-manager. So what if he had never managed? He took the position because he needed the extra cash.

In Roswell, Home Run Bob the player put up solid numbers. He hit twenty-eight homers and batted .365. As a manager, Crues was miscast. He grew impatient with his teammates, seemed oblivious to strategy, and didn't communicate well. The Rockets finished dead last, thirty-seven games out of first place. Even the Vernon Dusters, never a spectacular club, did better. So bad were the Dusters that year that Monte Stratton, a former major league pitcher who lost part of one leg in a rabbit-hunting accident, was brought on to attempt a comeback. Stratton's return failed, but later that year a movie about his life, *The Stratton Story*, starring James Stewart and June Allyson, did extremely well at the box office.

• • •

From 1950 to 1953, Crues went back and forth from Longhorn League teams to West Texas–New Mexico League teams, never coming close to duplicating what he had done with Amarillo. He ended his playing career on July 13, 1953, at Borger, where he had started out thirteen years before. Crues was batting a paltry .195 for the Gassers and had hit just four home runs when he walked away for good with barely a word. A first baseman now, like Bauman, he had played only eleven games that abbreviated season and had recently hurt his back leaping for a line drive. He was thirty-four years old, a youngster on the Borger team compared to a forty-eight-year-old gunk-throwing character named Lloyd "Gimpy" Brown, who seemed ageless. Brown batted .299 that year for Borger, hit the same number of home runs as Crues, and won thirteen games as a pitcher.

• • •

As Crues's skills declined, Joe Bauman's only got better. Nicely set up as he was in Elk City, an offer from Earl Perry, an Oklahoma friend now running the show for the Artesia Drillers in the Longhorn League, was tantalizing. Perry wanted Big Joe in Artesia the way Suitcase Bob wanted him in Amarillo. Joe and Dorothy made a visit and liked what they saw. As swell as Elk City was, the money Artesia dangled won them over. Joe would get a grand a month from the Drillers, plus another thousand to sign. Perry helped to buy Joe's contract with the Braves, releasing Big Joe for good from the damnable reserve clause. Not that it would really matter, for Bauman knew at age thirty no major league club was likely to come knocking.

As giddy as Perry was to get Bauman, he was not at all happy with how out of shape Big Joe was. Perry had been a terrific high school athlete in Tulsa, then a tough Marine who saw all the action any man would want in the Pacific. He pushed Bauman like a rented mule during that spring training of 1952 in Mineral Wells, Texas. The idea was to get Bauman to pick up where he had left off with the Gold Sox in 1947. It worked. Playing first base, Big Joe lofted fifty home runs that year. The crowds at Artesia's Brainard Park grew to capacity. All by himself Big Joe became the gate. He added fifty-three home runs the next year. It's possible he might have had more home runs that second season, but he relieved Perry as the Drillers' skipper halfway through. Much like Home Run Bob had been in Roswell, Bauman felt about as comfortable managing as he would wearing a tuxedo.

Earl Perry had gone to Roswell as general manager, and over that winter he talked to Big Joe about coming up there. You won't do any managing there, Perry promised. The deal was sealed when Bauman learned that a Texaco filling station was up for sale in Roswell. Big Joe had worn the Texaco red star proudly and he wanted to get back in that line of work. He had plenty of screen money from Artesia to do it. As much as he appreciated the Artesia fans, the decision to move forty miles up the highway in 1954 was for Bauman as easy as shelling peas.

Soon baseballs were coming off Big Joe's bat—a Vern Stephens model—at a steady clip. Coincidentally, Hall of Fame shortstop Stephens was a native of McAlister, New Mexico, a crossroads 130 miles northeast of Roswell. Quickly Bauman had twenty home runs, then thirty, then forty as a Rocket. Once vulnerable to lefties, they now didn't seem to bother him, not even San Angelo's Audie Malone. Malone, a tireless Mississippian who pitched for seven different teams in the leagues, normally delivered right-handed. Because he threw tolerably as a southpaw, he used that arm in an attempt to stymie the Roswell slugger. Bring it on, Big Joe said. The ploy didn't work; the round-trip canters continued. All of a sudden, it seemed, he had rung up fifty.

When Bauman's soaring shots at Roswell's Fair Park Stadium passed over the right-field fence, they often plopped into the rodeo arena of the Eastern New Mexico Fairgrounds. Young fans there gave chase, paying no nevermind when they stepped in a waiting cow patty. So much screen money—at times $800 a night—came Joe's way, he started divvying it to teammates. He did the same with the ham-for-every-homer agreement he had with Glover's Packing House in Roswell.

Unlike some ballplayers today, not once did Bauman pause at the plate to gaze in wondrous delight as one of his cowtailed blasts climbed toward the heavens. "Never show up a pitcher," Big Joe advised years later. "Even if he's piss poor."

Big Joe crushed his sixty-fourth home run, a four-hundred-foot clubbing over the center-field wall, on August 30, 1954. Appropriately, it came on Joe Bauman Night. When he missed a homer in the seventh inning and had to settle for a walk, most of the twenty-five hundred fans on hand got up and left. The next night, Joe made up for things in a big way. Thunk! Thunk! Thunk! Thunk! Thwack! He filled the firmament with four home runs and a double as the Rockets showed no courtesies to visiting Sweetwater, winning 15–9. He now had sixty-eight home runs. After that game, Roswell manager Pat Stasey put Big Joe in the leadoff spot to get as many at-bats as possible. On September 2, Ralph Atkinson, a Midland lefty and long Joe's nemesis, held Bauman hitless until the eighth inning. That's when he launched a 375-foot bomb to deep right with two men on.

In downtown Roswell, two miles from Fair Park Stadium, you could hear the cheering. Big Joe now had sixty-nine home runs, tying Home Run Bob and Unser Choe. "It felt good," he told Bob Green of the Associated Press. With four games left to play, the Rockets went on a road trip. *Life* magazine had already started to dog Big Joe the way rival *Look* magazine had tailed Crues. The constant clicking of shutters and blinking of flashbulbs got into Big Joe's head. On September 3 and 4 at Big Spring, a small ballpark where Bauman had never done well, cameras closed in and pitchers gave him nothing to hit. Joe came up empty as a broken bowl, even as the Texas fans urged him on. The *Life* crew wondered if its pursuit was a boondoggle, as *Look*'s had been.

On the last day of the season, Sunday, September 5, 1954, Bauman, still stuck at sixty-nine, rolled into Artesia for a doubleheader with the NuMexers, formerly the Drillers. Brainard Park, the Artesia ball yard, was 350 feet down the line in right. No barrel shoot there. The pressure was palpable. More than twenty-six hundred fans had come out for one reason: to see Big Joe break the record. Joe's parents were among the crowd, but they did not tell their son for fear of adding to the tension. Dorothy was also there, of course, and Joe knew it. For the last week they had not said word one to each other about home runs or records.

The first time Bauman came to bat, the NuMexers' Floyd Economides asked where he wanted the pitch. Big Joe looked down at the catcher everyone called "Greek" and said, in words that echoed Bob Crues's assault on seventy home runs in 1948, "I don't want none of that soft, easy bleep, Greek. You tell him to throw it like always."

Only Big Joe could talk to Greek that way. Economides, a bruising sort who had fought in the snows of Korea with the U.S. Marines, took grief from no one. Some seasons before, a base runner had collided viciously with Greek, who was blocking the plate. Greek made the tag and jumped right back up. The base runner, sprawled prone in the dirt and in great physical pain, could not stand. He had broken his kneecap—on Greek's forehead.

The pitch Greek ordered from José Gallardo was a fastball, sneaky swift and low. Big Joe stayed with it, and up and out it went, easily clearing the 350-foot mark. He had seventy; he had the record. He had now socked more home runs in one season than any ballplayer in any league at any level. On the same September day exactly forty years earlier in Toronto, Canada, Babe Ruth, wearing the uniform of the Providence Grays, hit the only home run of his minor league career. Then a pitcher, he tossed a one-hitter that day, winning 9–0 to defeat the Maple Leafs in an International League contest.

In Artesia, players from both teams gathered to greet Big Joe, to shake his hand as he trotted around third base and headed for home. This time Bauman told Bob Green, "That was like getting a piano off my back."

In the second game of that day's doubleheader, feeling no stress at all, Bauman added two more home runs to his coffers to reach seventy-two. The game turned into a rout as Roswell waltzed to a 17–0 pounding.

Joe Bauman played two more seasons with Roswell, including a final one in the Southwestern League in 1956. That last stand bore great resemblance to Crues's wrap-up. Dressing out for a couple of months, Big Joe made eight errors and struck out forty-three times. Taking ill-advised swings, he batted below .300 for the first time. "I can't pick up the ball anymore," he told his friend Jim Waldrip. The poor lighting in many ballparks didn't help him. Nor did a bum ankle that had nagged him since he was nineteen. Never a speed demon, Bauman had slowed now to a saunter. On June 8, 1956, amid little fanfare, Big Joe, thirty-five years old, called it quits. He wound up with 337 home runs during his nine years in the minors.

Against his better judgment, Big Joe came out of retirement in 1959 to briefly manage the Roswell Pirates of the Sophomore League. Miserable every minute, he left after a few weeks. Short as that stint was, it made him one of the few people to have worn baseball uniforms in all four of the minor leagues in the Southwest.

· · ·

Joe Bauman Texaco, located on West Second Street in Roswell, the busy highway that leads west to the Ruidoso racetrack and high, cool mountain air, turned into a lucrative business. Many motorists filled up on gas as an afterthought. They pulled in just for Big Joe's autograph or to say hello. Joe told his station workers that if any cute gals from Texas came by, be sure to tell him and he'd check their fluid and oil levels himself.

Things were going so well that Bauman opened another station in Roswell. At one point he had half a dozen people on the payroll. He and Dorothy were so comfortable now they moved his parents down from Oklahoma. Big Joe joined the Roswell Elks Club and Dorothy got involved with Beta Sigma Phi, a service sorority. They would go out to eat often, usually for chiles rellenos, and take frequent automobile trips. Joe played some golf, showing no pity to the little white ball.

For Bob Crues, life after baseball turned into a relentless challenge. When he lived in Amarillo, he was the toast of the town. He was given jobs, none of which lasted long. He worked for the Graham Home Plow Company—"Plows all depths to eighteen inches." He sold cars and jockeyed gas pumps. When the job offers slowed, he returned to Roswell, where he crossed paths once more with Bauman. Big Joe helped him get a piece of a Texaco station in town. The Crues family has sweet memories of the two gas station owners playing catch on a Roswell street. Crues worked there for a time, only to stop and go back to Amarillo for something else. He and Billie had four youngsters now, and they all needed to eat. Home Run Bob drove a beer truck in Amarillo, then motored for a moving company. Not satisfied, he returned to Roswell. He acquired jobs the way he had batted: not choosy, he took anything that came along.

In the late 1950s, Crues moved his family to Albuquerque. He signed on with a roofing company, then left that to rise to foreman of a lumber yard. He'd then hear about a more promising situation in Roswell, move back there and find one more rental house for Billie and the boys. When Roswell didn't work out, Home Run Bob went back to Albuquerque, where he joined forces for a time with his eldest son Ronnie. The two would go on "belly dumps." Driving a dump truck, they'd pick up a load of dirt from what would become Interstate 40 and haul it to piles in Tucumcari or Santa Rosa. His father talked on these nightly runs, Ronnie remembered, but not about himself. "He would never really open up."

Big Joe operated his filling stations until 1967, the year Walker Air Force Base, a Strategic Air Command facility, closed. The shutting down of the base sent Roswell into economic upheaval. Joe and Dorothy relocated to Hobbs, where they ran a package store for a short time. Soon, however, they returned to Roswell. People there remembered Big Joe fondly, and he was rewarded with a good post as sales manager for a liquor distributor. He retired from that after fourteen years.

In his retirement, Bauman stayed close to his home on Roswell's Deming Street. Once a week Dorothy would remind him to mow the lawn. His phone number was in the Roswell book, and always had been, so now and then he fielded telephone calls from reporters asking him to relive those seventy-two home runs.

A good time for Big Joe was catching a Braves game on television. Though he had long before spurned the organization, cursing the reserve clause that had hogtied his future, he was curiously faithful to the team, just as he was to Texaco. On rare occasions regret came his way. He would fret over his decision to go with Elk City and take himself out of commission for a major league look for three years. But such thoughts were fleeting. As he had neared the home-run record in late 1954, he did hear talk about a big league club being interested in him for pinch-hitting duty. When nothing came of it, he dismissed the thought. For the most part, Big Joe lived in the present. Only when reporters called did he dwell on the past. He'd patiently tell the writers that in that 1954 season the baseball looked so dang big. Sometimes he'd say big as a cantaloupe, other times big as a grapefruit or even a pumpkin.

• • •

Still struggling to feed his family, Bob Crues in 1965 suffered the first in a series of strokes. He was only forty-seven. He started walking with a cane and kept to himself. "He fell apart," Ronnie Crues said. "Dad considered himself a has-been and went into a shell." Crues had long been a drinker. In Amarillo, most every ballplayer drank beer in the dugout during games. So many players smoked that the dugout at night looked from a distance like the aurora borealis. Bob Crues now drank beer and smoked Lucky Strikes as if a condemned man. "Him and Mom would go through a twelve-pack every night," Larry Crues remembered.

The bad habits caught up with Home Run Bob and he developed heart problems. Even so, he moved from want ad to want ad, city to city. He pumped gas at a Shell station, then a Texaco station, then an Atex station. That done, the family would go off and hunt up something in Roswell. He kept on drinking, just like old Hack Wilson had. He came back to Amarillo and landed a job at Charlie's Package Store, hardly the most appropriate place.

What you saw with Big Joe and Home Run Bob was what you got. But after baseball, what you got with Crues was a dark side. He appeared to be battling demons. His sons say being an orphan ate at him. He seemed to believe he hadn't measured up as a ballplayer, as a man. Whatever the source of his woes, he didn't reveal it. This much is known: Home Run Bob deeply regretted not getting that seventieth round-tripper. People had told him if he had gotten it, he'd be on the front of a zillion Wheaties boxes. He didn't think anyone respected his RBI record. Someone hits, someone scores, fans clap a little, big bleepin' deal. RBI were like bases on balls, he told Billie. Who cared?

Life after baseball for Bauman and Crues eerily echoed more Mantle and Maris comparisons. When he stopped playing, Big Joe, like Maris, worked for a beer dealer. Home Run Bob, as Mantle had for done for most of his career, drank in excess.

Now and then Crues emerged from his funk. In 1975, he was inducted into the Panhandle Sports Hall of Fame, which for a while gave him a lift. But the struggles continued. More and more gas stations were becoming self-service; they didn't need him. He and Billie decided to retire in 1977— in Amarillo. They had spent their happiest days there. The feeling was, maybe some of that happiness might return. It never did. His spirits low, Home Run Bob got high on spirits. Billie would usually join him. "Every night was a party," Ronnie Crues said. The Crueses' children, now grown, suffered. Bob and Billie's youngest son, Lynn, died at thirty of what some believe was sleep apnea. Their second youngest, Mark, wound up homeless on the streets of Amarillo.

The day after Christmas 1986 found Home Run Bob sitting in his big easy chair, watching TV in the family's house on Crockett Street. A Lone Star beer can rested on a side table, a Lucky Strike between his fingers. He was waiting up for son Ronnie to arrive from New Mexico with his family. Billie was nearby, waiting up too, when her husband slumped forward.

Home Run Bob's heart had finally had enough. He was dead at sixty-seven.

The obituary for the most exciting baseball player in the history of Amarillo ran nearly hidden on an inside page of the *Amarillo Daily News*.

• • •

Fifteen years later and 225 miles from Amarillo, Joe Bauman was parked in his recliner in front of the television at his Deming Street house when Barry Bonds hit his seventy-third home run. "I ain't upset," Big Joe told friends. "Heck, I'm surprised the dang record lasted this long."

Big Joe didn't have much to say to reporters regarding steroids. He didn't understand them. In his day, all a ballplayer needed for a pick-me-up was a cold Miller High Life—in a bottle. It should be noted that he drank in moderation.

Bauman went on to suffer a stroke himself, in 2003. He too had to use a cane to get around. Fair Park Stadium, where he had his greatest season, was to be renamed in Bauman's honor, in August 2005. Big Joe, stove up now, was reluctant to attend the ceremony. In the end, he agreed to go.

His good friend Jim Waldrip had told the people who had planned the dedication that Joe would need help walking. That help did not appear fast enough; Bauman slipped and fell. A loud cracking noise sounded as his large body struck the concrete podium. In great pain and his hand quickly bandaged, Big Joe somehow got through his thank-you speech. That done, he wanted to go straight home. Waldrip urged him to go to the hospital instead. Big Joe said no, so Waldrip drove him to Deming Street. When they got there, Joe couldn't get out of the car. Waldrip immediately summoned an ambulance, which took Big Joe to Eastern New Mexico Medical Center. X-rays showed a fractured pelvis.

Big Joe never left the hospital. Dorothy was at his bedside when, on September 20, 2005, he died of pneumonia, a complication of the fall he took at his ballpark. He was eighty-three.

Joe Bauman's obituary, which extolled his home-run-hitting feat, ran on the front page of the *Roswell Daily Record*, above the fold.

• • •

Even in death, that Great Leveler, the two sluggers found common ground. Bob Crues's family had made arrangements with an Amarillo funeral home for his burial, but apparently there was a mix-up and his grave was not placed where the family had requested. In time, weeds covered it over. Only at the family's protests some while later was the marker retrieved for viewing.

Unexplainably, Dorothy Bauman had bought a plot for Joe at a resting place mainly meant for indigents. There Joe lay, beneath a grassless, shadeless plain whose owners soon went bankrupt. When Dorothy died in 2011, her remains and Joe's were placed in the large, well-tended South Park Cemetery, at the south end of Roswell.

Decorating Joe Bauman's handsome tombstone is a drawing of a baseball player swinging a bat. The figure, however, is batting right-handed. Everyone knows that Bauman, who had trouble with curveballs—especially those that dropped down and to the outside—batted from the left. It was Home Run Bob Crues, Big Joe's equal in so many ways, who batted right-handed.

· ·

VOICES: TOM JORDAN

1949: catcher, Roswell Rockets
1950: catcher, manager, Roswell Rockets
1953: catcher, manager, Albuquerque Dukes
1954: catcher, pitcher, manager, Albuquerque Dukes
1955: catcher, pitcher, manager, Artesia NuMexers
1956: catcher, outfielder, first baseman, pitcher, manager,
     Roswell Rockets, Carlsbad Potashers
1957: catcher, first baseman, Carlsbad Potashers

I played with and against both Joe Bauman and Bob Crues. I think Joe was more consistent about the way he went about things. Crues is definitely forgotten. Joe would be forgotten, too, if he hadn't hit those seventy-two home runs.

They both had holes in their swings, and a pitcher who had good control could get them out. Joe was pretty weak against lefties. There didn't seem to be many lefties then. Now, they're all over the place. In this country, it wasn't that hard to hit a home run. The wind blowed out and blowed hard. Amarillo was only about 310 to left and right. Heck, one year Amarillo had a pitcher who hit home runs in double figures.

Joe didn't get no free ride as a batter. He played in Artesia, where it wasn't easy to hit a home run. Home plate was northwest, and when the wind blowed in from right field, in the southeast, it didn't help Joe much. Fair Park in Roswell was not that easy down right field. I think Joe got all those home runs in 1954 because he got hot and everything came together. That year he was never injured, if I remember, which is kind of rare.

Joe was a good friend of mine, but I think when Roswell won the Little League World Championship in 1956 that was a bigger deal than Joe's seventy-two home runs. The whole town celebrated. Those were our kids. When those kids came home from Williamsport, people came out to meet the train, several hundred people. A big deal was made of it, and it was big.

I managed Joe for Roswell in 1956. He played part of the season until his legs and knees got bad. That was about it for him.

People ask me about Pete Domenici. I managed him when he played one summer with Albuquerque, in 1954. He was right out of college. I don't think he played more than two months. He was really wild. He throwed pretty hard, but he couldn't get the ball near the plate. He only pitched in two or three games, as I recall. I saw where Domenici said he batted against Joe Bauman. That couldn't have happened, because Albuquerque in 1954 was in the West Texas–New Mexico League and Roswell was in the Longhorn League. I remember Domenici come through Roswell one year to campaign for senator. He remembered me and said hello. I didn't vote for him; I'm more of an Independent. If I think people done what I thought they ought to do, then I vote for them.

I played three seasons in the major leagues. I done all right. I could have kept going, but I quit because I could make more in the minor leagues. The St. Louis Browns optioned my contract to Roswell. My arm was hurting some, but mostly I quit because of money. I made $8,000 a year as the player-manager in Albuquerque, and the most I made in a season in the majors was $6,000. You had that fence money, too. It could really add up.

I was running a farm in Roswell all those years. That was another reason I wanted to keep playing in the minors in the area. Me and my brother had about four hundred acres. We farmed cotton and alfalfa, watermelons and cantaloupes. Had a few cows, too.

I was a player-manager several times and it worked out pretty well. My teams won quite a bit more than they lost. We finished first or second most years. I was right out of the major leagues and I was a lot better than a lot of the players in the Longhorn or West Texas–New

Mexico Leagues. I never had trouble with players listening. I was probably more a player's manager than an owner's manager. Owners, they figured they could get two for one with a player-manager. That didn't always work out. Doing both jobs never affected my skills. I don't think I could have been a better player if I just played.

When I think back to those days of the 1940s and 1950s, I miss them. Texas used to have seven or eight minor leagues. Now the only minor league there is the Texas League. New Mexico doesn't have any true minor leagues. We don't have the fan base here.

I started playing minor league ball in 1938, with the Class D Abbeville A's [Athletics], in the Evangeline League, down south. I was eighteen years old. I was still playing ball when that league died, in 1957.

A few of the old ballparks in West Texas and New Mexico where I played are still being used. They have something there now called the Pecos League. It's an independent league for high school and college kids. The scores are always pretty high. One game I saw written up showed two teams together had scored more than eighty runs. Those kids are hoping for a scout to come by, and one or two players might be signed out of that. There just are not many places for professional players to play anymore. It's kind of sad. When Little League and PONY League came along, they hurt the minors leagues. People had a good reason now to come out to the ballparks and see their kids play. You can't blame 'em. Baseball has always been a kid's game.

. . . .

voices: Jim Heller

1947: pitcher, Amarillo Gold Sox
1948: pitcher, Amarillo Gold Sox

Joe Bauman and Bob Crues, they should have been in the major leagues. Especially Bauman. No ballpark in the world would hold what he hit. We were in the playoffs in 1947. Amarillo is high up, people forget. The pitcher on the other team threw nothing but hanging curveballs. Our first four players up to bat—Crues and Bauman among them—hit home runs.

Crues bought a house in Amarillo with his fence money. He'd pull out five- and ten-dollar bills from the fence. He'd hand the money to Bob Decker, who would put them in a box. I think he made close to ten thousand dollars. Every home run, he gave Decker a case of beer. Decker kept track of Crues's bats to see nobody used them or stole them.

Crues and Bauman were married, so I didn't hang out much with them. Bob Decker was my closest friend on the team. A very good second baseman and a great two-strike hitter. From Tarrytown, New York, Bob was. They used to call him "Double Decker" because every time he came up it seemed like he hit a double with two strikes on him. He later became a scout for the New York Yankees. He's dead now.

When I wasn't playing ball, I used to go to a small bowling alley in Amarillo, eight lanes I think, a block or so off Polk Street. I was a good bowler and you could get in matches there they called "spares." Someone would set a couple of pins and you bet whether you could get a spare by knocking them down. I never heard of that before. I would eat breakfast at the alley, which was dinner for us ballplayers. You could get a T-bone steak, two eggs, bacon, toast, and all the coffee you wanted for a dollar.

It's always windy in Amarillo, and that could be tough if you were a pitcher. On the way out to the ball field each day, I would always check this big flame that was blowing off excess gas. If the flame was blowing one way, it meant the wind was blowing that way, and vice versa. At the ballpark, you always wanted to pitch when the wind was blowing in.

Trouble is, the wind was usually blowing out. This was bad for fastball pitchers, and most of the pitchers back then were strictly fastballers. I did OK because I threw mostly sinker balls.

Early in the war I was playing for Bradford, Pennsylvania, in the PONY League. Casey Stengel, then the manager of the Boston Bees, which later was the Boston Braves, came down to scout me and some others. The hotel we were staying in kept an eye on us because the year before ballplayers there had knocked up three girls. Anyway, Casey stayed at the hotel. Casey was a loud snorer. You could hear him down the hall. So me and a couple of other guys rigged up a big bucket of water on the transom of the door to his room. When he opened it, the bucket would fall on Casey. He came down for breakfast that day, his hair all wet, said he was going to work us out till we dropped and fine everybody ten bucks. He never did any of that.

I hadn't been out of the army that long when I got to Amarillo. I was a combat engineer in Europe, a demolitions guy. My job was to blow up German pillboxes. I got a Bronze Star for valor and they offered me a commission, but I wanted to get home. I left the service a PFC. What happened? I wasn't a good soldier. I was a poor soldier. I went AWOL over there. I went on a three-day pass and stayed a few extra days. I got loaded and met a girl. The war, it was sometimes fun. But a lot of the time it was scary as hell.

Now Amarillo, that was fun. The highlight each summer in Amarillo was Waddy Week. You had to wear everything western. You couldn't wear white shoes or loafers. Only boots, Levi's, and a western shirt and cowboy hat were allowed. If they caught you not wearing that, you got dunked in this big tub of water. One day during Waddy Week I happened to see our team's owner and manager, Bob Seeds. He didn't have western clothes on. I told someone in charge of Waddy Week and they went and found Bob and dunked him. Suitcase always blamed me, but he could never prove it.

What a player Suitcase was. At Buffalo one year he hit seven consecutive home runs and missed the eighth by inches. He married a wealthy woman from Amarillo. Her and Bob had a ranch with about ten thousand acres. Mostly they raised cotton. Bob's daughter was pretty good looking, I remember. Bob told me, "Heller, I don't want you around my daughter. If you go near her, I'll sell you to a team so far away you'll never find your way back." Bill Serena of Lubbock was another good hitter. He was a low-ball hitter. I watched other guys throw that stuff to him and get murdered. I got Serena out with high pitches. He never hit a home run off me. I had pretty good control and could change speeds.

I was originally signed by the Red Sox when I was eighteen. I went to spring training in Sarasota and I pitched to Ted Williams. I didn't get to meet him, but he greeted me. His hello was to hit a ball that went over the center fielder's head. There was no fence, so the ball must have gone a mile. I pitched to Jimmie Foxx there and he popped up. That same spring Johnny Pesky hit a line drive off my kneecap and I was out a week.

I liked playing at Lubbock because there was an old shoe cobbler there. Joe the Cobbler, he was called. Joe made special-made baseball shoes. They don't make them anymore. Today, players wear shoes a few days and throw them out. I needed a shoe with a toe plate, to push off. Joe the Cobbler did that. His shop was a little hole in the wall.

You had to always watch out for Grover Seitz, who managed at Pampa. One year he called me up and asked me to go dove hunting. "Come on out, you and Decker." Well, when we got there, Grover gave me a twelve-gauge shotgun. The stock had no recoil pad. I shot over three boxes of shells at birds that day. The next morning, I woke up and my shoulder hurt real bad. Then I realized I had banged it up firing at those birds. I had to pitch that day against Pampa. When I saw Grover, I said, "You did this to me intentionally." He laughed and said, "Jim, I didn't." "The hell you didn't," I said.

While I was at Amarillo, I would go up to Trinidad, Colorado, in the off season and take classes at the junior college there. It was one of the few places that offered gunsmithing to study. I had always liked guns. When I left baseball, I went back to my hometown of Honesdale, Pennsylvania, and worked as a gunsmith, but I couldn't make a living. So I got a job with the Katz Underwear Company. I was a mechanic for sewing machines and made parts for them. I stayed there thirty-seven years, until I retired. I still live in Honesdale. I am ninety-two years old, and most days I feel it. I have that macular degeneration thing. It's due in part to living so long. My vision is very poor. As a pitcher, I wouldn't be worth two cents.

CHAPTER TWO

A Shot in the Dark

With the toe of one sneaker, Chuck Tidwell scuffed a mark on the ground. "I'm pretty sure this is where home plate was," he said. Tidwell began walking to the west, counting the number of his steps as he moved across a weed-choked pasture decorated with prairie dog holes and the occasional doubled-over beverage can. The temperature this afternoon on the east side of Carlsbad is a withering 104 degrees. That's about average for mid-August in this arid corner of New Mexico, where the empty, thirsty scrubland goes on forever and a day.

Tidwell stopped walking and looked around. "First base was here, I'm thinking." He pointed to the north and beyond, where, behind a cinder-block wall sat the back yards of houses. "The center-field fence was maybe 390 feet. Left-center was about 360. That's where that gol-durn baseball flew over."

A slight man with a high-pitched drawl, Tidwell was talking about a prodigious home run detonated into the night sky here more than half a century ago. Many believe no one has hit one farther. The empty, sun-baked plot that Tidwell traipsed around was so quiet you could almost hear the lamentations of Frank Sinatra. *There used to be a ballpark right here . . .*

Right here, during scorching summer nights of 1959, Tidwell worked at a ballpark named Montgomery Field. He was an "inside shagger" for the Carlsbad Potashers, a Class D subsidiary of the Chicago Cubs that belonged to what was known as the Sophomore League. Potash, an alkaline-potassium compound and the main ingredient in fertilizer, is, along with Carlsbad Caverns National Park, a staple of Carlsbad's economy. In the

1950s, there were six potash mines in Carlsbad. Only two of the old holes continue to produce.

As an inside shagger, Tidwell waited at Montgomery Field's front gate for one of the two "outside shaggers," youngsters who patrolled beyond the fence, to hustle over and hand him baseballs that had been hit for home runs or long foul balls. Tidwell was eleven that drowsy, end-of-the-Eisenhower-era summer of 1959. Gasoline was thirty cents a gallon and only knockabout sailors and carnival workers wore tattoos. Facial hair for the most part belonged to beatnik bongo players and the barnstorming House of David ball club.

Tidwell had slogged away at Montgomery Field since he was nine, most of the time earning fifty or seventy cents a night. He later put in thirty years in the potash business, laboring above ground, operating machinery that dried liquid potash. Like many males in Carlsbad, he followed his father to the mines. Boyd Tidwell, a chemist, worked forty years on top.

"I really wanted to be an outside shagger," Chuck Tidwell said. "They made a dollar fifty a game. But I was too young, too small. Mr. Montgomery said you had to be fourteen."

Montgomery, the overseer of all things baseball in Carlsbad, wanted older, bigger boys who could run like a streak to retrieve baseballs. An inside shagger, Tidwell remembered, was really a glorified delivery boy. He'd receive the baseballs from the cooler, more grownup outside shaggers then take the balls to Charlie Montgomery, the owner of the team. Montgomery sat plank stiff each night in a box seat behind third base, just back of the Potashers' dugout. No souvenir baseballs found their way into the hands of spectators at Montgomery Field. Montgomery saved every ball, for all would be used again. In Carlsbad, he had a reputation for being tighter than the lid on a pickle jar.

Charles F. Montgomery grew up in Arkansas and moved to Carlsbad in 1917 to work as a bookkeeper. In 1931, he purchased an insurance agency and eventually expanded into real estate. He became one of the wealthiest men in the community, though his house on Lakeside Drive, only a block from the Pecos River, was quite modest. Montgomery had fallen in love with minor league ball as a boy. To him, the Arkansas Travelers, the mighty Travs, were God's gift to the national pastime. During the 1952 off season, Montgomery purchased the Vernon Dusters, a sagging, Class C Texas franchise that had finished forty-two games out of first place in the Longhorn League. He renamed the team the Potashers. Santa Fe Park, a nothing-fancy ballyard, already stood in Carlsbad, just east of the railroad tracks. Montgomery leased the place from the railroad and did a minimum amount of remodeling. The single amenity: one small changing room with a couple of enter-at-your-own-risk shower stalls.

Damned if the new owner was going to add on a second clubhouse to his ballpark. This forced visiting players to put on their uniforms at the Crawford Hotel in town before games and ride back to the hotel afterward in dirty, sweat-soaked, all-wool jerseys. Montgomery's one splurge in life was to travel to spring training and back each year to watch the Chicago Cubs and perhaps get a look at a future Potasher.

On the night of August 11, 1959, Chuck Tidwell showed up at Montgomery Field about six o'clock. "You're on the scoreboard, Tidwell," ordered Montgomery, who liked to shuffle his boys around. Tidwell never found a lot to like in tall, somber-looking Charles Montgomery. "He wasn't your friend," he said. "He had money and he watched that money. He would sit here in his box always wearing a dark suit, dark necktie, and dark hat. He was very businesslike and a bit of a grouch."

Montgomery's wife, Hettie, sat alongside her husband at every game. "Little itty-bitty short woman," Tidwell recalled. "Never said much."

Two hundred and fifty or so fans came to Montgomery Field that summer evening, a typical crowd for a venue that could seat twelve hundred. In what was considered just another game in a season of 126 of them, the Potashers that night faced the Odessa, Texas, Dodgers. Interest perked when those in attendance realized Odessa's pitcher, right-hander Wayne Schaper, had a 6–0 no-hitter going into the seventh inning. That all changed when Carlsbad's Gil Carter, a herculean left fielder, doubled in a run. In the ninth, with the score now 6–1, Carter came to bat once more.

He had already broken the club's home-run record that summer and would go on to hit thirty-four for the season. Carter thought Schaper might try to brush him back, punish him for busting up his hitless game. The Potasher slugger, who batted right-handed, stepped back slightly in the box. The first pitch, a fastball, came in, surprisingly, not at him but over the plate, about waist high. Years later Schaper admitted that indeed he had wanted to plunk Carter, but the pitch got away from him. Carter leaned in and swung, dispensing a warthog-like grunt as he did.

Jerry Dorbin was reporting on the game that night for the *Carlsbad Current-Argus*. Dorbin recollected a loud snorting sound and a collective "Oooh!" from those around him as the struck ball began to rise quickly. This was no cinchy pop-up or sleepy high fly. Both the left fielder and center fielder for Odessa sprinted toward the fence but soon stopped. The arc was much too substantial for the ball to drop in fair territory or to permit an outfielder to make a leaping snag at the rim of the wooden barrier. Indeed, the ball topped the fifty-foot light poles that stood just on the other side of the fence. Still soaring, the ball carried a stand of pecan trees in the backyards of residences as if they were creosote bushes. It passed handily over elongated television antennas fixed to some houses so their owners could receive a signal from what was then the closest source, El Paso, Texas, 160 miles southwest. Still speeding, the pale orb continued to wing forward until it disappeared into the desert dark.

An outside shagger immediately took off in pursuit. In his box seat, Charles Montgomery waited patiently for the ball to be brought in, his long, bespectacled face impassive.

When the game ended, and the ball was not found, Chuck Tidwell put away the scoreboard numbers in a wooden box and locked up the box. That done, he got on his bicycle and went home. "I was so young it didn't register to me how far the ball went. I didn't think it was that big a deal. And it was late, so I left." The next day, he went looking for the ball with a buddy but had no luck.

· · ·

"Tape-measure jobs." That's what sportswriters have long called blasts that land deep into upper decks or sail with ease over towering stadium walls. Of course, very few people stop what they're doing and grab a tape to see how far such shots have gone. Bill West, the Carlsbad-Odessa game's official scorer that night in 1959, as well as the public-address announcer, eyeballed the distance of Carter's clout and scribbled "600 feet." Clearly, a ballpark figure.

Baseball is filled with notable moments, imagined and real. American humorist James Thurber in 1941 wrote a memorable piece of short fiction titled "You Could Look It Up." Told in the vernacular, the yarn features a midget who played in one professional baseball game.

Ten years after "You Could Look It Up" was published, Bill Veeck, the showman/owner of the old St. Louis Browns, sent three-foot-seven-inch Eddie Gaedel to the plate against the Detroit Tigers. The wild-hair stunt worked. Gaedel walked on four straight pitches, was replaced by a pinch runner, and strolled right into the record books, retiring from the game with an on-base percentage of 1.000. Gaedel's plate appearance is one of the most looked-up facts in baseball.

Estimating how far home runs have traveled is replete with tales, some tall, some not. New York Yankee great Mickey Mantle hit what many believe are two of the longest home runs. On April 17, 1953, at Griffith Stadium in Washington, D.C., Mantle hoisted a pitch that journeyed approximately 540 feet, according to previous calculations and in revised data that author Jane Leavy uncovered. On September 10, 1960, at Briggs Stadium in Detroit, Mantle clubbed one 643 feet, a mark also repeatedly authenticated. Supposedly, Negro League star Josh Gibson socked a home run a whopping 911 feet. That's three end zones, end to end. Information on this feat is particularly sketchy. The baseball was said to have journeyed 668 feet in the air alone. There was no fence to clear, so the ball bounced and then rolled into oblivion.

• • •

The 1959 game in Carlsbad ended 6–2 in favor of Odessa. Meanwhile, search parties continued to look for the ball. The hunt concentrated on the front- and backyards of houses along both sides of Mariposa Street, the first street north of Montgomery Field. News about a long home run spread quickly in Carlsbad. The following day someone said that a woman who lived on Mariposa had found the baseball beneath one of her peach trees. Or maybe it was a pear tree. Someone else said a woman had brought a baseball to the park that night and presented it to Gil Carter. No one remembered these women's names, but this was known: a yard on the north side of Mariposa Street was judged to be about 650 feet away.

• • •

Gilbert Marion Carter lives outside of Topeka, Kansas, and has for most of his eighty-two years. "I'm a country boy," he said during a series of telephone conversations. "Grew up cutting wood on my granddaddy's farm. My granddaddy, Alvin Marshall, he was real strict. I had to cut wood every morning for the cook stove and the heat stove. Had to feed the animals and do all these chores before I could walk to school a half-mile away." Weekends he had to shoulder hay bales, shovel cement, and lug bricks. In the summers, he pushed a plow to garden.

By the time he reached the Carlsbad Potashers, Gil Carter stood six feet and weighed 210 pounds. His muscles were said to rise like tiers on a wedding cake.

Carter was always a long-ball hitter, always batted in the cleanup spot. Not especially nimble with the glove, he was immensely strong. Country strong. As a teen in the early 1950s, he played on a fast-pitch softball team. One game took the team to Springfield, Missouri, where, Carter said, he hit two home runs in an afternoon. A good way beyond the park's left-field fence stood a mental hospital, which had bars on the windows. Both of his home runs hit those windows. The softballs didn't shatter the glass. Instead, they became stuck in the bars.

Major league scout Tom Greenwade happened to be at that game, according to Carter, and afterward he buttonholed Carter. Greenwade, a baseball legend for half a century, possessed terrific skills at sizing up a hopeful. He had found New York Yankee greats Mickey Mantle and Bobby Richardson, among others. Why Greenwade was attending a softball game is unknown, though he did grow up nearby in Willard, Missouri, and he bird-dogged the territory from time to time. In fact, he discovered Mantle swatting baseballs out of sight in nearby Baxter Springs, Missouri. Greenwade, who died in Willard in 1986, apparently thought Carter's brute strength in softball might somehow translate to professional baseball. He invited the raw youngster to a Yankees rookie camp in Mount Kisco, New York. Carter went but soon left, he said, after hearing too many racist remarks by too many people.

Later, Carter boxed in heavyweight fights across the Midwest. Baseball tugged at him, however, and he eventually contracted with the Negro League, brought there by the esteemed Buck O'Neil. After Carter put in a few good seasons, O'Neil told the Chicago Cubs about this husky, power-packed kid who hits the ball a country mile. The Cubs signed him in 1958 and sent him to their Class D team in Carlsbad, New Mexico.

The Sophomore League, which lasted only four years, was set up to give young ballplayers, mostly promising nineteen- and twenty-year-olds, a head start on finding a place on a major league roster. At twenty-seven years of age in 1958, Gil Carter did what several players in the Sophomore League did: he fibbed about his age. Though far older than most of his Potasher teammates, he shared their dream.

• • •

Under a dog-day sun that showed no mercy, Chuck Tidwell led the way to Mariposa Street, the first street north of where Montgomery Field once stood. Tidwell said the story he always heard growing up was that the ball had landed on Mariposa. Arriving there, Tidwell positioned himself in the middle of that street, fronted on both sides by small, frame tract houses. The area was developed by Charlie Montgomery, right after World War II, and the neighborhood is still known as the Montgomery Subdivision. Tidwell peered through the trees in a backyard to the south to line up where the left-center fence of Montgomery Field would have been. Tidwell also had heard that the ball had been found in a back- or frontyard on the north side of Mariposa. He proposed that he and a visitor focus on 404 Mariposa. The owner of that house, a gray-bearded gent named Carl Vinka, answered the door. After introductions and explanations, Vinka didn't appear at all puzzled. He said, however, he wasn't living in the house in 1959. Moreover, he didn't know of any peach trees in the area and thought such trees wouldn't last long in this part of New Mexico. He suggested talking to Leon Collier, who lived four doors down, at 306 Mariposa. "Leon's been here forever."

Collier, a retired potash miner nearing ninety, was not at home. Carl Vinka had said Collier's wife was in a nursing home and that her husband visited her often. Later, when Collier was reached by telephone, he said he had lived in his house on Mariposa since 1949. He did not remember any baseballs plopping into his yard or anyone else's yard. Yes, he knew of the Potashers, but he had never gone to one of their games. With that he hung up.

· · ·

On the day following the 1959 game, Jerry Dorbin, in his column in the *Current-Argus*, Punching the Wind Bag, revealed that he too had scavenged the area around Mariposa Street the night before without success. "We'd be happy to hear from residents of Mariposa Street or the vicinity who have reliable evidence as to where the ball landed," Dorbin wrote.

No one telephoned the newspaper. Instead, more rumors about the baseball's whereabouts circulated. A youth had found the ball and sold it to a pal. A homeowner, irked by the damage the ball could have done, threw it away. The ball had caromed into a chimney and disappeared. The latter seemed especially hard to swallow, for no homes in the area had chimneys.

On August 13, 1959, the United Press International wire service issued this report: "Local observers said the ball could have gone more than six-hundred feet." Finding the baseball, the story concluded, would surely help in pinning down the precise distance.

Jerry Dorbin said that two days after the game a woman had telephoned Charles Montgomery. She knew him, for she lived in the Montgomery Subdivision. She told the owner of the Potashers that she had found a baseball in her yard and it might be the one people were looking for. Montgomery was suddenly curious. When he arrived at her house, he inspected the ball. It apparently was marked as an official minor league baseball, the kind Montgomery recycled. Then the woman showed him where she had found it: at the base of a peach tree, not a pear tree, out back. Some branches of that tree had been disturbed, the woman pointed out, probably by the descending baseball. Unripe peaches lay nearby. Other peach trees appeared unaffected.

No one wanted this story to end there. A private pilot, who kept aerial photography equipment in his small plane, offered his services to an old friend, the publisher of the *Carlsbad Current-Argus*. Jerry Dorbin, who had been a photographer in the U.S. Navy, volunteered to accompany the pilot. Dorbin snapped several photographs that showed the ballpark and the neighborhood to the north. The best photo was taken to a conference room in Charles Montgomery's office and there placed upon a long table, alongside several plats that showed all the streets in the Montgomery Subdivision.

Montgomery knew the dimensions of his ballpark as well as the proportions of every lot and every street in his housing development. An exacting man, according to Dorbin, who stood by that day and watched, Montgomery triangulated the distance from home plate to the spot in the woman's backyard. He determined the measurement to be 730 feet.

There was absolutely no reason for Montgomery to fudge that figure, Dorbin said. It wouldn't be in the man's character. Using a grease pencil, Dorbin had drawn a line of dashes on the photograph to show the ball's path.

Microfilm of the *Current-Argus* for August 1959 clearly shows Dorbin's aerial photograph and his dashes. Easily missed is the small type beneath the photo that identified the landing spot as 317 East Church Street, the street to the north of Mariposa.

For some reason, the name of the woman who found the ball never was published. Such a fact, Dorbin said, did not seem important at the time. Certainly not as important as today, when fans who scramble to scoop up a significant home-run ball are often subjects of lengthy profiles and even follow-up stories years later. According to the 1959 Carlsbad city directory, Joseph and Florence Horton lived at 317 East Church Street. No occupation is given for either. Several Google searches failed to provide further clues.

The older sections of Carlsbad are marked by alleys. These dirt paths were set down years ago so sanitation trucks could make their weekly pick-ups unnoticed. Indeed, you can see an alley beyond the outfield of Montgomery Field, still used by Mariposa homeowners. A dirt alley separated 317 East Church from the yard of the house to the south, on Mariposa. That house belonged to Leon Collier. Would Collier remember Joseph and Florence Horton? In a phone call, Collier said, clearly irritated now, that the Horton name meant nothing to him. *Click.*

The current residents of 317 East Church did not answer a knock on the door. The 2012 Carlsbad directory revealed the residents' names and phone number. Several calls to that number over several weeks did not produce a response. Nor did a letter requesting information about a baseball that more than half a century ago fell onto a peach tree in the backyard of the house where they now live.

• • •

When Chuck Tidwell learned that the baseball did not set down in a yard on Mariposa Street, as he had always believed, he asked where they found it. "Good grief!" a stunned Tidwell gasped when told the ball fell in a backyard on East Church Street. "That's gol-durn farther than I thought."

Immediately after the 1959 game, several Potasher players gathered at Ping Wong's China Lantern, a Canal Street restaurant in Carlsbad favored by the team for its inexpensive sweet-and-sour pork and cold beer. Carter, of course, was the center of attention that night. He had always been well liked by his teammates. On long, unceasing bus trips, across vacant flats and many miles into Texas, Carter would make up funny poems and recite them aloud for entertainment.

"Ol' Gilbert, he was a real nice feller," remembered Murray Hall, a first baseman on that '59 team who now resides in Taylors, South Carolina. "You may not know," Hall said, "but Gilbert hit one ball that year that went straight up and out then got lost in the dark. Nobody could find it, but they awarded him a home run anyway. You ought to ask him about it."

Carter laughed at the recollection. "That pitch came in high," he said. "Head high. Normally I wouldn't swing at something like that."

• • •

The story of the August 11, 1959, home run, though known by some in Carlsbad, remains mostly unknown everywhere else. In 1980, Jerry Dorbin wrote a freelance article about the event and *Sports Illustrated* published it. But not everyone saw that piece. The story gained legs in the late 1990s, when it began to be mentioned on the Internet.

Divorced for several years, Gil Carter lives alone. He has five children, four grandchildren, and two great-grandkids, and he remembers all their names. "It was just a regular game at the time," he said. "When I hit it, I could feel my bat give about a half-inch. The bat bent a little bit. I took a full cut, got all of it. I knew it was gone when I hit it, and I stood and watched it for about five or six seconds. I knew it was special. It went over everything." Some confusion still surrounds the ball Carter hit. Carter said that a middle-aged woman from the neighborhood came up to him the following night and gave him the ball. She had found it her yard, she said. Carter did not remember her name. Yet in a 2006 interview with an MLB.com writer, Carter said a man gave him the prized baseball. He has a ball, *the* ball, he said, in a glass case at his Topeka home, along with the bat he used—an S182 Louisville Slugger. "Skinny handle, big barrel."

No bonus from Charlie Montgomery went to Carter for hitting the home run. However, in the long-ago, home-run tradition of minor leagues of the Southwest, appreciative fans stuffed folding money into a sheet of chicken wire affixed to the backstop. Carter said he received $633 in $1 and $5 bills that night. It's believed that even Montgomery contributed a few bucks.

• • •

Gil Carter played two years at Carlsbad. His 1958 season was cut short by a broken ankle. Though he led the Sophomore League in home runs and RBI in 1959, he also had more strikeouts and errors than anyone. "With ol' Gilbert, it was all or nothing," Murray Hall said.

The Chicago Cubs were impressed enough with Carter's slugging statistics to promote him in 1960 to the Class C St. Cloud Rox of the Northern League. Carter hit twenty-one home runs during his one season in Minnesota. He said he should have had three more there. "Those cold Canadian winds, they huffed and puffed and blew back in three balls I hit out." According to Carter, he turned one of those blown-back balls into a double. He wound up on third base with another. An outfielder caught the third ball. During a road game in Winnipeg, Carter said he hit a baseball that sailed four hundred feet.

In spite of Carter's long-ball achievements, Cubs management decided he did not fit their future plans. It's quite possible the Cubs were on to his true age. There has never been a big demand in professional ball for a twenty-nine-year-old rookie. "I didn't get no breaks in baseball," Carter said. The words were not of someone bitter. They came matter-of-factly.

After St. Cloud, Carter returned to Kansas. He drove a city bus in Wichita and then drove eighteen-wheelers. For a time, he played semipro baseball. While performing for the semipro Wichita Dreamliners, he said he hit a home run off Satchel Paige in Wichita's Dumont Stadium. The ball, Carter said, came to rest 430 feet away. He played slow-pitch softball, too, well into his sixties. Even at that age, he offered, he could whomp a ball, a softball, four hundred feet.

In good health, Carter is happy to relive his Potasher days and that celebrated home run. In fact, the home run sometimes appears to be his entire life. He will talk to anyone about it. Strangers often hunt him down for a chance to hear the story. "I tell any naysayers I hit a ball seven hundred feet," he said. "If they don't believe me, I tell them to get on their computer and punch up 'Gil Carter' and see what they find."

Carter has tried to get the feat into the *Guinness Book of World Records*. "I keep telling Gil that it's a lot harder to make the Guinness book than it used to be," said Jerry Dorbin, who has remained close to Carter. "You don't just fill out a piece of paper. There are a lot of hoops to go through."

Despite Charles Montgomery's meticulous calibrations, skepticism over the 730-foot mark remains. The *Minor League Encyclopedia* says the ball traveled 650 feet—on the fly. Other sources attest the record in minor league ball belongs to Joey Meyer, who in 1987 hit a 582-foot home run for the Denver Zephyrs at Mile High Stadium. Then there are those faithful polishers of the glittering crown worn by Mickey Mantle. Not a one of them wants to see Mantle's 653-foot clout tarnished by some backwater bush leaguer.

"Can't do nothing about any of that," Carter responded. "My record is what it is."

Carter spends many of his days telephoning old friends to rehash the highpoint of his baseball career. It's as if keeping in touch keeps alive what he did. Ruben Flores served as a batboy for the Potashers and that night was among those who searched for the ball. Flores said Carter calls him, incredibly, once every two weeks. What on earth does he find to say after all this time? "Oh, how am I doing, that sort of thing," Flores said.

Carter also speaks frequently to Wayne Schaper, the Odessa pitcher who served up the 1959 blast. Schaper lives in the Houston area and updates

Carter on his grandson's progress as a ballplayer. From time to time Carter checks in with Dorbin, who lives in Santa Fe. Retired from a twenty-one-year career as a stockbroker in New Mexico's capital city, Dorbin writes limericks, among other hobbies. Recently he dashed off one about the reputed longest home run:

> The length of the shot was notorious;
> The measurement really laborious.
> Seven hundred thirty feet
> Was the distance, complete
> And you could say *sic transit glorious*.

• • •

The Carlsbad Potashers played a part in three different minor leagues during their nine years of existence. The team always kept the same nickname, a rarity in those leagues. At the end of 1961, the Sophomore League, reduced to six teams, shut down. With no league for the Potashers to play in, Charles Montgomery called it quits too. For a while Montgomery Field remained in use, and one year it hosted the New Mexico High School Baseball Championships. The spot later served as a youth soccer field before a fancy new soccer complex was set up elsewhere in town.

Charles F. Montgomery died April 12, 1972. He was seventy-four. Hettie Montgomery followed six years later. The Montgomerys did not have children. What Charles Montgomery did have, among other holdings, surely were some strong memories—of a team, a ball field, and the longest-ever home run. Don't believe the last? You could look it up.

• •

VOICES: JOE CAMMARATA

1960: second baseman, left fielder, third baseman,
    Alpine Cowboys
1961: second baseman, left fielder, third baseman,
    Alpine Cowboys

A lot of stars came out of that Sophomore League. Jesús Alou had a ton of hits for Artesia and went on to the Giants. Willie Stargell was at Roswell. José Cardenal was like seventeen years old when he was in the league, but you could tell he was going to be good. He played, what? Twenty-some years in the major leagues, I think. Gene Michael, remember him? He later managed the Yankees and worked in the Yankees front office for a long time. Once upon a time he was a very good shortstop for Hobbs.

When I played mostly second for Alpine, Texas, Jim Fregosi was at shortstop. Jim didn't do that well, but he did later on. The Sophomore League was set up for young guys who signed for bonuses—you know, bonus babies. You were sent to the Sophomore League to play against guys your own age and experience, so you wouldn't get discouraged. Class D baseball. It was like today's Rookie League.

At Alpine, we played at Kokernot Field. God, what a gorgeous ballpark. There was no advertising on the walls; they were clean as a whistle. Every park you went to had signs, you know, like "Hit this sign and win a suit." Not Kokernot. I read somewhere it was called the "Yankee Stadium of Texas." Fregosi used to say Kokernot was the nicest ballpark he'd ever played in.

For a kid from Boston, Alpine, Texas, was like something you saw in a John Wayne movie. Blink and you'll miss it. It was that little. There was nothing there but desert and cactus. The majority of the population was Mexicans. There was a college, but Alpine was away from things, I'll say that. That's Big Bend country. Pretty but desolate. Nearby was Marfa, Texas. That's where they filmed *Giant* a couple of years before I got there.

Alpine was part of the Red Sox chain. Mel Parnell, the Boston great when I was growing up, was the manager at Alpine when I was there. I heard Norm Cash and Gaylord Perry played at Alpine way back, but that was when Alpine had a semipro team.

This guy, Herbert Kokernot, owned a big ranch and the team and the ballpark. A millionaire easy. Each year he threw a barbecue and we got to meet him. He was about sixty then. Great guy. He used to drive around in a gold Lincoln Continental with big steer horns on the hood. He wore a white jacket and had long hair. His ranch was something like thirty square miles.

Mr. Kokernot had wanted the players to live on the ranch and pay nothing, but the Red Sox said no. None of the other teams could do that and the Red Sox wanted everything to be on the up and up. I wound up sharing a small cottage with a couple of other players. It was out near this steakhouse on the edge of town.

There was nothing to do at night in Alpine. Nada. Not even miniature golf. There was a movie house, with a new movie every week or two. Most of us guys weren't old enough to drink anyway. I stayed in and wrote letters home. On Sunday, I went to Mass with the Spanish players at a church across from the railroad tracks. Beautiful church. I didn't understand a word, nada. But I knew what was going on.

The ballpark, that's what I remember. It was immaculate. It was supposed to be modeled after Chicago's Wrigley Field. This was my first year in pro ball and I had never seen anything like it. Kokernot had a crew that did nothing but take care of the park. There was a warning track in the outfield. I don't know if any other minor league park had that. If the grounds were wet, supposedly a helicopter was used to dry them. It was 330 down the lines, 415 in center. The walls, they were made of these rocks from a nearby quarry. The walls were about thirty feet high. Down in right field there was a place you could park your car and watch the game. Like a drive-in theater. Wrought iron and tile were everywhere. Here's something strange. The clubhouse didn't have any amenities. Basically, a shower and lockers. No whirlpools like they have today. It was like you were bivouacking in the army.

The first year I was there we traveled in an old bus. The second year, an airport limousine. We took some long trips, let me tell you. Alpine is near nothing. It's about five hundred miles to Albuquerque. Seven, eight hours to get there. We played in a lot of places that were dumps. Carlsbad was a dump. The fence at Artesia was falling over. In Hobbs, you needed a flashlight to see the ball. The lighting in our ballpark was top shelf.

When the Sophomore League died, the Sox moved me up to their Class C team in Pocatello, Idaho. The Pioneer League. It had rained during the day of one game there, and as I rounded first, my spikes got caught in the mud. I tore a muscle in my right thigh. A doctor told me, "You'll be lame if you keep playing baseball." So I quit. I became a freight conductor on the railroad for forty years. I never saw Alpine again. No need, really. I had seen it all before.

· ·

1946: pitcher, Lubbock Hubbers
1947: pitcher, Lubbock Hubbers

Bill Serena had a better year in 1947 than Bauman or Crues. He was one of the stars on the Lubbock team. An infielder, he hit fifty-seven home runs in 1947 and led all of professional baseball with that number. In the playoffs that season, he added thirteen more. So he had seventy in all. If you hit a home run at home, a clothing store in Lubbock would give you a pair of pants. Serena had plenty of pants to give to us teammates. He got a lot of money from the screen, too—fence money that he would stick in a pillowcase. One night after I pitched, Serena got close to $400. A fan yelled, "Herky, you ought to get half of that." So Serena divided the money with me.

That's what I was called, "Herky." People have always called me Herky. I was taking a Greek class in prep school and the teacher asked me to talk about Hercules. Suddenly the class ended. I stood up and flexed my bicep and said, "Just call me 'Herky.'" I am eighty-eight years old and I'm still called that.

I was still a student at Concordia Seminary in St. Louis when I went down to Lubbock in July 1946. Detroit owned my contract; I had signed with them the year before. Concordia is a Lutheran Church school—Missouri Synod—and I was studying for the ministry. My father was a Lutheran minister. You can imagine what players called me in Lubbock. "Pitchin' Parson," "Squeakin' Deacon," "Holy Thrower." You name it.

When I got to Texas I was twenty years old. It was hot and dry, with low humidity. My curve didn't break as well. I stayed with it and finished ten and six that year. After the season I went back to Missouri to continue my studies.

In 1947, I did better. One game I struck out nineteen, a league record. Everyone did better that year. We had picked up some pretty good players and we showed right away how improved we were. Though we were only Class C, we became one of the great minor league teams of all time. At least that's what I've heard. The Lubbock Hubbers. Hubbers because Lubbock was the "hub" city on the South Plains of West Texas. We were winning every other day, it felt like. By the time the season

ended, we had ninety-nine wins. We lost fewer than half that number.
Nobody could stop us, not even in the playoffs.

Serena had almost two hundred RBI in 1947, if I remember. Just an
outstanding year. He went on to play for the Cubs. But there were other
guys, too. Seven or eight players on our team batted more than .300.
Our pitching was strong as well. I won nineteen games, counting one in
the playoffs. Everybody on the staff finished in double figures for wins.
I had two different curves. I threw a two-seamer and a four-seamer.
The four-seamer broke further, and the two-seamer broke sharply. I
threw a slider and also two fastballs. My two-seamer went faster, my
four-seamer rose.

I didn't like all the cursing that went on in Lubbock. It got worse as
I rose higher in baseball. Guys had the same two adjectives and that
was all they used, over and over. Swearing is part of baseball, I'm well
aware. I tried to tune it out.

We won a lot of games in 1947 by stealing signs off the other team.
For instance, the catcher might not be closing his legs enough. Or a
shortstop would move over to his left if the pitcher was going to throw a
curve to a right-handed batter.

We were a smart team. Jackie Sullivan was our manager, and I respected him. He played second base. He used me a lot to try to figure
out other teams signals. Sullivan said, "Herky, go sit in the stands and
figure out what he is throwing." I saw that the guy blew up his cheeks
as he was about to throw a fastball. When he threw a curve, he put his
jaw off to the side. The other team caught on to us quickly, but that happened a lot. You tried to beat the other team by outthinking them.

We'd only give signs when a guy was in scoring position. Otherwise,
the other team would catch on what we used for our signs.

I took my golf clubs to Lubbock and I played during the day on the
city course when we were at home. When we traveled, I brought my
clubs along. I played at Albuquerque, Clovis, Abilene—all the places
with a public golf course. We went by bus. There was a long seat in the
back on which you could stretch out on. For road trips, the player who
was pitching the next night got to have that seat. It came with a pillow.
One night Bill Serena thought he should have it. He'd just played another great game and was the best hitter on the team, after all.

Eventually I moved up—to Double A and Triple A. In Lubbock, you
had maybe one or two really good players on a team. In Double A or
Triple A, you had good guys at every position. You had to know to throw

at different speeds or they'd kill you. In 1948, my contract with Detroit was declared illegal by the baseball commissioner because Detroit had too many players under contract. I signed with the New York Yankees, but in 1950 I was drafted from the Yankees by the Boston Red Sox. The following year, 1951, I went up to Boston. I was not going to play that year; I was going to finish my education. I had come down with a sore arm. When I finally was able to throw, I relieved. I got into four games with Red Sox, a little more than three innings.

Even so, I was on the Red Sox. That meant I was invited to the one hundredth anniversary of Fenway Park in 2007. The Red Sox flew my wife and me to Boston. Two hundred and twenty former Red Sox players showed up. I was with Boston not quite a year. There were about fifty people behind me in terms of service. One guy had been in the majors only twelve days. I was the fourth oldest. I was the only one of those four who was able to walk out on the field. The others, like Johnny Pesky and Bobby Doerr, they were pushed out in wheelchairs.

It took me four years to finish my last two years of seminary. But after baseball, I had something to go to—a career. A lot of guys didn't plan ahead. I spent thirty-six years in the ministry. I built Lutheran churches in South Carolina and in California. I spent twenty-one years building a church in St. Louis. People would tell their friends, "That's Herky's church."

CHAPTER THREE

Storm on the Way

The harsh, unnerving honking of a siren. That's what Glenn Burns re-membered most. A cacophonous, air raid–like warning, the noise con-tinuing for several minutes that afternoon. Something is wrong, thought Burns, the left fielder for the San Angelo Colts.

A native of New Salem, Pennsylvania, Burns, brawny and bull-necked, had a ball game to play that night, Monday, May 11, 1953. He looked for-ward to it. On Sunday afternoon, the day before, against the Carlsbad Potashers, Burns had slammed two home runs over the left-center wall of Guinn Field. His Colts were due to play the visiting, league-leading Potashers again that night. Burns couldn't wait to get started. Then that terrible siren went off.

"Mary, my wife, she was scared, real scared," Burns recalled. "We turned on the radio and somebody was saying a tornado was coming right at us, right at San Angelo."

• • •

If you played baseball in the leagues that stretched across the Southwest, you got used to weather extremes. Winds lashed with such punch they would grab short, piece-of-cake fly balls and gust them into triples. Hail-stones that were not quite baseball-sized clumps of bullet-hard ice would send players and fans fleeing for shelter. Nasty dust storms could fill your ears, nose, and mouth with grit and turn the lenses of your eyeglasses into sandpaper. In 1953, swirling sand squalls wiped out all opening day play in the Longhorn League in Texas and in New Mexico. Early April blizzards in the higher elevations scratched games almost every season. Come summer, the heat could be wilting. Officials canceled a contest between Midland and Vernon, Texas, on July 22, 1951. The temperature at game time was 104 degrees.

Lightning was as familiar as yesterday. On April 28, 1950, a bolt struck Pampa Oilers catcher Jim Martin during a game at Abilene. The jolt knocked his mask twenty feet past the pitcher's mound. Martin received a hefty shock but recovered to play the following night. Several days of drubbing rain in May 1951 brought severe flooding to northwest Texas and washed out games in Pampa, Amarillo, and Borger.

News of a tornado was a constant. But those sorts of tempests always occurred somewhere else, it seemed. Until that Monday in May, no one recalled a twister touching down in Tom Green County, Texas, and certainly never before, during or after a professional baseball game.

There were omens about this one in 1953, to be sure. Howling dust storms with winds up to fifty miles per hour had whipped the Texas Panhandle late Saturday, May 9, and more of the same were said to be headed in the general direction of San Angelo. Such disturbances, however, had a history of being fickle. They often petered out and went elsewhere, never to be seen again.

Even so, many San Angeloans wanted some kind of lesser storm because the city needed rain. During the drought-stricken Texas of the early 1950s, scattered showers had sat at the top of ten thousand prayer lists. Droughts had kept the parched land dry as a stick, and by 1953, 75 percent of Texas was experiencing record low rainfall.

Rain requests aside, San Angelo had been the target of so few tornados that nobody really gave much attention to the possibility of one occurring this May. Vicious tornados belonged to the north shoulders of Texas, to Wichita Falls and to those places that hugged Oklahoma. Not here, not in west-central Texas.

Tracking tornados in the 1950s was nowhere near as sophisticated as it is these days. Nonetheless, San Angelo had some years before installed a warning system—the jarring klaxon that troubled Glenn Burns. The city tested the siren every month or so, but because this was Burns's first year with the Colts, he had never heard it before.

• • •

The notion that a tornado might be in store for San Angelo did not particularly resonate in the mind of *San Angelo Standard-Times* sports columnist Bob Milburn. His column on Sunday morning, May 10, was all about the game that would take place that afternoon at Guinn Field. The Carlsbad Potashers, who had joined the Longhorn League that season, were not only playing superb baseball but also drawing a great number of fans at home. Much of the latter had to do with the excitement of acquiring an organized baseball team in Carlsbad. The *Carlsbad Current-Argus* treated the new team as if it were the Seventh Wonder. Win or lose, the daily headlines set atop baseball stories in the newspaper were the type size you generally found only during world wars. That rush of enthusiasm had carried the Potashers into first place on May 10.

"The Potashers haven't limited their power just to the field of play," Milburn wrote. "The Carlsbad fans have been storming the gate and for the first in many years San Angelo may have a serious contender for the season attendance lead."

The forecast for Monday, May 11, was thunderstorms and possible tornados for San Angelo and surrounding communities. Weathercasters had said similar things before Sunday afternoon's game. Not a droplet of rain had fallen, and the Colts ran over the Potashers, 13–4. That's the game in which Burns hit his two home runs at Guinn Field. San Angelo had pounded out fifteen hits that afternoon. The team wanted to stay on a roll this night and catch up with Carlsbad in the standings.

● ● ●

Glenn Burns is something of an odd duck. He quit pro ball early in his life to mine coal. Two months later he decided coal mining was too dangerous and he returned to the diamond. And yet after he hung up his spikes, he took a job in a dynamite plant.

Firmly fixed in the lower echelons of baseball, Burns hit 196 home runs and had a .337 lifetime batting average in nine seasons, most of those with Class C teams. In addition to playing for San Angelo, Burns put in time with Lamesa, Abilene, Wichita Falls, and Midland. As a Midland Indian, he batted .400 in 1955. Midland then attempted to sell him to the Ponies of Plainview, Texas. Peddle a .400 hitter? Midland team officials said he was error prone and couldn't bunt a lick. Burns said he wasn't fast afoot, but he got to most fly balls. And he was sure he bunted on base several times that season. One story had it that Burns refused to go along with the sale because at Plainview someone told him you had to split your home-run money. When the sale fell through, Burns reportedly was to go to Albuquerque, but Albuquerque, he said, never contacted him. Whatever the truth may be, Burns at age twenty-six did not play baseball again.

Strange as his story seems, what happened to Burns was not that unusual back in the low minor leagues. Young men could be hard to reach,
especially in the off season. Maybe they were picking tomatoes and living in a rooming house. Without e-mail, cell phones, or any phones at all,
communication with a player broke down now and then. Suddenly a player
found himself without a team and without an explanation.

Back in New Salem, Burns had never seen crazy weather, aside from
a winter blizzard now and then. He spent his first year in the Southwest
in the East Texas League, with the Longview Texans. There Burns met
his wife, Mary. She was a waitress at the Hollywood Café and he was a
ballplayer with time on his hands. "I think I got about $300 a month," he
recollected. "I had money in my pocket."

· · ·

Sometime on the afternoon of May 11, the Burnses heard a radio weather
report say that tornados were now more than a possibility. Indeed, word
came that a snarling storm extended along a line from San Angelo to Waco,
Texas. Just after 4:00 p.m., Burns, who lived a mile or so from the ballpark, went next door to see his neighbor, with whom he shared a duplex.
First baseman Carlos Galina, from Mexico and called "Charlie" by his
teammates, didn't know what was going on either. Apprehension gnawed
at both men. The siren was no longer being tested but was blowing for real.
Neither Burns nor Galina had been through a tornado. They had no idea
what it would be like or what they should do. They finally decided to stay
home.

The Carlsbad Potashers, meanwhile, were staying in the five-story Naylor
Hotel in downtown San Angelo. They were worried too. "We all were won-
dering what the heck was going to happen," remembered Carlsbad's second
baseman, Carroll "Goldie" Gholson, who now lives in Bivins, Texas. Gholson played eight seasons in the minors, three in Carlsbad and one each in
Vernon and Amarillo. "I kind of miss it, but not that awful day."

The San Angelo tornado—today it would be classified an F4, or vio-
lent storm—hit with a thunderclap close to 4:15 p.m. The twister whipped
through a residential area on the northwest edge of the city. It ravaged a
two-square-mile middle-income neighborhood known as Lake View.

"It got real dark and then it got real rainy," Bob Gregg said. A San Angelo southpaw, Gregg had pitched Sunday afternoon and won, raising his
record to four and one on the season. On Monday afternoon he drove to

downtown San Angelo with his two-year-old son Michael in the seat beside him. It was the Greggs' habit to attend all home games as a family. To do that, Gregg, with little Michael in tow, would pick up his then-wife Jean after she finished work at a downtown insurance company. Gregg parked the family's Buick sedan that day and waited for Jean to come out of her building. Even in the presence of a tornado, Bob Gregg, at twenty-three, had only one thing on his mind: playing baseball. He turned on the car radio to get a weather update. As he did, people began coming out of buildings and looking up wide-eyed at the black sky. "It was all pretty eerie," Gregg remembered.

The moment Jean Gregg got in the car, the rain fell as if dropped from a dump truck. The Greggs managed to work their way to the ballpark anyway. At that point, Bob Gregg was not sure if the tornado had hit the ballpark. When they arrived, Guinn Field was standing. Several ballplayers and media people stood outside the park under a shelter from the pouring rain. The Greggs sat in their car and passed the time. After about an hour, Gregg left his wife and small son in the car and went into the clubhouse. It was about 6:30 p.m. That's when he heard officially that the game had been called off. Guinn Field had not been damaged, but the incessant heavy rain had left lakes across the diamond: the team did not have tarpaulins big enough to cover the field. The Greggs headed off for their rental house.

• • •

To the north of San Angelo lay North Concho Dam, a seven-mile-long earthen fortress that sat directly in the path of the tornado. Going over that dam had taken the strength out of the tornado and made it go elsewhere, initially to the west. The dam, still in the process of being built, in essence turned the tornado away from downtown and Guinn Field. But it stayed long enough in the city to cause serious damage.

On Tuesday morning, May 12, a National Guard spokesman announced that the public would now be allowed to enter the Lake View area, hit hardest by the storm. Pat McLaughlin, the manager of the Carlsbad Potashers, rounded up the team's bus driver and any interested players who might want to inspect the scene of greatest destruction and give help where needed.

McLaughlin had pitched in thirteen games in the major leagues over a three-year, up-and-down span. Finally, when he wasn't wanted in the majors again, he returned to the minors for good and became a lifer. A native

Texan, man-sized and square-jawed handsome, McLaughlin looked as if he belonged in a John Ford movie. On top of that, he stood out for being the rare college man—he had studied at St. Edwards University in Austin. McLaughlin pitched fifteen seasons in the minors and never complained. He managed in the minors for six years. He loved the game, no matter the level, and he loved his fellow man even more. McLaughlin dearly wanted to do something for the people of San Angelo. San Angelo remembered his offer. Two years after the tornado, the Colts hired him to be their manager.

"The wreckage was bad," said Goldie Gholson, who rode in the bus to the site with several Carlsbad teammates. "I saw a car that was up on its end leaning against a tree. A semi had a load of hay, and about half that hay was off the truck still stacked on the ground. A horse looked like it was trying to get to its foal. I don't know how the horse got there unless the tornado moved it around. I am eighty-two years old. I felt lucky then and lucky now to be standing above ground."

• • •

The first sighting of the tornado had been at Chester's Package Store on the Big Spring Highway shortly after 2:00 p.m. The storm's path originally was west of the city. Then it moved south and east across the dam. There it whirled through the Rocket Drive-In Theater, the state fairgrounds, and the Lake View School before veering due east, toward Waco. One of the first damage estimates was $3,000, but that of course rose within minutes and soon climbed to $100,000. An early aerial photograph showed the grounds of the popular Rocket Drive-In, built in 1948. The screen and snack bar had been swept clean by the tornado. The big parking lot that once held rows and rows of car speakers lay blank as a sheet.

The death toll for San Angelo in the beginning was said to be 8. Then 10, then 13, then back to 10 again as some of the missing turned up, then finally 13. More than 120 people were injured, but that figure grew too, to almost 160. Scores were left homeless. The storm demolished 288 frame houses, and losses to these homes amounted to almost $1.5 million.

Ninety-six other houses were 70 percent destroyed, for a total loss of $300,000. In all, 143 vehicles were gone, including 29 trucks. A million more dollars in damages to businesses and a brick school whose roof collapsed brought the final losses to $3.2 million.

That the tornado of 1953 missed San Angelo's downtown was a blessing, for surely much of the city would have been laid to waste. Waco, however, was not so fortunate. When the twister left San Angelo, it covered the 190 miles to Waco briskly, as if summoned by the devil.

Downtown Waco took the brunt of the storm's fury. Buildings in a two-mile-square area were lifted by the funnel cloud and tossed back like toys to join mountains of broken bricks, splintered wood, and crushed plaster. Tons of glass shot through the air like glimmering darts.

Within a minute or two, Waco's business district became a giant pile of rubble. Close to two hundred buildings were demolished. When the dust cleared, the city bore strong resemblance to Dresden, the German capital left in ruins from bombing raids near the end of World War II. A total of 114 people in Waco were killed and 597 injured. Damage estimates came in at more than $51 million.

Not that San Angelo escaped suffering. The casualty list was published in Tuesday's *San Angelo Evening Standard,* and specifics were provided when known:

Debra Ann Baer, five months, cuts on head and body, also shock.
Ben McNeal, head injury and fractured leg, critical condition.
Mrs. W. W. Adney, 420 East Fortieth Street, head injury, very poor
   condition.
Mrs. T. F. Yount, Route Four, heart attack.

Stories of those who died also appeared, with no details spared:

Mrs. T. F. Hall, 59, was found on the Electric Hatchery Road. Her
husband is in the Shannon Hospital in a critical condition. Mrs. Hall's
body was found along the roadside. It was not certain whether her
home was completely demolished or not. Johnson's Funeral Home,
which picked up the body, said Mrs. Hall was dead when found. Mrs.
Hall's neck was broken.

• • •

What can a sportswriter find to say when surrounded by such sadness? Darnell Peacock's *San Angelo Evening Standard* Sporting Comment column for Tuesday, May 12, put things in perspective. Peacock, who generally wrote six-hundred-word pieces, turned out fewer than one hundred words. "Sports columns," he wrote "are quite often pains in the neck, especially to the writer. The reader (bless him) has the advantage of being able to ignore them. Sportswriting can also be full of emptiness. Following Monday's di-saster at Lake View was a prime example. At such a time, and following it, sports events are really very minor. The great thing was the heroism and cooperation of the many local and area people when disaster struck. So with your permission, we, too, will ignore 'Sporting Comment' today."

• • •

The rescue efforts and relief aid came almost immediately to San Angelo. Everyone, it seemed, wanted to help. National Guard troops, Marine Corps reservists, and Red Cross workers slogged through deep mud and flooded streets with flashlights in hand. Searches through the debris went on through the night until dawn.

Pat McLaughlin had been unable to get through to Carlsbad by tele-phone. He wanted to report what things looked like from the seat of the team bus. When he finally obtained a working phone line, he called the *Carlsbad Current-Argus* newspaper. "It missed us by one mile," he told the sports edi-tor. "We got the rain part of it and all, but the big wind didn't get us."

McLaughlin told the newspaper that riding the team bus that toured the tornado's worst site was an experience he would not soon forget. "I saw sheep killed and houses twisted into kindling wood. Big brick houses were just flattened. The thing just knocked over the top of the schoolhouse in Lake View with lots of kids inside. We offered our services, but the air base was already there with its ambulances."

• • •

A tornado of any size and strength is no laughing matter. Yet after a week of sorrow and grieving in San Angelo, sportswriter Bob Milburn recog-nized the welcome need for a smile. In his Sport-O-Scope column for May 17, Milburn came up with this: "Seems that one of the fellows living in the Lake View area stepped away from his house or what was left it after Monday's tornado, viewed the wreckage for blocks around and then com-mented: 'Darn, there goes the ballgame tonight.'"

Baseball had resumed in San Angelo on Thursday night, May 14. The rain had finally departed, leaving behind frigid air. Only 432 fans turned out to see the Colts beat the Artesia Drillers, 4–1, at dried-out Guinn Field. Meanwhile, the Carlsbad Potashers had already arrived in Big Spring for a series there. Life in the Longhorn League went on.

• • •

Before the San Angelo–Artesia game, Jackie Price put on a show for those brave enough to sit through the damp chill. Price's place in the small circle of what might be called minor league entertainers was overshadowed by Max Patkin and Al Schacht. All three were anointed "Crown Prince of Baseball," but Patkin and Schacht, who specialized in slapstick zaniness and comedic mimicry for minor league fans, are far better remembered. Patkin is best known for having a cameo in the popular *Bull Durham*, considered the quintessential minor league baseball film. When Schacht wasn't performing on the road or appearing on *The Ed Sullivan Show* on television, doing his imitations of famous baseball players and managers, he made his name as a restaurateur in New York City.

Jackie Price did not deliberately seek laughs. Instead, he filled his act with amazing feats. For instance, he would throw three different baseballs simultaneously to three different catchers and all the balls would land in the gloves that Price said they would. With one man waiting on the pitcher's mound and another covering second base, Price would stand at home plate and throw two balls with one hand, one going to the pitcher and the other to the second baseman. Both were perfect throws. Price's forte, a stunt that always drew the loudest applause, was to hang upside down from a trapeze erected over home plate. He would ask a pitcher to fire fastballs toward the plate. Somehow, Price would hit those pitches, often for long distances. "I hit nearly .300 this way," he told San Angelo Colts fans. "That's better than I was ever able to do upright in my playing days."

Price had been a respectable minor league shortstop, playing six seasons, mostly in Double A ball. He wound up batting .267. In 1946, a stint with the Triple A Oakland Oaks of the Pacific Coast League earned him a call-up from the Cleveland Indians. Cleveland kept him for a week or so and then let him go. Price's playing days were over. Out of the professional ranks, he yearned to stay in the game somehow. That's when he came up with his one-of-a-kind routine of circus catches, phenomenal throws, and singular batting displays. Well remembered is Price shooting a baseball out of an air gun then jumping into a Jeep and racing after the ball to eventually snare it. Beginning in 1946, Price drove forty thousand miles each summer, back and forth across the country, to minor league ballparks large and small, many of them in the Southwest. Now and then he would take his show to Canada and Cuba. He kept up this grinding pace until 1960.

Tired of all the travel, Price settled in San Francisco, where he tended bar. The regulars there enjoyed the pourer in the flashy suit who told of catching fast-moving baseballs in his uniform shirtfront with his eyes closed. But behind the colorful neckties and wild stories was a man who had a drinking problem, which he apparently used to battle depression. On the night of October 2, 1967, Price left work and went home. There he wrapped one end of a leather belt to a light fixture and the other around his neck and hanged himself. He was fifty-four years old.

Jackie Price's fee for the San Angelo–Carlsbad game was $200, his standard charge for a Class C league contest. When the Colts' management presented him with the check, Price shook his head. He had heard all about the deaths and the destruction the tornado caused that week. He asked that the money be given to the storm's disaster fund.

• • •

A little more than a month after the tornado, Carlsbad returned for a series against the Colts. Bob Gregg pitched the first game. The contest turned out to be a tense pitcher's duel, with Gregg striking out eleven batters and Carlsbad's Marshall Epperson seventeen. In the last of the ninth inning, with the game still scoreless, San Angelo's John Tayoan reached first base on an error.

Up stepped Glenn Burns. The first ball he swung at sailed over the light pole in left field. Burns's walk-off home run gave San Angelo a thrilling 2–0 win. "The place went crazy," said Gregg, who that night pitched the only shutout of his professional baseball career. Afterward, Burns, holding the bill of his Colts cap in one hand, pulled out close to a hundred dollars from the wire screen behind home plate and dropped the cash in his cap.

Once again he had money in his pocket.

. . . .

VOICES: LARRY KELCHER

1953: pitcher, Abilene Blue Sox, Borger Gassers
1954: pitcher, Borger Gassers, Odessa Oilers, Lubbock
    Hubbers
1956: pitcher, Lubbock Hubbers, Clovis Pioneers

Those spring winds, that's what I remember. Borger, Texas, is way high up in the Panhandle. When the wind came in hard there, and someone hit a fly ball, the outfielders didn't bother to turn around. They knew it was going out.

How did I get to Borger? I was pitching for a town team, the New Athens Merchants, in Illinois in 1953. One day during a game, a guy came up to me, right out to the mound, and said, "Do you want to pitch in the minor leagues?" "Sure," I said. He said, "Then be on the train tomorrow, to Abilene, Texas."

So that's where I landed, in July of '53. I had just turned nineteen. After I pitched in my third game in Abilene, the player-manager, Hersh Martin, pulled me aside. "I just bought your contract," Skip said. "We're both going to Borger." Three weeks after I signed my first contract, I was sold!

I remembered Borger when Abilene had played there earlier that summer. I started to smell something when we were a few miles away. It was terrible; I could hardly breathe. "What's that smell?" I asked. "Oil," someone said. "Gas," someone else said.

For better or for worse, I was now a Borger Gasser.

When we had stayed there before, as visitors, we stayed at the Borger Hotel, a big red-brick building, the tallest building in the town. I remember waking up there to a noise and outside my window was an oil pump, one of those pump jacks, working away. The home team lived in the Desoto Hotel. How can I put this? It wasn't a Hilton. If you stood in the lobby, you could stretch your arms out and almost touch the walls.

Borger is all about oil and gas. There was a giant Phillips Petroleum refinery north of town. It was supposed to be the biggest refinery in the world. There were also two carbon black plants, one owned by Phillips and one by Huber, just west of town. Carbon black is a substance then used in ink and paint. The town's nickname was "Smokey City." When you'd lay out your clothes at night, they'd be black by morning. People there told me I would get used to the smell and the soot. I never did.

We had some characters at Borger. None was nuttier than Windy Eldridge. The owner of the Borger Gassers had two very attractive daughters. They always sat right behind our dugout at Huber Park. You couldn't help seeing them every time you left the dugout or came back into the dugout. Windy wanted to see a lot more of them. So what he did was drill a hole in the bottom back wall of the dugout. That way he could look right up those girls' skirts. On the road, Windy would take a corkscrew with him. He always knew what room the prostitutes were staying in our hotels. So he would ask for the room above it. He'd post someone by the elevator to be a lookout. Then in his room he would drill a hole in the floor to see all the action below. That Windy, he was crazy.

Another teammate, Patricio Lorenzo, or Pat to us, was a big strong guy and a good hitter. Pat thought he should be a great hitter. Lots of times when he struck out or grounded out, he would get mad and break his bat over his knee. Never saw anyone else do that.

One time at Borger we were playing the Plainview Ponies at their place. Plainview that year had some great hitters. Don Stokes, for instance. They called him "Pappy." He was older, I guess. Frosty Kennedy was another top hitter. He always played with a full chaw of tobacco in the side of his mouth. His sleeves were cut off at the shoulders, just like Big Klu's, Ted Kluszewski. The team batting average for Plainview was over .300.

For some reason, one night the Plainview manager decided to pinch-hit for Stokes, who was leading the league in hitting. I think our skipper and theirs dreamed this up. Plainview puts in a pinch hitter who hadn't got a hit all season. The fans are screaming and howling. Hersh goes out and tells our pitcher, "Let this guy hit the ball." On the first pitch the Plainview guy swings and misses. The crowd goes wild. He takes a second pitch down the middle. The third pitch the guy swings and barely scrapes the ball. It bounces off the face of the rubber. Their guy is running to first and our guy is making like he can't field the ball. Somehow, the Plainview batter got an infield hit. People are filling the screen behind home plate with money. Lots of money. They're even passing the hat in the stands for more money. Apparently they loved the guy. He took home $316 that night. What a haul. I was making less than that a month. Two-fifty, I think.

The sidewalks in Borger were wooden. I never had seen anything like that. The ballpark in Borger was a hoot. It was near the carbon black plant. The field had metal fences so the ball made a heck of a noise when it hit. *Bang!* There was a flag pole in dead center field, inside of the fence. If the ball hit the flagpole, it was in play.

At the end of my rookie season in pro ball, I was oh and six. Not a good beginning. Hey, when you're that young, you always think you can do better. You always think you'll be playing baseball forever.

In 1954, I reported to spring training—in Borger. Why there? Much cheaper, only way I could figure. Spring training hadn't yet finished when I found I had been optioned to the Odessa Oilers. In Odessa I got to pitch to the great Joe Bauman. That was the year that Joe hit seventy-two home runs. The first time I faced Joe, the manager told me, "Don't give him anything but junk." I struck him out. The second time up, I thought I knew better. I gave Joe a pitch right down the middle—a fastball. He hit a towering fly to deep right. You could see the ball bouncing on an asphalt parking lot far, far away. It might still be bouncing.

Few of the teams then had two clubhouses at their ballparks. When we went to Roswell, all the Odessa players changed into our uniforms in one room before we went to the ballpark. We would leave the clothes there and shower there—all done to save money for another night. That night, while we were at the ballpark, someone must have been on to us. They robbed that room. I had put sixteen dollars in my shoes and covered it with socks. It was gone.

After about a month in Odessa, I found out the Oilers had returned my option to Borger. When I arrived back in Borger, this guy said, "We've sold you to Lubbock." I asked, "Why couldn't you tell me this when I was in Odessa?" I turned around and drove down to Lubbock. When I got there, they said they no longer had room for me because I was no longer a rookie and was now on limited service. In those leagues, if you played two years, you were classified a limited-service player. After two years, you were classified a veteran. A team could only have two or three veterans play. And a team was allowed only four or five limited-service players. After that, you could have as many rookies as you wanted.

Lubbock had optioned me to Hot Springs, Arkansas, in the Cotton State League. So now I had been on three teams that season. I had not played on two of them and I was about to join my fourth team. That's how the low minor leagues operated in those days.

I was with the Hot Springs Bathers for about a month. I got in six games and had no wins or losses. Then I screwed up my back again. I had injured my back in high school by trying to throw a ball from the outfield to home plate—throwing it behind my back. Real stupid, I know. At that point Hot Springs optioned me back to Lubbock. In February 1955, I went to spring training at Midland, Texas, with the Lubbock team. After spring training, I was released. I went home to Illinois and did nothing. In 1956 I had a tryout with the Dallas Eagles of the Texas League, and they signed me to a Double A contract. Then they optioned me out to Clovis. I got in some games at Clovis until someone realized I had played professional ball for two seasons. They had never asked me. Clovis released me.

I remember calling up my mother and telling her I had been

released—again. "Get a job," she said. "But Mom," I said. "Get a job," she said. So I did. I went to work in Lubbock for Olin Matheson, the chemical corporation out of Houston. One day I noticed a poster advertising this pretty woman who was playing the organ at the Caprock Hotel in Lubbock. I went to the hotel and asked her out. We've been married for fifty-four years now.

Not a very inspiring career, I have to admit. As a pitcher, I tended toward wildness. I was six feet five inches and weighed 220 pounds. There were no speed guns then, but I think I could throw it in the mid-nineties. You would think I might intimidate batters. Trouble is I hit more guys than they hit me. I walked more people than a school crossing guard.

Bottom line, I won zero games and lost nine in three seasons. In my defense, the four teams I played with were in last place when I arrived. Then again, I didn't help any of them out of the cellar. But it was fun, really. Not every guy can say he played professional baseball. Those minor league teams shuffled me around like a piece of meat. Would I want to play on those teams again? In a New York minute.

· ·

VOICES: KAREN BLOODHART

1952: umpire's daughter, Longhorn League
1953: umpire's daughter, Longhorn League
1954: umpire's daughter, Longhorn League

I had never been in West Texas before we moved to Big Spring in 1952. I was real small then, and I announced one day that I wanted to play outside. Everybody thought I was crazy. I went outside, and in just a few minutes my legs were all scratched up from the blowing sand. Every day it seemed as if people in Big Spring, Texas, were sweeping sand out of their houses.

My father, Al Sample, always loved sports. So being an umpire seemed a natural thing for him to do. Dad grew up in a little place called Bazetta, in northeastern Ohio. Bazetta no longer exists; it's been incorporated into Cortland, which is north of Youngstown. Dad didn't play baseball, as far as I know, but he did play basketball in high school. When World War II broke out, he enlisted in the army and fought in the Battle of the Bulge, where he was wounded.

Right out of high school Dad married his sweetheart, Jeanne Hargate, and I came along in 1945. I never knew my mother; she died giving birth to me. After the war, Dad remarried and took odd jobs when he could get them. At some point in there he came up with the idea of being an umpire.

In 1949, he applied to and was accepted by Bill McGowan's Umpire School in Daytona Beach, Florida. We all went with him, meaning me and my stepmom, Leah. Bill McGowan was an umpire in the American League for more than twenty-five years. He was an impressive man, from what I heard, and was elected to the Hall of Fame. In the 1930s, he started the second umpiring school in the United States. He ran it for sixteen years, until he died in the 1950s.

When Dad graduated, the school helped him find a job in Pittsburg, Kansas, in the Kansas-Oklahoma-Missouri League, a Class D league. Soon after Dad got there, he ran into a problem. I was pretty young, but I can remember the incident. It was a game in Pittsburg. Mom—she was my stepmom but the only mother I really knew—was with me. Two women were sitting about three or four rows behind us. I remember this game as "Kill the Umpire Night." The women kept calling out to my father, "Are you blind? Do you need glasses? Were you injured in the war?"

Well, that last crack sent Mom over the top. She turned around and told the two women that the umpire was her husband and they should be quiet. I was too little to remember what the women said, or if they said anything.

About a week later, my father received a letter from the president of the Kansas-Oklahoma-Missouri League. It said something like, "If you cannot contain your wife, please leave her home." The point of the letter was, the customer is always right. Fans paid for their tickets, they can say what they want. Baseball after the war was still trying to get itself going. It needed every fan it could get.

The following season my father was sent to the Longhorn League, which was a move up from Class D to Class C. So it was a promotion, I guess. The league told umpires where they had to live. Not the house, but the town. We were told to move to Big Spring, Texas. The first Big Spring house we rented had mice. We found another house to rent. We went to all the home games in Big Spring. If a game was played in, say, Odessa or Midland, the umpires traveled together.

After a season in Big Spring, we went back to Ohio. My father could not take a year-round job because he needed the summer to umpire. We always rented houses wherever we went. So we wintered in Ohio and summered in New Mexico, which doesn't make sense if you know about weather.

The following year we moved to Artesia and to another rental house. It was in Artesia that I learned how to keep score. I was not allowed to run around the ballpark, as kids today are. I had to sit still. Dad, I think, gave me a scorebook, and people sitting near us said, "Do this, Karen, put a 'BB' here in this box for 'base on balls.' Write 'K' over there because he went down swinging. That man who just hit a triple, go ahead and mark in that box '3B.'"

I got to know Joe Bauman in Artesia. The thing I remember most about him was that he was big. Real big. I had never seen anyone that size.

One night in Artesia I remember a base runner was sliding into home plate. Dad bent down and called "Out!" in a loud voice. As Dad was saying that call, his front-teeth plate flew out of his mouth and landed in the dirt. The next day in the newspaper there was a photograph of the player sliding into home and this little headline: "He's out and they're out."

Some people who knew my father said he was called the "Whistling Umpire." Apparently, he used to whistle to himself while he umpired. It was, he told one reporter, a way to relieve the stress he felt during a game. I never knew this, but I heard that in one game fans threw rocks at my father. Listen, in our little corner of the state, in places like Hobbs and Carlsbad, there are some real angry people.

Maybe Dad whistled to control his temper. He had a terrible temper, in fact. He'd always been this way, as long as I could remember. The thing is, you don't want to have a temper if you're an umpire. In high school, he was playing an important basketball game that would lead to the state championships. A member of the opposing team was at odds with Dad, elbowing him and pushing him. Dad couldn't take any more. He turned around and decked the young man. My grandfather sat in the top of the bleachers and saw it all, Dad told me. Dad walked off the court. He'd had enough.

Dad was able to hold his temper on the ball field. He had an unusual sense of fairness. That kind of worked against him in his second year at Artesia. Umpire scouts were in the stands that game and Dad knew it. They were there to check him out, to see if he should be elevated on up to a higher level. I can recall this well. A base runner was on first base, and when a ball was hit, the runner took off, passed second base, and headed for third. Only two umpires were working those games. My father was behind home plate and the other umpire was back of second base. My father ran up to third base to make the call and gave the safe sign. The other umpire called the runner out. Though Dad had a temper, he didn't argue. It was his call to make and he was maybe two feet away from third. He knew the scouts were in the stands and he didn't want to make a scene. So he let the other ump's call hold up. After the game, the scouts told him, "You didn't stand your ground."

That was the beginning of the end for Dad as an umpire. He was almost thirty-three years old. That was too old to be where he was, even then. He didn't want to spend another year or two in Class C. I don't think he was having any fun at it, either. Baseball in any capacity should be fun—not stressful and not work. After all, umpires are the ones who say, "Play ball!"

Dad knew a man in Roswell named Harry James. Not the trumpet player, but the owner of the Roswell Laundry. Harry was a huge baseball fan, and he helped Dad get a job in charge of cadet services at the New Mexico Military Institute. Dad would be over the post office, the laundry, the bowling alley, the PX. He retired from the institute in 1983 as a full colonel. Dad died in 1992. He was coming back from Meals on Wheels, where he volunteered, and drove his car into a tree. He didn't have a stroke, but they did find a blood clot on his brain. The accident left him semicomatose for nine months, with only slight communication. He was seventy.

During his time at the institute, Dad refereed a lot of basketball games. As far as I know, that game at Artesia was the last time he umpired baseball.

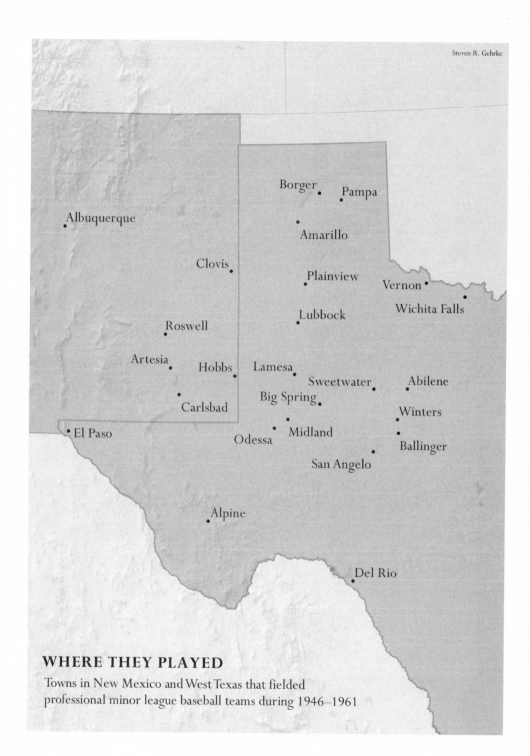

Steven R. Gehrke

Albuquerque

Borger

Pampa

Amarillo

Clovis

Plainview

Vernon

Wichita Falls

Lubbock

Roswell

Artesia

Hobbs

Lamesa

Sweetwater

Abilene

Big Spring

Carlsbad

Winters

El Paso

Odessa

Midland

Ballinger

San Angelo

Alpine

Del Rio

WHERE THEY PLAYED

Towns in New Mexico and West Texas that fielded
professional minor league baseball teams during 1946–1961

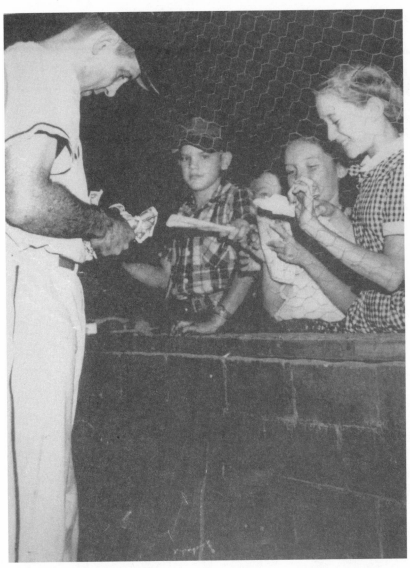

Joe Bauman played only three years (1954–1956) for the Class C Roswell Rockets. During that time, fans of all ages and from across eastern New Mexico and West Texas came to see him bat—at his home field of Fair Park Stadium or at ballparks on the road. (Jim Waldrip collection.)

A shoulder injury caused Bob Crues, who had started out as a
good pitcher, to turn himself into a remarkable hitter. In 1948,
he batted in 254 runs in 140 games for the Amarillo Gold Sox.
The major league mark, set in 1930 in 156 games, is 191. (Crues
family collection.)

ARTESIA DRILLERS — 1953

TOP ROW— Left to Right: Earl Perry, Gen. Mgr. — Joe Bauman, Mgr. — Joe Fortin, Len Royle, Bill Haley, Bob Presley.
SECOND ROW—Left to Right: Jackie Wilcox, Les Mulcahy, Paul Halter, Vince DiGiantomasso, Andy Alonso, Joe Calderon.
THIRD ROW—Left to Right: Pat Monahan, Fidel Alvarez, Mike Carrier (Batboy), Armando Sanchez, Herminio Reyes.

Before he joined the Roswell Rockets in 1954, Joe Bauman (*standing second from left*) played the previous two seasons with the Artesia Drillers. Bauman was brought to Artesia by Earl Perry, the fellow wearing the straw hat. With Artesia, Bauman served notice of what was to come when, in 1952 and 1953, he hit fifty and fifty-three home runs, respectively. (Jim Waldrip collection.)

(across) In 1946 and 1947, the Amarillo Gold Sox sent to the plate two exceptional minor league sluggers in Joe Bauman and Bob Crues. Inconsistent pitching kept the Gold Sox from winning the championship those two seasons. In this 1947 photo, Crues is standing fourth from left and Bauman stands second from right. (Steve Lagomarsino collection.)

SPORTS

SCREEN IN ARTESIA, N. MEX. AFTER HITTING RECORD-BREAKING 70th HOMER, JOE BAUMAN FILLS HIS FISTS WITH MONEY PUSHED AT HIM BY FANS

When a batter or pitcher did particularly well during a game, obliging fans in the Southwest minor leagues upheld a time-honored tradition of sticking folding money in a screen behind home plate. Few ball players picked more money out of the screens than Joe Bauman. It wasn't unusual for Bauman on some nights in 1954, the year he clubbed a record seventy-two home runs, to pull out several hundred dollars. (Jim Waldrip collection.)

During the three seasons he played for the Roswell Rockets and after he retired from baseball, Joe Bauman owned and ran a Texaco gas station on West Second Street in Roswell. Many fans pulled in just to shake his hand or to get his autograph. (Jim Waldrip collection.)

Dorothy Ramsey stood a foot and half shorter than Joe Bauman when the two began dating in high school in Oklahoma City in the 1930s. Back then as well as later, Dorothy was always Joe's biggest fan. (Jim Waldrip collection.)

Few pitchers relished seeing Joe Bauman in the on-deck circle. Though he batted left-handed and pulled many pitches over numerous right-field fences, on occasion he sliced baseballs past opposite-field fences. In nine minor league seasons, Bauman hit 337 home runs. (Jim Waldrip collection.)

During the late 1940s, Bob Crues could put palpable fear into opposing pitchers. In 1948, Crues socked sixty-nine home runs, which then tied the record for professional baseball. Joe Bauman, Crues's former teammate at Amarillo, broke that mark in 1954 while playing with the Roswell Rockets. (Crues family collection.)

An infantryman in Europe during World War II, James Heller in 1947 and 1948 won a total of thirty games for the Amarillo Gold Sox. (Jim Heller collection.)

In August 2005, Roswell's Fair Park Stadium was renamed in honor of one of minor league baseball's greatest stars, who also happened to be a longtime resident of Roswell. (Toby Smith photo.)

(right) Charles F. Montgomery is considered the godfather of baseball in Carlsbad, New Mexico. Montgomery, who ran real estate and insurance businesses in southeastern New Mexico, owned and operated the Carlsbad Potashers, from 1953 to 1961, through three different minor leagues. (*Carlsbad Current-Argus*.)

(below) Carlsbad Potasher players share batting tips prior to the 1957 opener. *Left to right*: Eddie Reed, Bill Williams, and Roy Niccolai. Reed wound up hitting .300 over nine seasons in the minor leagues. (Nearlovingsbend.net.)

CHAPTER FOUR

Base Brawls

Fistfights are in the blood of baseball players, and periodically that blood is spilled. For some reason, ballplayers like to tangle. An errant pitch or a testy remark can serve as battle cries for entire rosters of grown men. Those who did a hand's turn in the bottommost leagues of the Southwest took such cues to heart.

When the Rawlings gloves came off, the roundhouse punches took off. Fists flew on the pitcher's mound, at home plate, in the stands, and in the dugout. There were no water coolers in the 1940s and 1950s, but there were drinking fountains—on the field. On June 12, 1955, in a fit of rage, Albuquerque Dukes outfielder Larry Segovia kicked a water fountain next to the dugout so hard he broke a pipe at the base of the device. Soon a geyser rose sixty feet and soaked fans in the adjacent stands. It took almost five minutes to shut the water off.

There have been more bench-clearing brawls in baseball than you can count, sending more ballplayers down, some for the count. Nowhere is it stipulated, but brawls must always be bench-*clearing* affairs. Almost never will you read, hear, or speak of, say, a bench-evacuating brawl.

Such slugfests are not under the proprietorship of Major League Baseball. A memorable fracas in the leagues took place on June 12, 1951, a warm Tuesday night. While that uproar can hardly be compared to the bloody warfare then going on seven thousand miles away, on the scarred hillsides of Korea, the Albuquerque free-for-all provided action that the fans present had not paid for.

The tussle had ballplayers seeing stars and stars seeing ballplayers. It had limbs that required stitches and fans who left in stitches. The fight—actually, there were two mix-ups that evening—sent journalists reaching for *Roget's Thesaurus*. Employed in newspaper accounts over the next few days were the following synonyms: "donnybrook," "clash," "scrimmage," "rumble," "rumpus," "ruckus," and "rhubarb."

The Albuquerque Dukes and the visiting Abilene Blue Sox had, as the old saw goes, no love lost between them. With five hundred miles separating the cities, members of the two teams in the West Texas–New Mexico League never were pen pals. Only a month before the June 1951 brawl, a messy dustup occurred when the teams played each other in Texas. Umpires that night gave three players the heave-ho for fighting. On two different occasions, the Dukes' second baseman, Dom Chiola, attempted to use a bat on Abilene pitcher Jim Melton's head. Abilene's manager, Hack Miller, was also thrown out of the game. Twice. After his first ejection for arguing with an umpire, Miller changed into street clothes and slipped back in to Blue Sox Stadium. Spotted in the stands, this time Miller took his leave in the company of two policemen. The Dukes won by the lopsided score of 16–3, which may help to explain some of the outbursts.

The feud between Albuquerque and Abilene had been simmering for a lot longer than one month. In June 1950, the two teams met in Abilene, an encounter the *Albuquerque Journal* described as a "near riot." Toward the end of that contest, the plate umpire asked Dukes pitcher Steve Lagomarsino to exit the premises. Declining to do so, Lagomarsino then "laid hands upon umpire Frank Crain," according to the Associated Press. More than likely Lagomarsino was not trying to impart a spiritual healing, for the two men proceeded to punch each other—the blows euphemistically described as "pokes" by the wire service. If spectators were keeping score, the round went to Lagomarsino and the game to Abilene, 12–8.

Later, during that same 1950 season, the Dukes swept a three-game series from the visiting Blue Sox, amassing twenty-four hits in one of those contests. Piling on was prevalent in that hitter's league. But that night's score and the headline the next morning in the *Albuquerque Journal* displayed an acute feeling of savagery:

Dukes Murder Blue Sox, 26–8

By the middle of the 1950 baseball season, every team in the West Texas–New Mexico League looked forward to crossing paths with hapless Abilene. The Blue Sox finished graveyard-dead in last place, some forty games behind. The Dukes in the meantime bested all comers in their claim of the pennant and the playoffs.

Baseball players carry grudges in the same way they carry bubble gum. The 1951 season for Abilene definitely had the look of payback. This time it was the Dukes who were slumping. When Abilene rolled into Albuquerque that June for a three-game set, the Blue Sox were four games in first place. They quickly dispatched of Albuquerque in the first two encounters.

The final engagement would be held on a heavily promoted Albuquerque Night at Tingley Field, the Dukes' park southwest of downtown. Visiting teams typically liked to travel to Albuquerque. The biggest city in the West Texas–New Mexico League offered places to go, things to do. Moreover, the ballpark, with the Sandia Mountains as a backdrop to the east, looked vastly different from the fritter-flat towns in the rest of the league.

Tingley Field took its name from Clyde Tingley, governor of New Mexico during the 1930s. A chest-thumping Democrat, Tingley called himself "mayor of Albuquerque" when such a title did not officially exist. Porky, semi-illiterate, and full of himself, Clyde Tingley loved baseball. In fact, he placed his name on the new ballpark before one nail there had been pounded. The site was pleasingly handsome, if a bit odd. A light pole stood inside the outfield fence, and beneath the stands was a room with beds for unmarried Dukes players. All in all, it was a likable arena, handy to Route 66 and the bright lights of downtown.

It's not known if the ballpark's namesake was among the nearly five thousand fans who jammed into Tingley the night of June 12. Celebrities, however, did not go wanting. Actors Kirk Douglas and Jan Sterling had arrived in Albuquerque late that afternoon, their appearance coinciding with the world premiere of the movie *Ace in the Hole*, to be shown at three theaters in the city the next day. The Hollywood stars faced a busy agenda that following day, with a parade, a barbecue, a visit to the city's veterans hospital, and a luncheon with the rotary club among their stops. A baseball game topped the stars' to-do list on their arrival night.

The summer before, a good portion of *Ace in the Hole* had been filmed in Albuquerque and at various spots across New Mexico. Oscar-winner Billy Wilder produced, directed, and shared in the writing of the screenplay. In the film, Douglas plays cynical, ethics-poor newspaper reporter Chuck Tatum, who coincidentally is a worshipful fan of the New York Yankees and of Yogi Berra in particular. Canned by papers in New York City, Chicago, and Detroit for such infractions as drinking on the job and bedding the publisher's wife, Tatum yearns to get back in the limelight.

Flat broke when his car breaks down in New Mexico, he hires on at the *Albuquerque Sun-Bulletin*. Bored as all get-out from being handed mundane assignments, he manipulates a breaking news story about a man trapped in a cave. Tatum is certain the event will return him to the big time. Sterling plays Lorraine Minosa, a sultry café waitress stuck in an unhappy marriage. The film's bang-bang dialogue drips with sarcasm:

TATUM: When they bleached your hair they must have bleached your brains, too.
LORRAINE: I've seen hardboiled cases, but you, you're twenty minutes.

That a retinue from Tinseltown would be attending a ball game was not accidental. Minor league teams of that period always were on the lookout for publicity angles, Albuquerque pitcher Jesse Priest said, and he should know. The Dukes once arranged a photograph of Priest pretending to read a book on the cover of which someone had hand printed "How to Pitch." The photo turned up on the sports page the day Priest was to take the mound. A steady, power-pitching right-hander, Priest did not need much instruction or hype. He won nineteen games for Albuquerque in 1951 and again in 1952.

"Teams did whatever it took to get fans to come out," Priest remembered. Much of what owners did was to keep a close eye on attendance figures. This was especially true in the 1950s, when empty seats in the minors were becoming all too common. If it enticed more spectators, the Dukes' management was more than happy to embrace whatever Paramount Pictures, the money behind *Ace in the Hole*, had in store.

Paramount had many things in mind. The ballyhoo began moments after the airplane that carried Douglas and Sterling landed in Albuquerque. Nothing would be left to chance. The two actors, attending the first movie premiere in their young careers, had been given lessons on how to step off an airplane: where to look, how to smile, how to wave, what to say.

Accompanying the stars was a phalanx of cameramen, newsreel producers, press agents, and studio publicists. Traveling in a five-car motorcade led by police cars with sirens blaring, the group headed down Central Avenue to the Hilton Hotel to change clothes. That accomplished, the motorcade proceeded to Tingley Field.

When word spread that Douglas and Sterling would be at the ballpark that night, fans mobbed Tingley's ticket window. So squeezed in were spectators that food and drink vendors could not get through the ballpark's aisles. "Overflow crowd" is frequently used to puff up the attendance at sports events. The crowd at Tingley Field was so large it actually overflowed onto the field. Fans stationed themselves along the foul lines and against sections of Tingley's outfield fence. If anyone had had the nerve or skill to shinny up one of the park's light poles, a perch there would have been claimed.

At minor league games today, the public regularly takes part in zany skits on the field between innings. To draw more fans, teams sixty years ago had ballplayers be a part of the entertainment *before* games. Footraces that matched each team's speediest member were a common sight. Every July 4 in Pampa, Texas, Gray County sheriff Rufe Jordan would show up at Oiler Park atop his palomino, Yellow Dog, and put out a challenge to ballplayers with the Oilers, or whoever they were playing that holiday, to race across the diamond. No one in Pampa can remember a runner ever besting Rufe Jordan on Yellow Dog.

Prior to the June 12 game in Albuquerque, members of the Dukes and the Blue Sox took roles in such shenanigans as a wheelbarrow race, an egg-throwing competition, and a base-walking contest. Today's ballplayers earn too much money to risk getting hurt in activities that have little to do with the game itself.

The two principals in *Ace in the Hole* were not simply going to be guests at Tingley. Paramount worked it so that Douglas and Sterling had promi-nent functions in the pregame festivities. First Douglas kissed the wives of all the married players. Sterling, whose attractive, blonde presence brought the expected wolf whistles, then presented the men with wrapped gifts.

Requisite speeches extolling the virtues of New Mexico were delivered, followed by one of those we-hope-you-like-our-movie-and-be-sure-to-tell-all-your-friends-to-see-it pitches. The final diversion was a sketch surely hatched by Paramount's PR department. Sterling pretended to pitch to Douglas, who stood at the plate. Douglas pretended to hit her pitch. Hands on hips, Sterling frowned as Douglas grinned and rounded the bases. Fi-nally, Douglas touched home plate, but the umpire called him out. The two argued wildly, or pretended to. Though it was a far cry from *The Red Skelton Hour* or *I Love Lucy*, the top TV shows that year, the skit generated raucous laughter and waves of applause.

• • •

Astute baseball followers were aware of the hostility between Albuquer-que and Abilene. However, it's likely no one expected what would happen that June night in 1951, especially after all the gaiety that had preceded the game. The blowups came early. In the last half of the second inning, without warning, manager Hack Miller leaped from the Abilene dugout and barreled like a daft steer into Dukes catcher Al Cuitti, who was behind the plate. Cuitti (pronounced "Cute-ee") was an edgy young Californian, never at a loss for words. Apparently, some of those words that evening had struck Miller, always a cranky sort, the wrong way.

Hack Miller, it was said, emerged from his Mama's belly pissed off. As a catcher, he would regularly throw handfuls of dirt on top of a batter's shoes. If a player were wearing just-polished spikes, Miller liked to spit tobacco juice on them. Never once did he veer away from a player when he slid into a base. As a manager, he did not stand quietly in the third-base coach's box. In an attempt to distract the opposing team's third baseman, Miller would frequently unload a steady stream of foul-mouthed insults.

Built like a tombstone, his face a perpetual scowl, James Eldridge Miller was fifteen years older than Cuitti. But that didn't keep Miller from taking a swing at the Dukes catcher. The umpires put a stop to the clash, but not before a good lick by Cuitti closed tight the Abilene manager's left eye. Things happened so quickly that Jesse Priest, more than half a century later, did not have a clear memory of the initial fistic fury.

The real fireworks, what the press later termed the "second round," opened the third inning. Pitcher Steve Lagomarsino sprung from the Albuquerque dugout and started wrestling with the Blue Sox's third-base coach, Jim Melton. "Aw, Melton kept pointing at us, you know, agitating us in the dugout," is the way Lagomarsino recalled it. The takedown by Lagomarsino triggered an ugly chain of events. Players on both benches swiftly entered the fray, which spurred at least five hundred fans to leave their seats—or their spots on the field—and hurry to the upheaval around third base. Most of the ticket holders were not interested in taking part in the pushing, shoving, and grappling, it soon became evident. They were there because they wanted a front-row seat to what had become a knockdown, drag-out battle royale.

Jesse Priest had been one of the first players to arrive at the Lagomarsino-Melton scuffle. Priest was Lagomarsino's buddy on the team, and Priest wanted to offer his friend a hand. The two pitchers coincidentally went into law enforcement after their minor league baseball careers ended. Priest became a Texas Ranger and Lagomarsino wound up as a top officer with the New Mexico State Police. On this night, however, Priest soon found himself not helping his teammate but lying helpless at the bottom of a stuffed sandwich of baseball players. "A person can get hurt real bad when that happens," he said recently from his home in Midland, Texas. "Lord, there were four or five guys pressing down on me." Somehow, he worked his way clear without being harmed.

Lagomarsino suffered a loose tooth and a bruised lip in the brawl. "Nothing major," he said. Melton's jaw swelled to almost twice its size. Six policemen on hand that night did not have it easy as they worked to pull apart the combatants. Two sergeants were struck by blows, a ballplayer's spikes tore into one patrolman's shoe and ripped at his shirt, and a fourth cop was gashed on the leg by a player's spikes.

"The Dukes put up their dukes," Al McPherson's story began the next day in the *Albuquerque Tribune*.

"Quite a night," Lagomarsino remembered. He put the blame on that unpleasant game between the two teams the month before. "That stuff just kept going. Both of us were in a pennant race." The melee lasted approximately ten minutes. When order was restored, umpires told both teams that any player who was not officially involved in the game had to remain in Tingley Field's changing room. One of those players was Jesse Priest, who would pitch the following night.

Priest said that brawls like that happened more in the minor leagues than in the big leagues. "Little things were always causing younger guys to pop off. Temperatures were high out there, and so were tempers. A lot of it was due to inexperience, I think." Lagomarsino, who retired to Albuquerque, agreed. "Mouthing off was always part of it."

Though never discussed, some managers in the leagues were known to egg on players to start fights as a means of drawing more spectators to the ballpark. If, say, a player collided purposely with a fellow from the other team, that player was encouraged to continue the incident the following night. Such mock fights bore more than a little resemblance to choreographed professional wrestling matches, which were at the time beginning to show up on television.

"You didn't really know what was fake out there and what was real," Priest said. "All I know is managers wanted to win. They got riled up because they wanted to keep their job or they wanted a better job for the next year. So they did everything they could to win."

For all the extracurricular action, the June 12, 1951, game turned into a pitcher's duel, with the Abilene Blue Sox winning 5–4. Afterward, reporters cornered Hershel Martin, the manager of the Dukes, for a reaction. Martin shrugged and called it "just another rhubarb," surely the greatest understatement of the night. To those same reporters, Cy Fausett, who owned the Dukes, could not stop smiling. After all, the night's crowd was the largest in the history of professional baseball in Albuquerque. "I am very happy," Fausett said, surely the second greatest understatement. To a reporter, Kirk Douglas delivered to a group of Dukes players what may have been his best unscripted line: "Does this sort of thing happen every night?"

Surprisingly, no fines or suspensions were handed out to those participating in the fisticuffs. Ten days later, as Albuquerque got ready to play a three-game series in Abilene, the president of the West Texas–New Mexico League ordered the Blue Sox to refrain from rowdiness and demanded that the team have adequate police protection during the series. A report circulated in various newspapers that Blue Sox players had threatened the Dukes the next time the two teams played. No details concerning that alleged threat were made public.

The hoopla in Albuquerque could not save *Ace in the Hole* from being a box-office disappointment. Paramount executives early on had worried about the movie, believing it to be too dark. That concern may be why so much attention was paid to the film's premiere in Albuquerque. Just before the film was released nationally, and without consulting Billy Wilder, the studio changed the title to one it considered more viewer friendly, *The Big Carnival*. That name stuck until the movie went to videocassette in the 1980s, when the original title returned. Redemption soon followed as movie critics such as Roger Ebert began calling *Ace in the Hole* a film-noir classic.

Douglas and Wilder went on to become legends in the movie industry. A series of forgettable pictures defined the remainder of Jan Sterling's career. Some film historians say she did her best work in *Ace in the Hole*.

Following its execrable 1950 season, Abilene also found expiation. After the June 12 game, the Blue Sox continued their winning ways. Abilene won the league's pennant that year and added a championship by capturing the playoffs. The Dukes finished second. *Albuquerque Journal* sports editor J. D. Kailer praised the "hustle" that Blue Sox manager Hack Miller, hired part way into the season, had contributed. Miller's nasty disposition clearly didn't hurt the team.

• • •

The Albuquerque Dukes are history now, as is Tingley Field. Departed too is the term "rhubarb." As a baseball word—and it never caught on in any other sport—rhubarb, like "four-master" for a home run, belongs to another era. The source of the word is not rooted in the sweet pie, as one might think. *Sports Illustrated* reported that in 1938 a Brooklyn Dodgers fan shot and killed a New York Giants fan in a barroom beef over the outcome of a ball game. The bartender, whose name no one remembered, described the incident to baseball writer Tom Meany as a "rhubarb." What the barkeep meant by that is also lost. Radio broadcaster Red Barber heard the tale, liked the word, and began to say it frequently on his play-by-play of the Dodgers' baseball games. Barber had a large audience and the word subsequently passed into the language. The popularity of "rhubarb" grew such that in 1951 the word became the movie title for a screwball comedy about a pet cat named Rhubarb who had been willed ownership of a baseball team.

The current application of the word on air generally falls to older baseball announcers, such as Vin Scully or Ralph Kiner. Rare is the day "rhubarb" is heard on ESPN. On June 13, 1951, however, the morning after two wild brawls erupted in one baseball game, everyone was using the word.

Sometimes a base brawl involved two people you would never think might be fighting with each other. In the second inning of a Sunday afternoon game, on June 5, 1955, a batter on the visiting Artesia NuMexers beat a throw to first base, according to umpire Bill Frank. The five hundred or so fans vehemently disagreed. Big Spring second baseman Bob Martin was so angered by the decision that he began exchanging words with Frank. That discussion ended with Frank pointing Martin in the general direction of the Steer Park showers.

In the fifth inning, Artesia attempted a double steal. The runner at second base advanced, but the one on first was called safe by Frank. Again spectators expressed their disapproval via a cascade of loud boos. One fan standing behind a fence in back of first base began shouting at Frank, who had made the call at second. Frank did nothing until the fan reportedly invited the umpire to come closer so the two might confer. Frank unwisely did so and soon the pair were trading punches. Players and the police stepped in to stop the boxing match. It's not clear who won that match, but the NuMexers won the game, 6–3. Evidently, no fines were imposed.

Sports writers were not immune from the fray. Larry L. King, later a celebrated author (*Confessions of a White Racist*) and playwright (*The Best Little Whorehouse in Texas*), in 1951 worked the sports desk for the *Midland Reporter-Telegram*. Former major leaguer Zeke Bonura played a painfully poor first base for Midland. After one game in which Bonura committed five errors, King, who earned extra money as the official scorer, wrote that Bonura fielded "as if both feet were buried under anvils." The next day, an enraged Bonura, nicknamed "Banana Nose," showed up at the newspaper office and rushed at King. Fellow reporters intervened.

Though King managed to escape an angry player, Max Odendahl, another journalist, wasn't as fortunate. Odendahl was the *Roswell Daily Record*'s one-person sports staff in the mid-1950s. He too served as the official scorekeeper. Before games, Odendahl would go down to the field to get the lineups from the two managers. As he did so on the night of July 29, 1956, Ralph Buckingham, a pitcher for the Roswell Rockets, began yelling in the reporter's face. Furious, Buckingham accused Odendahl of charging Rockets pitchers with too many wild pitches.

"No one else is bitching about that," Odendahl responded. The argument became so heated that Buckingham suddenly took a swing at the writer, but missed. The two grabbed at each other and fell to the grass. Team members on the Rockets had to pull them apart.

Buckingham had been a good prospect until he developed control problems. He had eleven wild pitches that season and believed mistakes were costing him a chance to move up.

"I'm not proud of that incident," Odendahl remembered. "I was a young kid, I didn't know all that much about baseball. I wasn't quite sure of the difference between a wild pitch and a passed ball. So many of Buckingham's pitches hit the dirt before they got to home plate."

Buckingham was fined fifty dollars by the Southwestern League and shipped off to Amarillo, then part of the Western League. He pitched in just eight more games as a professional, with no record. He died in 2009. Odendahl never did a column or story for his newspaper about the brief scrap. "I guess I could have written that Buckingham threw a punch like he did a baseball," he said. "But I felt sorry for the guy. That thing kind of ended his career."

· ·

VOICES: BOB LAPHAM

1946: visitors' batboy, Abilene Blue Sox
1947: visitors' batboy, Abilene Blue Sox

Oh, gosh, yes, Hack Miller liked to stir up trouble. He would fight anybody, anytime. He was one mean little so-and so.

I was ten and eleven years old when I worked at Blue Sox Stadium in Abilene as the visiting team's batboy. One night, this was in 1946,

Hack, who was managing Lubbock then, came to Abilene. He really got into it with an umpire. The umpire tossed him out. Hack refused to go. The umpire would not start the game unless Hack left the field. "I ain't budging," Hack said. Finally, Howard Green, who owned the Blue Sox, told Hack to go or he would call the police and have him removed. Hack stood his ground. Finally, three cops showed up and lifted up Hack and carried him out. He kicked and yelled the whole way.

My two seasons as batboy, Abilene's manager was William Hayden Greer, known to all as "Stubby." Stubby was a feisty shortstop. He had a temper, too, but nothing like Hack Miller. Stubby and the Blue Sox second baseman, Len Glica, formed a great double-play combination. Stubby went on to coach and manage and play a lot of years. Len was killed in the Korean War in early 1951.

Here's how you became a batboy for the visiting team: A bunch of us kids would wait outside the ballpark for the visitors' bus or station wagons or whatever they arrived in. As soon as we would spot the manager, we would make a mad dash toward him. It might be Grover Seitz from Pampa or Bob Seeds from Amarillo or someone else. We knew who all the managers were in the West Texas–New Mexico League. We would battle each other to see who got to the manager first. It was grab-ass kind of deal. When you grabbed his shirt, the manager said, "OK, kid, you're the batboy." And for the next three-game series, you had the job.

Gordon Asbury was the batboy for the home team, the Class C Blue Sox. We thought he had the greatest job in the world. I think he had some sort of connections. Seems like his father was a lawyer, maybe a friend of the owner.

Blue Sox Stadium was an all-wood affair. Rough, rough pine wood. It's gone now. The stadium sat about five hundred people. The outfield fence was six feet tall and it had all these signs on it that said, "Hit me for five dollars," "Hit me for ten dollars." If you didn't get the visiting batboy job, you made a beeline for the scoreboard in center field. First one there got to run the scoreboard, the next best job.

Danny Ozark was the star of the team in 1946, his only year with Abilene. His hand was pulling money out of the chicken wire a lot that summer. Some people used to think Danny was from the Ozarks. You know, because of his name and the goofy things that came out of his mouth. Danny was the guy who said, "Half the game is 90 percent mental." The truth is Danny grew up in Buffalo, New York, and his real name was Daniel Ozechowski. Danny had a long career in the minor leagues, but never made it to majors as a player. He did become a manager in the big leagues, and a good one, taking the Philadelphia Phillies three straight times to the league championship series.

As a kid, I idolized Danny, and so did my friends. We even learned where he lived. One time a bunch of us were hanging around on a Saturday morning. We started arguing who of us had the nerve to go to Danny's apartment and knock on his door. I was chosen. I didn't think that Danny had played a game the night before and might be asleep. It was about ten o'clock when I reached where Danny lived. It was one room, which he shared with Ed Krage, the center fielder for the Blue Sox. I knocked, and when Danny came out in boxer shorts, he was ready to strangle whoever was at the door so early. Many years later, I was the sports editor of the *Abilene Reporter-News* and I did a telephone interview with Danny. I told him the story about the early morning wake-up call. He laughed and said he didn't remember it.

The owner of the Blue Sox put a hard-wire netting up and over the seats in back of home plate so balls wouldn't fall and hurt fans. But some balls sailed far over the netting and out of the ballpark. Those balls would every so often hit cars that were parked below. When your heard a crash or a loud noise, everyone would laugh and cheer. Some poor fan's windshield just got busted.

Abilene finished first in the standings of the West Texas–New Mexico League in 1946. We entered the Shaughnessy playoffs as a big favorite. The Shaughnessy system was invented in the thirties, I think, by a baseball guy named Shaughnessy. It was a popular system for the minors but has since pretty much disappeared. In the Shaughnessy, the best four teams had a single-elimination tournament. Number one played number four, number two played number three. Abilene fell apart in those playoffs. The Blue Sox performed sluggishly and we lost. I'm telling you, everyone in the city was crushed. People felt even worse when they found out most of the team had gone out and gotten drunk the night before.

You didn't get paid as the visiting team's batboy. What you received were used baseballs that had their covers almost falling off or a used bat. Not a broken or shattered bat, but a cracked bat. Almost every game I worked I would be given a cracked bat. I would take it home, to my father's workshop, and hammer in a small tack or two to close the crack. Then I would wrap the bat with black electrical tape.

Some of those bats were Hillerich & Bradsby Babe Ruth autograph models. Or H&B Ty Cobb models. I had about twenty of them when I stopped being a bat boy. I'd give my eyeteeth for one of them now. The bats I think went the way of my mother. As I grew older, she gave them away. That's what mothers do. They mean nothing by it, I know. Still, the bats were mine. They might be worth a lot of money now. I have plenty of good memories, though. I won't let go of those.

· ·

VOICES: LEN SANTI

1947: catcher, Clovis Pioneers
1951: catcher, third baseman, Clovis Pioneers

I never got in any fights, but I got mad once. I grew up seven blocks from Brooklyn's Ebbets Field. I played sandlot baseball as a kid. I thought I might be a catcher. I got behind some kids hitting batting practice and first thing I knew I had a bloody nose from being hit in the face by a foul tip. Or as we used to call it, a foul ticky. It hurt like crazy and I was plenty angry.

I sold the *Brooklyn Daily Citizen* newspaper, for two cents a copy. Sold the papers outside Ebbets Field. Newsboys were allowed to go into Ebbets Field after the sixth inning, provided we had sold all the papers we started with, which was twenty-five copies each.

I grew up watching Cookie Lavagetto, Peewee Reese, Roy Campanella. Campy was a catcher like me until he got crippled. Babe Herman was a great home-run hitter. One game I remember Babe Herman came to bat four times with the bases loaded and struck out the first three times. On the last lick he hit a home run, but we lost. I am ninety-seven years old, but I still look at the newspapers to see how the Dodgers, the Los Angeles Dodgers, are doing. You can't take Brooklyn out of the boy.

For fifteen years I played catcher for the semipro Plaza Cubs in Brooklyn. Rheingold Beer sponsored us. One day, Wiley Moore, a scout for the New York Giants, signed up me and Joe Moccio, a pitcher. We were to report to a Giants farm team in upstate New York, Class D—on March 15, 1942. I never got there. I was drafted by the air force on February 26, 1942.

I played baseball for air base teams in Colorado, Mississippi, and finally, in late 1942, at Clovis Air Field, which later became Cannon Air Force Base.

When I first got to Clovis, I thought, what a hell hole. There was dust flying everywhere, including into my mouth. People would say to me, "You're from New York, aren't you?" They could tell by the way I talked. I said "woise" instead of "worse."

I was standing out front of the Clovis BX one afternoon, playing catch with another guy, when this pretty girl walks by. She said I flirted with her, but I think she flirted with me, which she denies. Anyway, we introduced ourselves. She was Joyce Matlock, a local farm girl.

I started courting Joyce. One day when I went to her family's farm to pick her up, her father, Mr. James Matlock, he comes running out to meet me. He said he had a cow in the lot and she had a dead baby in her that needed to come out.

I grew up on the streets of Brooklyn. I didn't know a cow from a couch. "I can't stand blood," I said. I then told Mr. Matlock about getting hit in the face by that foul ticky.

Mr. Matlock wasn't listening. He couldn't care less. He handed me two ropes and said, "Come on, I need you to help me."

Mr. Matlock put one rope around the cow and tied the other rope around the legs of the dead calf. He pulled on his rope and I pulled on mine and pretty soon that dead baby came out. That's when I got sick. Oh, God, I thought, don't let me fall into cow shit. I leaned over a trough to spit up. Then I passed out.

For some reason, Mr. Matlock let his daughter go on seeing me. We got married October 8, 1943. When I got out of the service in 1946, I took out a loan and bought 320 acres of farmland. I knew nothing about farming, but I wanted to learn. I planted wheat and it actually grew. The best years of my life were spent on that farm in little Grier, New Mexico. We raised three children there. I learned to play dominoes in Clovis in the winter. In the fall, I went deer hunting. Where you going to do that in Brooklyn?

Before I came to Clovis, having a religious faith meant nothing to me. Mom took me to Sunday Mass in Brooklyn at 6:30 a.m. every week. 6:30! She put her fifteen cents in the plate. There were five of us kids. I was christened Leandro Jerome Santi, but it didn't mean anything to me. In New Mexico, I met the Lord. I joined the Ranchvale Baptist Church and became a born-again Christian. For a long time I didn't tell my mother.

In the spring of 1947, I read in the *Clovis News-Journal* that the Clovis Pioneers were having a tryout. I went out to the ballpark and I made the team. I was thirty years old. A sportswriter called me the "Grier farmer."

I remember Big Joe Bauman of Amarillo. Ray Bauer, too. Ray was popular in Clovis. They called him "Power Bauer." He settled down in Clovis after baseball and ran a business. He died a couple of years ago. One time in Albuquerque a cop stopped our team bus. He said we had run a red light. We argued with him, and the cop said, "You better shut up or you're all going to jail."

Bell Park, where we played, had low fences. You could almost look over them. The grandstands were OK, and there was a batting cage off the side. The fans were always good.

In 1949, I went to spring training, but the team had found someone else to be catcher. I went home. I didn't play for a while, then came back in 1951. They put me in at third base because I had bad knees. I'd been farming for several years by then, and you're moving the wrong muscles for baseball when you're farming. Bad knees and I couldn't bat anymore, either. When I bunted, I'd leave the ball on the ground. I was thirty-four years old. It was time to farm year-round.

We did well the first five or six years we farmed. This would have been 1949–1955. Then the droughts came. Things got so bad I was forced to take a civilian job at the Clovis Air Base. I worked there from 1955 to 1960. Then I took another civilian job at a base in Victorville, California. I stayed there for twenty years.

The people in rural New Mexico are some of the greatest people on Earth. In New York City, you didn't trust anybody. Out in New Mexico, if somebody needed help, you helped them. When I first got to New Mexico, people were tipping their hats at me or smiling all the time when they saw me. I became suspicious. Why were they doing this? What do these people want from me? I found out they were just being friendly. That's the way people are here in Clovis. If you needed someone, they lent you a hand. If they needed help, you jumped right in.

CHAPTER FIVE

Knights of the Keyboard

Sportswriters at the midmark of the last century, especially those who did the business of journalism in the leagues' small communities, typically were looked up to and liked, certainly much more than current practitioners. To read a few critical words about a pet team or favored player can send today's sports fan into an absolute froth. Yesteryear's reporters cheered openly and unabashedly for the home team.

In the ranchlands and farms along the east flank of New Mexico and on the open spaces of West Texas, where almost everyone subscribed to a thriving, daily newspaper, sports writing was once considered an honorable profession. Residents knew the local sports reporter well. They spoke to him by name in the grocery as he paid for a box of Oxydol. They exchanged greetings as he received a dollop of Wildroot from the town barber. They saw him shopping for a basin wrench at the Montgomery Ward or picking up a pack of Chesterfield at the Allsup's or singing "Fairest Lord Jesus" in the First Methodist Church, just like everyone else.

Citizens waved to him as they drove their Ford pickups down Main Street and listened to Hank Williams plead "Take These Chains from My Heart." At the ballpark, men touched the brims of their sweat-stained Resistols as he climbed the steps to the press box. Their wives hurried after to hand him homemade sugar cookies wrapped in wax paper.

A newspaper's sportswriter did not leave town when the baseball season ended, as so many minor league ballplayers were wont to do. Newspaper writing then was a full-time job, a year-round job. It was a respected vocation, a position of stature with a rosy future. Those who labored at it were seen as medieval knights, armed not with a jousting pole under their arms, but with a trusty Underwood at their fingertips.

. . .

Football, in both college and high school, drew the most readers to what used to be called the "sports page," even though sports stories generally took up two pages and sometimes parts of a third. That football ruled was especially true in the American Southwest, where gridiron stars such as Sammy Baugh, Bobby Layne, and Doak Walker held the spotlight. Minor league baseball struggled at times for room on the sports page. Those writing about the undermost stratums of baseball, Class C and Class D, struggled as well—with words.

Sportswriters of that day happily larded their stories with jargon. Readers did not appear to notice and seemed by all accounts to enjoy if not always understand this sometimes queer usage of the King's English. Because the standards of the journalism profession have since been elevated, such language now is considered passé and frowned upon. The current norm within the craft holds to the belief that if you do not use certain sports-centric words in conversation, there is no good reason to write them.

In the postwar years, such an edict definitely did not hold true. Consider if you will such antiquated baseball terms as "horsehide," "tilt," "skein," and "twirl." It would not be at all unusual to come across in a 1948 news-paper story the following sentence: "Maynard will be twirling the horse-hide at Tuesday's tilt, hoping to continue his skein." Baseball players were "tabbed" for a productive season, future games were "slated," victories "garnered," and tie scores "knotted." A double play was a "twin killing." Fans didn't buy tickets, they purchased "ducats." The "hot corner" enjoyed a long ride in stories as a synonym for third base. Taking things further, and in vogue for a while, was this curio on the physical bag itself: "hot corner hassock."

Phrases leaned strongly toward clichés, such as "nail in the coffin," "when it rains it pours," "inked a pact," "played their hearts out," a "nip and tuck duel," and so forth.

From whence did such language spring? One need look no further than the *Sporting News*. Founded and headquartered in St. Louis, the weekly tabloid billed itself the "Base Ball Paper of the World." It's no typograph-ical error that baseball is two words in that blustery designation. That was how the game was spelled in 1886, the year the *Sporting News* came into being. The newspaper, which covered the major leagues exhaustively, did not neglect the other layers of organized ball. Those who signed on with Class C and D teams in the Southwest soon knew their place within the *Sporting News*—notes bounded by ellipses, interred deep within the far back pages of the weekly. For a time, these brief, filler-like jottings could be found beneath the less-than-flattering column heading "Highlights of the Lower Minors."

That slight aside, if you reported on baseball for papers in the four leagues, the *Sporting News* was a pleasurable resource. As you thumbed through its many features each week, you grew used to seeing the *Sporting News* employ "portsider" for a left-handed pitcher, "hillock" for the pitcher's mound, and "slab" for the mound's rubber. In *Sporting News* speak, the first game of a series of a double header was a "lidlifter." Outfielders were "flyhawks," reliable pitchers were "flingers" who had sturdy "wings," a single was a "bingle," and a slugger was a "biffer" or even on occasion a "swatsmith."

In the manner of the movie industry's popular tabloid *Daily Variety* and its quirky headline nomenclature ("Sticks Nix Hick Pix"), readers of the *Sporting News* were seldom baffled by a headline that read, "Biffing Backstops Bolster Flag Drives" (hard-hitting catchers lead the way in pennant races) or "Socking Frosh Flyhawk a Glitzer" (rookie outfielder hits for great power). Both *Daily Variety* and the *Sporting News* are still around, but in digital versions only.

• • •

Across the Southwest sixty and seventy years ago, the sports departments of newspapers with modest circulations often were one-man operations. Reporters who covered minor league baseball also covered everything else in view. Plus they edited and laid out the sports page and even wrote shorter versions of stories to exchange with area newspapers. For a writer, the payoff for all this labor was not in money but in doing a column. Such columns bore standing titles, which usually were either greatly prosaic or cringingly cute. At some places, a column title was passed down to the newly hired sportswriter. At the *Roswell Daily Record*, for example, Riding Herd on Sports was used year after year by several different people. A photograph of a writer did not normally come with the column until a decade or two on. That didn't matter in, say, 1952. Everyday readers then knew what the man looked like. And columnizing then, make no mistake, was a male-dominated pursuit.

Having a column was like having your name on a marquee. A game story, that familiar, inning-by-inning review of the previous night, was too frequently numbingly dull beyond the first three paragraphs. A column was different. It was special, and sometimes personal.

But column writing was also one more piece of work for a paper's sports-writer, who already carried a wide load. Thus shortcuts were taken. Banalities in columns were scattered about like breadcrumbs to pigeons. Rather than searching for the appropriate word, a writer frequently took the easier, more-traveled road. On occasion, such a fellow would poke fun at the way he used English. As sports editor of the *Hobbs News-Sun*, Art Gatts produced copy under the title "Gab'n with Gatts." An April 1956 entry began this way: "You have to break out the clichés to aptly describe the Hobbs Sports baseball team. Here's a few to show what we mean: Never give up, fight till the last out, a scrappy bunch of ballplayers." Down a paragraph or so into the column, Gatts, without realizing it, took the hackneyed path himself: "Jose Dominguez might be the lefthander we need with a few games under his belt." The "we" in the column duly notes Gatts's allegiance, as do the words "under his belt." Of exceptional girth, Gatts often could be spotted at a table in George's, a crowd-pleasing eatery on East Main in Hobbs. It was rare for him to tuck into a dinner there without being interrupted by a local devotee who wanted to shoot the breeze about one baseball game or another.

Sometimes columnists used a word or more in the most confounding of ways, a bygone embellishment unimaginable in this century. Bern Gantner let readers of the *Clovis News-Journal* know what was on his mind via In the Background of Sports, the column he penned. Following an extended road trip taken by the Clovis Pioneers in the summer of 1954, Gantner came up with this oddity: "The good news is that the Pioneers return tonight to their wigwam." Did the team actually reside in a tent? Of course not. Yet no one questioned Gantner, for he was universally approved by readers, a characteristic all newspaper writers once desired that has mostly gone out of fashion.

Charles Stanfield, a predecessor of Ganter's at Clovis, wrote in Stan's Sports Slant that first base was the "gateway bag." When a batter stood in the box and readied his swing, Stanfield said the player "waggled the willow."

In Mopp'n Up, Bill Canino's recurring contribution to the *Artesia Daily Press* in the 1950s, a tough, hard-played baseball game for the Artesia Drillers was a "riot," the Longhorn League "the loop," a home run a "buster," and an inning a "frame." In Al McPherson's column Al About Sports, in the *Albuquerque Tribune*, a run was a "marker," the score a "tally," and a "can of corn" an easy fly ball. Strangely, McPherson's game stories were not cluttered with the familiar. In fact, he surely made readers scratch their heads. Of a pitcher, McPherson wrote, "He franked three batters intentionally." Of a batter, he delivered this head-scratcher: "He hit a grasscutter to center to bring in the calcimine removing run."

Harry Gilstrap of the *Amarillo Daily News* wanted readers to believe that his words had been set in type just for them. Thus he titled his column Between *YOU* and *ME*. The capital, underscored letters are his. So was this vocabulary: "chunkers" for pitchers and "tiffs" for games, except those played on Sunday, which always were "Sabbath games."

During the late 1940s, the well-intentioned Wilbur Bentley made up the *Albuquerque Journal*'s sports department. The poor fellow tried too hard in his column, Angle Shots. In fact, his style harkened to his 1920s forebears, when men were men and the prose was purple. Luminaries of the print world such as Grantland Rice called outfielders "gardeners" and baseballs "apples" and a simple game of ball "a conflagration of the sword."

Bentley, like many sportswriters of his time and station, never traveled with the team that he wrote about in his old-fashioned style. After a series of rainouts on a road trip he had not witnessed, Bentley let his imagination run. "If, when the Dukes get home today, and it is discovered that they have web feet and are sprouting water wings, we hope their duchesses will not be too greatly put out." Jerry Brown of the *Carlsbad Current-Argus* liked to blame a rainout on "Old Jupe Pluvius." Thank "Old Sol," Charles Stanfield of the *Clovis News-Journal* wrote of a bright, radiant day.

. . .

It was not uncommon for baseball writers to mix their sports. Too many scribes to count said of an injured ballplayer that he was "not up to par." When a new manager was rumored to be hired soon, which happened a good deal in the leagues of New Mexico and West Texas due to frequent firings, the replacement was about to "take the driver's seat." When baseball games entered the ninth inning, still knotted, "the clock had started to wind down." Joe Kelley of the *Lubbock Avalanche-Journal* never referred to doubles as anything but "safeties." Gil Rusk, writing in his *Carlsbad Current-Argus* column Fan's Fare, said early one season, "We've seen our Potashers now after the bell has rung and they leave little to be desired."

For Amarillo's Harry Gilstrap, winning in extra innings was almost always an "overtime victory."

No education requirement existed for reporters who covered minor league baseball in that period. Frank Deford, the eminent, Princeton-educated stylist who joined *Sports Illustrated* in 1962, the year after the last of the leagues disappeared, said that when people hear you're a sportswriter, they assume you're more interested in the sports part of the word than the writing part. Indeed, when it was learned that a sportswriter in the hinterlands of the Southwest had attended college, even briefly, he might gain a nickname from the players he wrote about. These monikers ranged from "Professor" and "Einstein" to "Smart Ass" and worse. William "Putt" Powell, a columnist for the *Amarillo Globe-News*, did not graduate from high school until he was twenty-one. Powell grappled with grammar and spelling for most of his career, but readers didn't seem to mind. Everyone loved Putt. Well, almost everyone. When told he had been hung in effigy for writing something critical, Powell said, "Where the hell is Effigy, Texas?"

J. D. Kailer, a savvy sports editor of the *Albuquerque Journal* for nearly a decade before leaving in 1959, held a bachelor's degree from the venerated University of Missouri School of Journalism. He had a second degree from the University of Illinois. Kailer came to Albuquerque well seasoned for the times. At Illinois he had written a column for the *Daily Illini* newspaper, and during World War II he served on the staff of the highly regarded *Yank* magazine, published for GIs across the globe. Worldly Kailer may have been, but he was not immune from embracing jargon in his column, The Scoreboard. Whenever a player set a league record, Kailer was apt to call the event a "circuit breaker." When a manager lifted a pitcher from a game, the man was "derricked," and a poor infielder was a "freebooter." To Carlos Salazar of the *Albuquerque Tribune*, the heart of a team's batting order was always the "heavy timber."

Minor leaguers in the 1940s and 1950s did not have the education that many do today. Today's professional ballplayers more often than not are drafted out of college. For decades, young players often came straight from hardscrabble farms or grim factories into organized ball. Even so, players were much closer to reporters then than now. Harry Gilstrap frequently joined Amarillo's Bob Crues for a drink. The two even went hunting together in the off season.

Some sportswriters drank too much alcohol, which today can bring an immediate firing. Buck Lanier, who toiled for papers in Clovis, Roswell, Carlsbad, and El Paso, among other stops in the 1950s, was good friends with Jack Daniels. Lanier stopped drinking, he said, when it got harder to get up at four o'clock in the morning. Employees of afternoon newspapers, which America once had in abundance but now are scarce as typesetters, generally came to work before dawn.

Columnists at that time rarely found fault, and if so, the carping generally was mild. Carlos Salazar filled his It Says Here column with information. Only seldom did he judge. On the other hand, J. D. Kailer, Salazar's chief competition in Albuquerque, didn't back down from making a strong comment. Indeed, Kailer was unafraid to write or speak the truth and it ultimately cost him his job. When Cy Fausett, owner of the Albuquerque Dukes in the 1950s, significantly upped the price of tickets even as attendance slipped, Kailer wrote, "The man has set baseball back five years."

Bob Milburn of the *San Angelo Standard-Times* so strived for impartiality he was awarded the Putt Powell Award, given annually to the best Texas sportswriter. Bob Gregg, who pitched for the San Angelo Colts back in the early 1950s, thought Milburn fair. "When I had a bad outing, he would say so. He might say something like, 'Although San Angelo won the ball game, Gregg showed his wildness streak.' That was OK with me, because he was telling the truth. But boy, my mother, who read the San Angelo paper each day, hated Bob Milburn."

• • •

It's probable that small-town sportswriters in the Southwest were aware of the East Coast icons of the mid-twentieth century, baseball craftsmen such as John Drebinger of the *New York Times*, Red Smith of the *New York Herald Tribune*, and Shirley Povich of the *Washington Post*. The local sportswriter may even have come across on occasion a column by one of those masters and yearned to be in the big time. But being a sportswriter out West was not a bad thing at all, and thus many men spent decades in the same community. Carlos Salazar labored fifty-two years in Albuquerque. Putt Powell put in sixty-two years at the *Amarillo Globe-Times*. He wrote his last column six days before he died of cancer in 1992.

Working in smaller communities may not have brought widespread fame and grand wealth, but the pleasures were many. Life in little places for a sportswriter moved at a first-gear pace. People there were friendly and you didn't need to lock your door at night, or any time.

Some reporters did move on to bigger things. Howard Green was a teenager when he joined the sports staff of the *Abilene Reporter-News*. In 1939, when the Abilene Apaches went out of business, the news broke Green's eighteen-year-old heart. He vowed to bring baseball back to West Texas. Green did, finally, in 1946, when with two investors he placed an expansion team in the West Texas–New Mexico League—the Abilene Blue Sox. That led Green to wear, improbably, two hats: general manager of a professional baseball team and beat writer for that same team. The "Boy Wonder," some called him. Green resigned from the *Reporter-News* in 1947 to devote himself to baseball. He founded two leagues—the Longhorn League, which was comprised of teams in both West Texas and New Mexico, and the Gulf Coast League, which had franchises in East Texas and Louisiana. Green continued running minor leagues until 1956, when he entered politics. He served several years in the Texas legislature. The Blue Sox disappeared in 1957, and Green died in 2005.

• • •

More than anything, sports reporters during this period were "homers," which in large part explained their popularity. Building up the home team in print and holding an absolute loyalty to that task was appreciated by newspaper readers and demanded by many publishers. Columns slamming players or teams rarely were published.

Bern Gantner of the *Clovis News-Journal* bubbled over with praise in his column when the Clovis Pioneers showed up in 1955 dudded out in new uniforms. "This year's Pioneers are a different bunch of players from those who have worn the livery of the Pioneers in the past," Gantner wrote. "These uniforms are the best that money can buy. Each costs more than half a century note, according to manager Grover Seitz. Fifty-two dollars to be exact." To certify the quality of the uniforms, Gantner quoted Seitz: "Those suits didn't come out of a Cracker Jack box."

Readers in the South Plains region of Texas always knew where Joe Kelly of the *Lubbock Avalanche-Journal* stood. No one root-rooted for the home team more than old Joe Kelly. In an August 1951 Between the Lines column, Kelly confronted one more mediocre season for the local nine, the Hubbers. "Lubbock fans tonight have a chance to show their appreciation for the fine job the players have done this year," he wrote. "They're a swell bunch of guys and deserve every good thing they can be given. They'll need all the support they can get with the invading Lamesa Lobos. Go out and let the players know you're for them."

On the other hand, J. D. Kailer would let the home team have it in the

Albuquerque Journal if he felt it appropriate. Though the Dukes in the early 1950s were losing money, the club's owner continued to count his nickels. "Thrifty doesn't begin to describe him," Kailer wrote.

Jerry Dorbin of the *Carlsbad Current-Argus* had entered journalism to write Great Literature. It was not unusual for Dorbin to turn out fine prose, even on deadline. After Gil Carter of the Carlsbad Potashers hit a home run farther than anyone at the time could imagine, Dorbin banged out this well-crafted lead for his game story: "Tuesday night at eight-forty-five p.m., using home plate at Montgomery Field for a launching pad and without so much as a countdown, a six-foot, one inch, 208-pound outfielder became the first man in history to put a baseball in orbit."

Many of the columnists of that period resorted to what became known as "three-dot journalism." Emptying a notebook filled with scraps and stringing them together, separated by ellipses, was a lot easier than writing a continuous narrative. Such a style is still used, but almost always at the very end of a reporter's story, not throughout it.

• • •

Sportswriters in the leagues of the Southwest did not always have it easy. Salaries were barely enough to support a family, and working conditions left a lot to be desired. Some ballparks in the leagues did not have press boxes and writers were forced to labor in the stands. Spring winds were apt to be fierce. Temperatures could turn cold in two shakes. Summer nights could be sweltry and bug filled. Lights in more than a few ballparks resembled candles, and some fans could be mean as snakes.

Just about everyone typed stories, of course, though lugging around a manual typewriter was not much of a pleasure. For some, the job was a continual test. Dave Smoker was a young sportswriter for the *Clovis News-Journal* in 1956. "I was also the official scorer," he said. "I had to put the score and the box score on the wire so those items would go all over. On Saturday nights it was nightmare. I had to rush back to the office and type madly on the wire to West Texas newspapers, because they wanted it right away. They had a deadline to meet for the Sunday morning newspaper. They were always screaming for my head. I was always praying that the ball game wouldn't go extra innings."

Though the scores of games changed, reporting on baseball games and writing a column shared a sameness. Sometimes there were memorable performances to put in the paper, but often not. In covering the Class C and Class D teams decades ago, sportswriters always knew the dust would get in their eyes and the sun would fry their necks. For just about every reporter, the job was worth doing. Buck Lanier perhaps said it best: "We had as much fun out there as a prairie dog in soft dirt."

. . .

Many members of today's media were once athletes. That is especially true of radio and television broadcasters. Few print journalists covering baseball teams now, as well as back in the day, played the game professionally. Royce Wilson Mills, who took photographs and occasionally wrote stories for the *Artesia Advocate*, was the rare exception. Mills did not just play a few ball games. He spent more than a decade in the minors, eight of those years in the leagues of the Southwest, splitting time between Lubbock, Borger, and finally Artesia, where he finished his career in 1952. He was not a run-of-the-mill athlete either. Mills is remembered as a pretty fair pitcher.

No one but the taxman called Mills "Royce." He was "Rooster" from an early age. As an adult, he stood five feet eight inches—slight but full of incessant energy. Definitely a banty rooster type. Nicknames, often bestowed by sportswriters, were a part of minor league baseball, and "Rooster" was surely one of the best known. In fact, Mills used the name in photo credits of pictures he took and taglines on the stories he occasionally wrote.

The record book shows Rooster began his baseball career in 1939, for the Tarboro, North Carolina, Goobers of the Coastal Plains League, but it is unclear whether he played in a game with the Goobers. In 1940 he joined the Longview Texans of the East Texas League and compiled a 13–8 mark. He followed that with Class C and D teams in Arkansas and Mississippi.

. . .

Like so many ballplayers, Mills was called into the service and lost four years of what would have been his prime baseball years to the U.S. Army Air Corps. He became a crew chief on a B-24 until the Germans shot down his plane in 1944. Captured, Mills spent six months as a POW. Rather than sit in a prison, he was forced by the Germans to march continually. The allies were moving in, and the only answer the Germans could find was to make POWs keep on the move by foot. Mills's daughter, Lynda Chambers of Fort Worth, Texas, said, "He had very little food and was always cold and I think that's where his physical skills diminished."

Rooster Mills returned a hero. His baseball career, however, seemed in jeopardy. He struggled at first playing at the B and AA level for Detroit farm teams. In 1948, with Lubbock, he went 13–6 and 16–3 the next year. His earned run averages were high, over 5.00, but so were the ERAs of many pitchers in the leagues. In 1951, his ERA soared above 7.00.

As all pitchers did then, Rooster batted and was a good enough slap hitter. Meanwhile, he was trying to raise a family of three children with no money in the bank. Before every game his wife, nicknamed "Cricket," urged him to hit a home run, because it would bring in backstop dollars. "We need the money!" Cricket often said as Rooster went out the door. But Rooster never was a payday hitter, and he ended up with only five home runs in his career.

Rooster took off-season jobs where he could find them. He served as a deputy sheriff in Borger, Texas, a position Bob Crues once held. He dabbled in freelance writing. He sold some articles to an archery magazine, a hobby he enjoyed, and he took photographs to go with his articles. He was self-taught in both pursuits.

In 1951, Rooster became the fifth manager that season for the Ardmore, Oklahoma, Indians of the Sooner State League. The Indians were pitiful. Between all five managers, the club finished with forty-nine wins and ninety-one losses. Rooster's name came up for managing posts in 1952 at both Borger and Lamesa, but neither job panned out. The following year, Earl Perry, manager of the Artesia Drillers, brought Rooster to New Mexico to shore up the pitching staff. At age thirty-two, he went ten and six, and the Drillers finished seventy-five and sixty-five, twelve games back. The saving grace that year for Rooster was that he became friends with Joe Bauman, also in his first season with the Drillers.

The Mills family stayed on in Artesia for the next two years. Rooster stocked shelves in a grocery, cut meat in a butcher shop, and did journalism. He eventually moved the family to Fort Worth, Texas, where he sold automobiles for the Mastin Motor Company, a DeSoto dealership. He liked talking to people, said his son, Scott Mills, and Mastin would give him a new DeSoto every year. Rooster died in Fort Worth in 1983. He was sixty-three years old.

One of the last photographs Rooster Mills took in Artesia brought him enduring fame, much more so than all his years in the minor leagues put together. The photograph, which was reprinted in many places, shows Joe Bauman smiling brightly and shaking hands as he comes across home plate. Big Joe had just hit his record-breaking seventieth home run.

· ·

1953: beat writer, Midland Indians, *Midland Reporter-Telegram*
1954: beat writer, Midland Indians, *Midland Reporter-Telegram*
1955: beat writer, Midland Indians, *Midland Reporter-Telegram*
1956: beat writer, Midland Indians, *Midland Reporter-Telegram*
1957: beat writer, Midland Indians, *Midland Reporter-Telegram*
1958: beat writer, Midland Braves, *Midland Reporter-Telegram*
1959: beat writer, Midland Braves, *Midland Reporter-Telegram*

When I started in this business, everyone used manual typewriters—and not the portable kind. Then typewriters got a little smaller in size. It took a while before we got to electric typewriters, which were better, except when they broke down. Computers were coming in when I retired, but they were mostly unreliable at first. When computers did arrive, they spelled the end of linotype machines and hot-lead printing. I miss all that, if you can believe it. I'm eighty-nine years old, which may help explain why I feel the way I do.

In 1953, my first year as sports editor in Midland, baseball in the Southwest was beginning to fade away. It was already fighting for its life. We still had rivalries in West Texas—Big Spring, Odessa, and Lamesa—and that was important. But people were finding other things to do. Barbecue grills had just come along and people stayed home to grill hamburgers. Teams in the minor leagues were always having financial problems during the 1950s. And I wrote about that all the time.

People still came to the ballpark, don't get me wrong. The George Bush family, who lived in Midland during the 1950s, would come out for Indians' games. They were just like everybody else in those days. Both George Bushes were big baseball fans, especially George W. He played Little League here in Midland.

The major leagues wanted nothing to do with those C and D teams. The players themselves could make more money down here with off-season jobs and under the table payments and with what we called "screen green." That was the money found stuck in the screen for a player after he hit a home run. Screen green was a very big deal here. At least once in the 1950s the leagues tried to get rid of screen green, believing it was hurting baseball. On the contrary, I think it helped.

The major leagues in those days were like plantations before the

Civil War. With the reserve clause, players were treated like slaves. The pay was not great in the majors, and if you didn't like it, too bad. Thing is, you could make as much money in the minors. That's why Joe Bauman stayed put in Roswell all those years.

We had a pitcher in the Southwestern League, Jim Heise. He had been a schoolteacher in Hobbs before he went to play for Midland. The Senators called him up as a free agent. He was so excited. He got three bucks here for meal money, and there he would be given eight dollars. He didn't do so well up there in one season and soon he was back in the minors, where he probably made more money and could move around.

I didn't travel to too many away games. Mostly Odessa and Big Spring. The road from Midland to Lamesa only got paved after I came here. Midland when I arrived had thirty-five thousand people. Today it has one hundred thousand. Teams in those early days had very small pitching staffs. Some guys would pitch doubleheaders and come back for relief the next day. That, of course, brought high scores. Strangely, pitchers never got sore arms. Or at least I didn't hear about it. Eddie Jacome, he was a workhorse at Midland. One season he pitched close to 340 innings.

I grew up in New Jersey and I watched the Yankees as a boy. One summer in 1947 or 1948, I got an internship at the *Albuquerque Tribune* and filled in for Carlos Salazar at Tingley Field. All I had known were ball games played at sea level. When I saw my first game at altitude, I couldn't believe how fast the ball left the park.

In almost all the parks in Texas and New Mexico, the prevailing wind was out of the Southwest. A pitcher tried to keep the ball down, but you still got a lot of home runs. The ball carried well in Midland. We're at two thousand feet. Joe Bauman's home runs would rise and rise and rise and then disappear. A fly ball down the lines here in Midland was always a problem because the lights were bad. The umpire would watch the foul line and if he saw the outfielder cross the foul line chasing the ball, he called the ball foul. Sometimes players wouldn't even try for fly balls They would pretend the ball was foul because they couldn't see it.

Screen green was different for every team. Some teams you had to split it. Some teams you got all of it. And sometimes you got very little. When Midland hosted the Longhorn League All-Star game one year, Glenn Burns, who was on the Midland team, hit a home run to win it in the tenth inning As soon as that happened, everyone hurried off to a picnic, a big All-Star bash. Poor Glenn. When he finished circling the bases, there were only a few dollars of screen green waiting for him. All the fans had left.

The first black in Midland was a pitcher, in 1954. Frank Pickens. Frank won twenty games that year. He was from Louisiana. After he was here, and did so well, people began accepting the blacks a lot more. Frank did less well the second year and was out of baseball. Two seasons he lasted.

Hogan Park was located outside of town. We used to have a ballpark in town, but then somebody built a shopping center and the park was put outside of town, which today is close in. Hogan Park was quite a place. One time when it was real dry, a game had to be stopped because of all the grasshoppers. Someone had to come out and spray. There were rattlesnakes in the outfield. I never saw them, but the outfielders would come in and complain about them.

If you were a baseball player and you served in World War II, you often lost your prime years. Players would come back from the war and not last long in the game. Jim Prince was an exception. He was gone from baseball for six years and came back in 1947. He hit .429 for Midland that first year back and .329 the second year. Then he tailed off. He eventually became a postman in Midland.

There were some wild games here. That was the feature of West Texas baseball. Lots of action, lots of screen green. I was always writing about it in Battle Scene, my column for the newspaper. Oh, I was the object of a gripe or two. Usually because I was the official scorer for all home games. I would sit up in the press box and someone would bring me a hot dog or soft drink. When I had to use the bathroom, I asked someone to watch things for me. You can't satisfy everyone. That's what I learned. If I wrote something a player didn't like or maybe wrote something that upset a fan, I think the worst I was called was "Yankee."

Sports writing was what I always wanted to do, and I stuck with it in Midland until 1989, when I retired. We had terrible hours and pitiful pay. We didn't see our families and we had to do the work of three people. Computers are a godsend. People don't have to write stories any longer; the form's done for you. It's a new world out there. I was born in the wrong century.

. . . .

VOICES: TOM MEE

1955: radio broadcaster, Clovis Pioneers
1956: radio broadcaster, Clovis Pioneers

I did Minnesota Twins' games on television for forty-seven years. I didn't just fall into that job. I had to learn how somewhere else. And that somewhere else was little Clovis, New Mexico.

I was doing basketball games in Lewiston, Montana, in 1955. The work was fine, but I was a baseball guy. So I answered an ad in the *Sporting News*. Station KICA in Clovis wanted someone to do their play-by-play for the Clovis Pioneers. I was twenty-six, twenty-seven then.

Clovis was a good baseball town. They drew about fifteen hundred a game, which was good for those teams playing D level. The owner of the station, which was about a thousand watts, had promised me seventy-five bucks a week. When I got there he said, "Rather than paying you extra to broadcast games, why don't I give you eighty-five bucks a week?" I said OK, and that's what I made for the two years I was there.

I would go to the station at about eight in the morning and work a board shift. I wrote copy, and the second year they added a television station to the studio. I did sports on the air and weather, too. I prefer to broadcast baseball on TV, but I think I'm better at radio than TV. When the team was at home, I'd get to the ballpark about four in the afternoon. I'd mill around during batting practice, talk to people. I loved it. I was busy all the time. My wife, Noreene, had twins—a boy and a girl— during those Clovis years. So I was busy at home too.

I never traveled to road games. We did re-creations. Everybody was doing them in those days. An older guy sat in the studio next to mine at the station. He would receive messages on Morse code about was happening at a game in, say, Lubbock. Then he would type what the dot-dash said. Every half-inning he would bring me what had taken place on the field. I would broadcast that, with timeouts to do commercials. Did I have an assistant? Yeah, ten fingers.

I wanted to make it sound live. Listeners had to visualize me sitting up in the press box, so I acted. I had gotten a degree in radio/speech at the University of Minnesota and had done some dramas on air there.

That helped me re-create. *"There's a line drive down the left-field line . . . it's back near the wall . . . Paskiewicz is rounding first and heading for second . . . here's the throw . . . he slides . . . he beats it! He's safe! A double for Hammerin' Hank!"*

A lot of radio guys would hit a piece of wood with another piece of wood to make it sound like a hit. I just gave them the voice. I put the adjectives in. Nobody ever knew I was recreating a game. They thought I was there. A few times I saw someone on the street who had heard my broadcast the night before, maybe from Amarillo. They'd say, "Why aren't you with the team?" I would tell them I had re-created that game. I'm not sure they knew what that meant.

The Pioneers were a very good team my first year, very lousy the second year. The second year, we went to the Southwestern League. The best hitter on Clovis was Lincoln Boyd. He could hit a ball clear into Texas. He was about six foot five. One game he hit two grand slams, a triple, and a single. Eleven RBI in all. He left us in July of 1956 and disappeared. One story had it that he got in trouble with some girl and had to leave town. I don't think he played professional baseball after that.

Clovis was in a dry county. No beer was sold at the games or anywhere in town. You could always smuggle it. After a lot of home games the players and fans would go to a restaurant on the road out of town. We'd have a party there. Jimmy Self, who was working as a disc jockey for KICA, was a musician from Plainview. Jimmy was a great fan of the team. He sang country western songs at those parties. His most famous song was one he wrote, "Blue Christmas." No alcohol at those parties. We didn't want to expose players to drinking and bring a scandal.

The best fans we had at the ballpark were two guys about thirty years old or so. Bobby Scott had Down syndrome and Norman Vohs had what they call spasticity. His movements often were spasms and he had trouble walking. Those two were both at the ballpark almost every night. The thing is, they didn't like each other and so didn't sit near each other. They did love baseball. The last game I broadcast there was the final game of the 1956 season, against Pampa. Before the game, our manager, Glenn McQuillen, asked Norman if he wanted to play in the game. You have to realize, Clovis was forty-some games out of first place. Nothing was dependent on that game. Anyway, Norman's eyes bugged out of his head. Mac put him in the game as a pinch hitter. I kind of knew that the two managers had worked something out. Norman was going to bat.

Vohs at the plate . . . takes the first pitch . . . he taps a dribbler . . . the pitcher can't find the handle . . . Vohs is making his way to first . . . the pitcher throws to the first baseman . . . oh, no, the ball went over his head and is rolling away! . . . Vohs is going to second . . . the throw goes into left field. Vohs takes third base!

At that point everybody is yelling and screaming. The fans love it. Bobby Scott is with me up in the press box and he's excited even though he's not Norman's friend.

Vohs is not stopping at third . . . he's heading toward home . . . the left fielder juggles the ball and here's the throw . . . it's off the line . . . it won't get there in time! . . . Vohs touches home plate! Norman Vohs has scored a run! Norman Vohs has scored a run!

What a game that was. Pampa won and the Pioneers used everyone on their roster, even someone who wasn't. You know, Norman Vohs is in the record book for his only plate appearance in the minor leagues. What a tremendous thrill. To me, it was the most fun I had in Clovis.

The decision to leave Clovis came in February 1957. I found out the Southwestern League was in dire straits. In fact, it folded after the coming season and baseball in Clovis disappeared. Mostly though, Noreene and I missed Minnesota. We're both from there. The experience in Clovis, especially with the re-creating of games, helped me land a job with the St. Paul Saints, a Triple A team in the American Association. I did games there for four years. Then I went to the Twins. Calvin Griffith was the owner, and I enjoyed every minute. It was a great career with the Twins and Clovis really set it up for me.

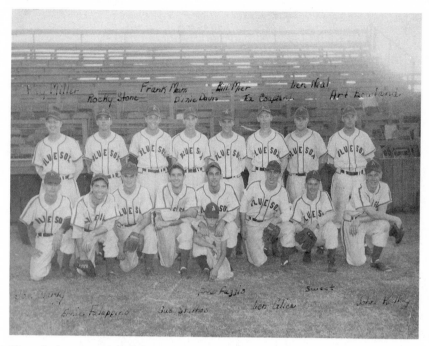

Though the 1948 Abilene Blue Sox finished with a losing record, a fan favorite was nineteen-year-old second baseman Len Glica (*kneeling third from right*). A Brooklyn Dodgers prospect, Glica moved up to Class B in 1949. In 1950, he entered the U.S. Army. Serving as a private with the 24th Infantry Division in Korea, he was killed in action on May 25, 1951, just four days after arriving in the war zone. The second professional baseball player to die in the Korean War, Glica was twenty-two years old.

Tingley Field, which opened in 1937, was the home for professional baseball in Albuquerque until 1968, when it was torn down. (Albuquerque Museum of Art and History.)

Minor league teams in the Southwest of the past played most of their games under the lights, a practice that continues. Day games in the 1940s and 1950s took place almost exclusively on Sunday afternoons. At many ballparks in the low minors like Tingley Field, the lighting left something to be desired. (Albuquerque Museum of Art and History.)

On the day before the world premiere of the movie *Ace in the Hole*, the stars of that film, invited to Albuquerque to promote the movie, watched as fisticuffs broke out on the field between the Dukes and the visiting Abilene Blue Sox.

Steady pitcher Royce Wilson Mills not only had a memorable nickname ("Rooster") but also had the distinction of being perhaps the only former player who took photographs and wrote articles for publication about games and former teammates. (Mills family collection.)

First baseman Willie Stargell became an icon for the Pittsburgh Pirates and was inducted into the Baseball Hall of Fame in 1984. Twenty-five years earlier, Stargell spent a turbulent rookie season with the Sophomore League's Roswell Pirates. The Pirates played their home games at Fair Park Stadium, the same venue where Joe Bauman had starred. (Jim Waldrip collection.)

As the sports editor for the *Albuquerque Journal* from 1950 to 1959, J. D. Kailer built a reputation as an admired journalist who did not hold back from telling what he believed, even if some readers did not like it. (Pat Kailer collection.)

Though Jackie Robinson broke the color line of Major League Baseball in 1947, de-segregation took time elsewhere. In 1951, when John W. Wingate set foot in Lobo Park in Lamesa, Texas, he became the first African American to wear a uniform in one of the leagues of the Southwest. Wingate took part in twenty-seven games for the Lobos that season. (Dan Pinto collection.)

When Vic Wertz contracted polio in 1955, he became one of the first major league players to come down with the disease. Unlike Frank Okrie, who played only in the minor leagues for Amarillo and Albuquerque and who was paralyzed for a time, Wertz had the nonparalytic form of polio. Wertz returned to the majors in 1956 and retired in 1963.

Almost everyone called Roy Woldt by his childhood nickname, "Deck." Deck Woldt was a fine hitter and gifted centerfielder, mostly for the Pampa Oilers. In his retirement he coached the Pampa High School baseball team for several years. (Roy Woldt collection.)

111

Minor league diamonds were not simply for baseball games. In times gone by, the fields were often used for weddings—of players. Here, Dean Franks and Alma Belle Messick enjoy their big night together at Roswell's Fair Park Stadium in 1949. (Joe Franks collection.)

Gary Young had a brief minor league career as a pitcher with the Roswell Rockets. Young did manage to squeeze in a wedding, to Ima Jean Long, before a 1952 game. (Courtesy Carol Hickman.)

After being married at Steer Park in Big Spring, Texas, on June 23, 1955, Huck and Emma Doe spent their second night as a married couple in the bridal suite of the Settles Hotel in Big Spring. The hotel still stands, though it has been greatly remodeled. (Emma Doe collection.)

A promising career was cut short when Jimmy Hugh Davis, nicknamed "Stormy," a first baseman for the Ballinger Cats, was beaned by a pitch during a game on July 3, 1947, in Sweetwater, Texas. A week later, Davis, only twenty years old, died.

Minor league baseball players liked to have fun. Here, two members of the Lamesa Lobos team in 1948 simulate an out-at-second-base play at Lobo Park in Lamesa, Texas. (Dan Pinto collection.)

During the 1940s and 1950s, minor leaguers in the Southwest often traveled in station wagons. Station wagons, such as this one being packed by members of the Lamesa Lobos, circa 1949, were often used for long road trips. (Dan Pinto collection.)

CHAPTER SIX

Invisible Men

In the spring of 1959, a polecat-shy, thermometer-thin first baseman reported to San Angelo, Texas, to begin a career in professional baseball. In the Bay Area of northern California, where the kid was raised in housing projects by a single mother, his high school abilities had impressed a Pittsburgh Pirates scout. Signed as a free agent for a bonus of $1,500, this prospect clearly revealed some rough edges. He didn't seem to know a pop fly from a popsicle. However, his quick bat and surprising power at the plate turned heads.

The Pirates took a chance and sent the youngster to a fledgling coalition in the Southwest. The Class D Sophomore League had been created the year before to nurture raw, young ballplayers, such as Wilver Dornel Stargell.

No sooner had Willie Stargell begun playing for the San Angelo Pirates than the team went bankrupt. This was not uncommon in the Sophomore League. A new home was found in New Mexico, and in a couple of weeks the San Angelo Pirates became the Roswell Pirates.

Willie Stargell went on to play three more years in the minors, each time advancing to a higher grade. He reached Pittsburgh for part of the 1962 season and gained full-time status with the Pirates the following year. As Stargell got on in years, Pittsburgh fans took to calling him "Pops." Pops grew to be as beloved a figure in western Pennsylvania as did another Pirate icon, Roberto Clemente. A twelve-foot statue of Stargell in his familiar, crouched batting stance stands outside the Pirates' stadium, PNC Park. In 1988, he entered baseball's Hall of Fame.

A bronze monument and a place in Cooperstown are a long way from the scruffy, oil-patch ball fields of the Southwest. Neither honor would have come Stargell's way if he had not stuck with the game that first season and overcome some accompanying rough moments.

Those hard times were documented in a book published in 1984. *Willie Stargell* was that rare autobiography written by two people. Tom Bird, once a Pirate public relations man and a close friend to Stargell, shared the writing. Presumably, Bird did most of the labor. The book told of Stargell's life up to publication. He died from complications of a stroke in 2001 at the age of sixty-one. Stargell's time in the Sophomore League is given 7 pages in the 247-page book. Most jarring was Stargell's eye-opening discovery that life in 1959 for a black man in the Southwest was just as bad and perhaps even worse than life for a black man in the Deep South.

Racism, according to Stargell, ran rampant in the Sophomore League. The league supposedly had a rule that a team could field only four blacks. Roswell had two African Americans, Stargell and John Mason, and two Latin players—a Cuban, Emiliano Telleria, and Julio Imbert from the Dominican Republic. In the eyes of Sophomore League administrators, Latins were the same as blacks. Stargell said all four men were segregated from the white players "at all times."

Stargell's color kept him from finding a place to live in Roswell. Finally, the team located a bed for him in a house rented by a black sergeant stationed at Walker Air Force Base. On road trips with the Roswell Pirates, a degrading housing situation frequently awaited him. The worst stop came in Artesia, New Mexico, where, he said, he was forced to stay in a reeking, boarded-up shack used to store fishing bait.

On occasion restaurant proprietors allowed Stargell to eat in their kitchens, but much of the time he had to wait on the team bus while the white players ate inside. Now and then one of his teammates would bring back to the bus a sandwich for Stargell. "Though I was deeply bothered by the racism, I hid the hurt inside me," Stargell/Bird wrote.

Stargell put up with white fans making remarks when he played, long after the color line in baseball had been broken. In fact, he grew accustomed to insults. Far more troubling was how black fans treated him, he said. He was fielding ground balls before one game in Hobbs, New Mexico. Behind him was the blacks-only section of the ballpark. Blacks that night let Stargell have it with a flurry of objectionable remarks. Despondent, Stargell walked slowly back to the dugout. "If anyone would console me, cheer me on, I thought, they would. I never felt so alone."

The low point came before a game in Plainview, Texas. Roswell that night was to play the Plainview Athletics. Instead of accompanying the team to the game on the bus, Stargell decided to walk to the ballpark alone from his hotel. On his way through town, Stargell said, a white man jumped out from an alley to block Stargell's path with a shotgun. Raising the gun, the man stuck both barrels against the side of Stargell's head. "If you play tonight, Nigger," he snarled, "I will blow your brains out."

Stargell continued on to the ballpark, but now deeply shaken. He couldn't talk to his white manager about this. No one wanted to listen to such talk, he decided. He thought about running, leaving town, leaving the Sophomore League behind. In the end, he stayed and played that night. When a car in the ballpark parking lot backfired, Stargell jumped. He finished the game as he had started it—knees knocking but unharmed.

The Plainview incident apparently served as a crossroads. "It strengthened my spirit," Stargell said. "I was ready for whatever lay ahead. I wasn't afraid of anyone or anything. . . . Not even when my life was threatened did I complain."

• • •

The man who threatened Stargell has often been identified as a Ku Klux Klan member, though how someone would know that is unclear. History does show that racism clearly existed in West Texas and parts of New Mexico during the 1950s. Though the civil rights movement in America got underway in 1955, desegregation in the area was slow to happen. In many places in the Southwest, up through the late 1950s, blacks could not eat in the same restaurants as whites, stay in the same hotels, sit in the same sections of movie theaters, or splash in the same swimming pools. In minor league ballparks, where blacks sometimes starred, their race was confined to a separate seating area.

Factual errors mar Stargell's book. For a period, Stargell's manager in Roswell also was once a Roswell first baseman. But Stargell and his coauthor fail to mention Joe Bauman at all, other than to misspell his name—Joe *Bowman*—and to write that he had hit a record seventy-three home runs back in 1954 for Roswell. The actual number, of course, was seventy-two.

• • •

Four years after the publication of *Willie Stargell*, journalist Bart Ripp interviewed Stargell for a story that circulated widely via the Scripps Howard

News Service. Stargell was about to enter the Hall of Fame, but the article focused entirely on Stargell's survival in the Sophomore League.

In Ripp's feature, Stargell added dramatic flourishes to his time in the Southwest. Stargell now had the Plainview redneck placing the barrels of the shotgun squarely between Stargell's eyes, not against his temple. Stargell did not merely wait patiently on the team bus while his teammates went off to eat in a restaurant he was not allowed to enter. "I'd watch the guys go in, laughing and slapping each other on the back," he told Ripp. "I'd stay on the bus and twiddle my thumbs." In Ripp's account, Stargell searched for food and found it in the most hideous places. "I would have to walk out back of a restaurant," Stargell is quoted as saying. "They would throw a piece of newspaper down on this huge chopping block. I'd eat scraps and leftovers on this block covered with flies, bloodstains and pieces of meat."

Two years before Stargell's autobiography came out, Danny Andrews, then editor of the *Plainview Herald*, did a phone interview with Stargell. Andrews said Stargell told him *two* white men showed up at Jaycee Park, the Athletics' home field, and threatened Stargell if he played that night. One of the men held a shotgun.

Two more books about Stargell appeared in the spring of 2013: *Pops: The Willie Stargell Story*, by Richard "Pete" Peterson, and *Willie Stargell*, by Frank Garland. Each goes over the same racial hostilities that Stargell faced during the summer of 1959, with slight variations.

• • •

Something definitely unnerved Stargell at Plainview. More important than finding the exact specifics of the incident is answering this question: Were blacks treated at midcentury the way author Ralph Ellison portrayed them in his groundbreaking 1952 novel *Invisible Man*? The African American narrator of that prize-winning novel said the white world sees right through people like him, that he is "socially invisible."

Racism is as much about perception as it is about ignorance, Charles Becknell, a professor in the Africana Studies Department at the University of New Mexico, said. When told what Willie Stargell wrote in his book, Becknell asked where Stargell grew up. Because Stargell came from the Oakland/Alameda area of California, Becknell said, where blacks had long moved with some ease among whites, Stargell would be looking at eastern New Mexico and West Texas with a different awareness. "It would be a

shock for anyone coming to these places when you hadn't experienced racism where you lived formerly," he added. "To black people who lived here
during that time, it was no shock if you went to Roswell or Texas or anywhere in the South. We knew how and we saw how blacks were treated."

As a football player at Hobbs High School in 1959, Becknell remembered
going to Roswell to play a game. "They threw Coke bottles at us, the thick-
glass, hard kind of bottles. Roswell I don't think was any different from
Carlsbad, Lubbock, or Clovis."

· · ·

Twenty years or so ago, Steve Whalen, a Roswell schoolteacher, read a
magazine profile about Stargell in which the writer asked Stargell to name
the worst place he had played baseball. "Roswell, New Mexico," Stargell
answered. That comment hurt Whalen. As a boy, he had worshipped
Stargell when he played in Roswell. In fact, Stargell had on different occasions presented Whalen with bats he had used and a glove that he had
scribbled his name on. In a story that echoes Babe Ruth–like lore, young
Steve one night asked Stargell to hit a home run for him. Stargell complied.
Years later, when Whalen read Stargell's disparaging words, he thought of
not only how he and a lot of youngsters had looked up to Stargell but also
how his mother, Virginia Whalen, would regularly bake bread and rolls
and give them to the Roswell Pirates. "Gosh darn, so many people in town
thought the world of him," Whalen said.

Steve's older brother, Tim, who also attended the Pirates home games,
felt the same way about Stargell during that time: "He was big physically,
but just so gentle to us kids."

Being older than his brother, Tim Whalen clearly recalled prejudice in
Roswell. He remembered a now-gone restaurant in the city named Wylie's,
which had a sign in the front window that read "We Do Not Solicit Colored
Trade." When his father explained what it meant, Tim Whalen, then a student at a Roswell Catholic school, grew confused. "The nuns were always
telling us that we're *all* God's children."

· · ·

Cuban ballplayers, particularly those with darker skin, did not have it
any easier. Julio Ramos, a pitcher who grew up in Banes Oriente, Cuba,
remembered prejudice in Roswell, where he played in 1955 and 1956.

Racism apparently was such a built-in part of the environment at that time that it was often overlooked. "There was one water fountain for whites, one for blacks and Mexicans," Ramos said. "There was no sign over which is which, but you knew. In the movie theaters there, blacks and Mexicans had to all sit together, and they knew where to go. There were bathrooms for whites and one for blacks. You got to know the one without asking."

In towns across West Texas, Ramos said, blacks on the team could not go anywhere to eat. Ramos was the designated food shopper among those who rode the Roswell team bus. "They would say, 'Julio, chicken!' They only wanted chicken. All the time, 'Julio, chicken.' I was lighter than the blacks, so I could go in the store and buy it."

Allowing only four blacks on a team, as Stargell's book said, would seem unusual for 1959, particularly since some teams in the leagues before 1959 had far more than four. Indeed, almost the entire roster of the 1949 Big Spring Broncs was Cuban, many of them "Afro-Cuban." Ramos was on that 1949 roster, and like many of his teammates and several dozen ball-playing Cubans across the country, he was signed to play by a fast-moving, fast-talking, rotund Italian.

• • •

Born in Messina, Italy, in 1890, Joe Cambria eventually settled in the Boston area, where as a young man he played semipro baseball. Later, he moved to Baltimore, Maryland, and started a laundry business and ran an amateur baseball team. At some point in the 1930s he became friends with Clark Griffith, who owned the Washington Senators. Cambria had visited Cuba earlier, and he told Griffith of the many fine ballplayers there, an untapped mother lode, he said, for American baseball teams.

With Griffith's blessing, Cambria began traveling regularly to the Caribbean island, as well as to South American countries, in search of baseball players who showed the ability to play in the States' minor leagues and perhaps one day go further. Beginning in 1934, Cambria opened a pipeline between Cuba and the Washington Senators. Things went slowly at first. However, when World War II ended, the floodgates opened wide, particularly after Jackie Robinson joined the Brooklyn Dodgers' Triple A team, the Montreal Royals, in 1946. Branch Rickey, the owner of the Brooklyn Dodgers, decided Robinson had to first pass a test with the Royals before he came to Brooklyn.

Robinson let the insults and death threats he received at spring training and afterward that season in the minors roll off him. When that happened, Joe Cambria went to work and began to send Afro-Cubans as well as lighter-complexioned Cubans to leagues across the nation. For Cambria, a fertile ground were the Spanish-speaking areas served by the West Texas–New Mexico League, beginning in 1946, and the Longhorn League, which came along a year later.

Some of the many players in the leagues of the Southwest who later rose to the major leagues were Camilo Pascual, who won more than 170 games pitching for the Senators and Minnesota Twins, Carlos Pascual, Mike Fornieles, Sandy Valdespino, and José Valdivielso. It is possible that Cambria told Griffith about a University of Havana pitcher named Fidel Castro. The young man has decent skills, Cambria may have said, but he did not have a major league fastball. Through the years, that story has evolved into Castro receiving a tryout with the Senators or the New York Yankees to even playing a few games with one or both teams. Another story has it that Castro was offered a spot in the Longhorn League, on the Big Spring, Texas, team, but at the last moment turned it down.

Cambria would sign players and frequently pass them along to Pat Stasey, a Texas native who, from 1947 to 1952, played and managed at Big Spring. Stasey's Broncs consistently were the team to beat. He later managed in Roswell and Hobbs but did less well there, likely because he had fewer Cubans. Cambria did not just concentrate on Cubans, however. Alex Carrasquel, a native of Venezuela, and one of Cambria's first signings, went on to pitch for the Washington Senators in 1939, the first of his nation to play in the United States.

• • •

In some ways it was harder for a black man to play baseball in the Southwest than it was for Jackie Robinson to play in the major leagues. Integration was not helped by a 1946 statement made by J. Alvin Gardner, president of the Texas League: "I'm positive you'll never see any Negro players on teams in Organized Baseball in the South, as long as the Jim Crow laws are in force." A large display advertisement in the *Amarillo Daily News* of May 31, 1946, reminded readers that three prominent banks in the city would be closed on June 3. That date marked the birthday of Jefferson Davis, leader of the Confederacy during the Civil War.

Four years after Robinson joined the major leagues, discussions about having a black man play in West Texas—in the *minor* leagues—finally began. A March 1951 article in the *Amarillo Daily News* revealed that Jay Haney, then the manager of the Lamesa Lobos, was considering having a black player on his team. Haney said that if permission were granted by the West Texas–New Mexico League, a black player "would not live with the whites and would eat in the back" (presumably the kitchen of a restaurant or beyond) when the team stopped for meals. "We aren't trying to break down segregation laws of the state," Haney added.

Haney said he expected attendance to rise if black players made the team. "People will come if for nothing else but to see what happens and to ride the players." A blacks-only tryout camp was scheduled to take place in Lamesa, Texas, in March 1951. Anyone who comes, said Haney, "must at all times keep his place with his own race."

The reaction to Haney's announcement resulted in a firestorm for the readers of the Amarillo newspaper. Numerous letters to the editor denounced the tryout. Haney, who owned a Humble gas station in Lamesa and was respected in the community, stood his ground and held the event. Walt Buckel, now ninety-one, worked in 1951 for what would become the *Lamesa Press-Reporter*. Buckel recalled that a local farmer, who never missed a game in Lamesa, vowed he would never return to the ballpark if the Lamesa Lobos suited up a black player.

Two black players, both twenty-three years old, stood out at the tryout. Each had played semipro baseball. Connie Heard was an outfielder, John Walker Wingate, a shortstop. When the season opened, Wingate made the roster. He played in twenty-seven games that season and batted .250. And that farmer who vowed to never return? "I won't tell you his name," said Buckel, "but I will tell you this. He kept his promise."

After serving two years in the military, Wingate returned to baseball. His contract with Lamesa was sold to the Sweetwater/Wichita Falls Spudders and then to the Roswell Rockets in 1954. In 1955, Wingate finished his minor league career with three teams in the Big State League in Texas. After baseball, he lived for many years in Beaumont, Texas, where relatives say he drove a beer truck. As the first black man to integrate baseball in the Southwest, he is nearly unknown.

"John Wingate was no Jackie Robinson," Jim Zapp, an African American and a fine outfielder and first baseman for Big Spring in the 1950s, said. Before they came to the Southwest, Wingate and Zapp both put in time in the Negro League, where Zapp starred. And both finished up with the Port Arthur Seahawks of the Big State League. "He was an average ballplayer," Zapp remembered. "Little guy. You didn't notice him. If

Wingate had been bigger and better, more people would have heard of him and know what he did."

Approximately the same age as Wingate, Len Tucker, who was signed by the St. Louis Cardinals, might have been a more acceptable choice than Wingate. Well spoken, and a college man, as was Robinson, Tucker played one year at Pampa, in 1956, and tore up the Southwestern League. He batted .404, collected 228 hits, and belted 51 home runs. Fleet afoot, like Robinson, he stole forty-seven bases. Tucker continued to play professionally through 1963 and saw duty on three different Triple A teams. Surprisingly, he never received the call from the big leagues. He taught school in Fresno, California, for more than twenty years. He died there in 2011 at age eighty-one. If he regretted never playing in the major leagues, Len Tucker did not mention it, according to relatives. Similarly, black pitcher Jim Tugerson threw forty-four consecutive shutout innings for Artesia in 1954, achieving a record of nine and one and a remarkable ERA of 1.50. Like Tucker, Tugerson too played AAA ball, but never made it to the big leagues.

. . .

Some whites stood up to the intolerance that blacks in the leagues faced. Thurman Tucker, who managed at Hobbs and Carlsbad in the 1950s, would frequently enter a café and announce, "We're going to eat here. We have a black center fielder, are you going to serve us?" If the café owner said no, Tucker took his team down the road to another place.

When Gil Carter played for Carlsbad in 1959, the Potashers began a three-game set at Plainview, Texas. In the first game, Carter hit a ball that struck the top of the outfield wall and bounced over for a home run. The next time he got up, fans yelled, "Strike out the Nigger." That's when Charlie Montgomery, owner of the Potashers, walked slowly to the pitcher's mound. Montgomery had accompanied the team to West Texas on that trip, which he did on occasion. Some Carlsbad players saw Montgomery as a grumpy guy who cared little for his players. Not that night. "If you say that again," Montgomery told the crowd in a loud voice, "I will put my team on the bus and we will never come back here."

"I wasn't sitting in the back of the team bus," said Lou Johnson of the 1954 season he spent with the Pampa Oilers. Texas hasn't changed, according to Johnson, who played minor league ball there for San Antonio and Paris, as well as Pampa. "The locations change, but not the racism." Johnson kicked around the minor leagues for thirteen years until he finally

made the Los Angeles Dodgers. He played three years there and partici-
pated in two World Series. He has worked in the Dodgers' front office for
more than thirty years, mostly in community relations.

His color kept him down on the farm, Johnson said. So did his attitude.
On the field Johnson was known as "Sweet Lou." Off the field? "I was a
mean son of a bitch. I didn't kowtow."

Herb Simpson, on the other hand, was mild as a May morning, on the field
and off. A black man who played for the Albuquerque Dukes in the early
1950s, Simpson nonetheless had an unofficial "bodyguard" on the team,
Joe Jacoby, another black ballplayer.

• • •

For every team in all four leagues in the Southwest, arrangements for black
players seldom varied. When a team pulled into town, in a bus or in station
wagons or sedans, the first stop was always the black section of that community, invariably called Colored Town. There, two or three or four black
players would be dropped off, at either a hotel or a private home. They
would eat there and sleep there. The team bus would then go on to one
of the whites-only hotels. The following afternoon, the bus would come
back and pick up the blacks and take them to the ballpark to play. To those
players who did not grow up with segregation, this always seemed strange
at first. Such separation was seldom talked about.

Segregation during the 1940s and 1950s was seen everywhere except Albuquerque. Because Albuquerque sat on Route 66, it depended greatly on
the travelers who came through, going east or west, no matter their color.
Albuquerque was clearly more liberal in terms of race than many of the
smaller towns where baseball was played. Most hotels in Albuquerque had
no problems with someone's color. Having in its midst the state's flagship
university and a large scientific laboratory gave Albuquerque a pronounced
worldliness. In addition, residing in the city was a sizable black community.
Blacks attended school with whites, blacks taught at white schools, and
blacks owned their own businesses. In the state's largest city, blacks were
not at all invisible.

. . . .

VOICES: RIGLER BROTHERS

1953: fans, Plainview Ponies
1954: fans, Plainview Ponies
1955: fans, Plainview Ponies
1956: fans, Plainview Ponies
1957: fans, Plainview Ponies
1958: fans, Plainview Athletics
1959: fans, Plainview Athletics

BRUCE RIGLER: I do remember Willie Stargell coming here, but I don't remember all the details. I'm sure that some KKK existed here, but it never had momentum. We had some come in to make it bigger, but the Plainview people weren't interested in it and it fizzled. I don't think we had a race problem here. We had some radicals on both sides, but basically we considered you be who you are, we'll be who we are, and that worked out just fine.

ROBERT RIGLER: I don't actually recall that Willie Stargell story. I do know schools in Plainview were segregated. That stopped in the early 1960s, I think. If the KKK was here, it didn't do anything in my time. Anyway, we were too busy milking cows and watching baseball. I think the first game I went to at Jaycee Park here in Plainview, Frosty Kennedy hit a home run. I am ninety-one years old and that was 1953. Frosty wanted to hit a home run on every swing. He didn't care about getting on base. He wanted the money in the screen.

BRUCE: I am four years younger than my brother, but I remember that first game, too. Frosty helped get the crowds here. He could hit the ball out of the park easily, but he hit in forty-odd straight games one year. He sold the team all by himself. Whenever he came off the field or went back out to third base or first base where he played, he'd stop to chew the fat with fans. I really liked that. He wasn't one of those players who said, "Don't bother me." He let people know he liked them. I only learned his real name was Forrest a few years ago, when I read his obituary.

ROBERT: I don't know where "Frosty" came from. He came here the first year the Ponies played, if I'm not mistaken. Then he went

somewhere else to play, which so many of them did, for more
money. You can't blame them. Then he came back here again.
Everybody was glad to see him once more. He hit sixty home runs
here the last year he played for Plainview. That was a lot of home
runs and still is. After he hit one, he'd take his chewing tobacco out
of his mouth, make a ball out of it, and then roll that ball toward the
other team's dugout. A show-off deal, I guess.

BRUCE: Frosty was kind of tubby. He had a paunch on him. Don
Stokes, our center fielder, he was an inch or two taller than Frosty.
He was a well-built fellah. A real good player to watch. So was
Jodie Beeler.

ROBERT: I think Don Stokes married a girl from Plainview. Or from
Hale Center. I saw Frosty in church a time or two. The First Presbyterian Church. Ernie Brock brought him there. Ernie was a fan
like we were, but he was much more involved with supporting the
team. He was the big push behind it. He had an insurance and real
estate business, and he helped get the money to put the Ponies
here. So did Bob Hooper. He had a car dealership in Plainview,
Dodge and Plymouth. He also owned some racehorses. Bob
Hooper, he loved putting money in the screen for Frosty.

BRUCE: Ernie had a piece of the ball club. He was a booster. He
was always selling Plainview. He would tell people, "You don't
have to go to Lubbock or Amarillo for something. You can get
it right here." He had a sign on the outfield fence at the ballpark
that advertised his business. I remember Ernie's sign and one for
Piggly Wiggly.

ROBERT: The park where the Ponies played was a nice place.
The high school boys' team plays there now. If the stands were
crowded, some fans stood out off the base paths. Or they would sit
in their cars, which they had parked up to the right- and left-field
fence. I heard a few windows get plunked. There were no dressing
rooms. You came ready to play and then you went home.

BRUCE: We usually sat on the third-base side. Somewhere between
home plate and third base. People could usually sit where they
wanted. I don't remember any reserved seats. Maybe there were
some close to the infield. It was a very relaxed thing. I think a ticket
cost about two and a half dollars. People didn't have big money,

but they had enough to go ball games. You knew everyone there. It was a social thing, a civic thing.

ROBERT: You would see the players around town. Frosty always said hello. They would eat a lot of times at Quick Lunch, which is still there, in the middle of town on East Seventh, right off the main drag.

BRUCE: Players might go to Robinson-Herring Drug Store or Camp's Drug Store. They served sandwiches there. You could get a light meal. The players stayed at the Hilton Hotel here. It is dilapidated now, and closed up, but back then it was nice. It was nine floors.

ROBERT: The Hilton, that was our skyscraper in Plainview. We didn't go to ball games every night, believe me. My brother and I ran a dairy farm. We had to get up early.

BRUCE: Our father had started the farm in 1916. There were ten children in the family, and when we come back from the war, my brother and I took it over. Nobody else wanted it.

ROBERT: I got up at 4:00 a.m. It was not easy to do that after a night game. If we got home after a ball game and there was dew on the ground, we'd bale hay all night.

BRUCE: My brother always beat me out of bed. I worked forty years without an alarm clock and got up every day at 4:21.

ROBERT: Back before professional baseball came to Plainview, softball was a big deal here. There was a world championship softball tournament here in the late 1940s, early '50s.

BRUCE: We're on the map for a lot of things. Jimmy Dean, the sausage man, he grew up here. Before he was selling sausage, he was a country singer. After the war we read in the newspaper that Jimmy Dean was going to sing somewhere. We said, "Who told that kid he could sing?" But he went to be a popular singer and star on TV. "Big Bad John," that was his biggest hit.

ROBERT: Jimmy Dean, he did a lot of things for the Wayland Baptist college here. He was back here two months before he died in 2012.

BRUCE: I'm sure when he came to visit in the 1950s, he went to Ponies games. Everybody went there at least once.

ROBERT: Or to see the Athletics, the team that took over.

BRUCE: The Plainview Athletics, they didn't have big-name players like the Ponies. We had young players with the Athletics, none that I can remember, like Frosty. I didn't go as often as I did go to the games when Frosty played. We got out of the dairy business in 1987. Sold our cows in a government buyout program. We had thirty or forty growing up, and when we stopped, we had two hundred head. We still live on the farm. Our houses are about seventy-five yards apart. My brother, I don't see much of him. He's off playing golf almost every day now.

ROBERT: Those who can, play golf. Those who can't, play anyway. That's me.

* *

VOICES: GIG BRUMMELL

1961: pitcher, Albuquerque Dukes

My best friend on the Dukes was my battery mate, Jerry Brooks. Jerry was black. I recall one time in Hobbs or Artesia a bunch of us, including Jerry, went to a bar for food after a game. The place was fairly busy, but the owner said, "We're closed." I knew he said it to keep Jerry out. I remember having conversations with Grady Wilson, our manager, about the treatment of blacks. Grady was from the South, but he was definitely not a bigot. "I don't like it one bit, Gig," he said. But there wasn't anything anybody could do.

When we went to play in Hobbs, we had to drop off the darker Latins on the team and the blacks on the north side of town. That's where there was a black community and that's where they would stay. This was 1961, and discrimination still existed, which surprised me. I had been around blacks growing up in Missouri and I didn't realize they were different.

There was a very noticeable friction with some of the darker Latins toward Anglos. Sort of reverse discrimination. They would talk Spanish around us. It wasn't blatant, but clearly the feeling was, We're just as good as you. That went away once we got on the field and played together as a team.

My real name is Bernard, but everybody called me "Gig" back then,

and they still do. My older brother had been nicknamed "Gig," and he
sort of handed down the name to me.

I came to the University of New Mexico on a partial basketball schol-
arship, but because I loved baseball—I was a pitcher—I played that
too. Doing two major sports in Division I wasn't so uncommon in the
1950s, but hardly anyone does that these days. It's just too hard.

In the summers I would go off and play baseball in the Ban Johnson
League, an amateur league mostly comprised of collegians. There was
no baseball draft in those days. Scouts picked you up and just kind of
stuck with you. Everybody had to start at the bottom and work their way
up. Almost never did anyone start with a Double A team or in Triple A.

I did well as a pitcher for UNM, and after my senior year I signed with
the Kansas City Athletics. I had the choice of going with different teams,
but I signed with the Athletics mostly because they played at Tingley
Field in Albuquerque. The Dukes, then an Athletics affiliate, were a
Class D club then, and that year was the last of the Sophomore League.

By the time I joined the Dukes, they were halfway through the first
half of the season. I didn't know anyone on the team. We had a lot of
Latins. Many of them said they were seventeen or eighteen years old
when they were probably twenty-one or twenty-two or more. I was
twenty-one when I signed.

What really stands out for me were the bus trips. We would end a
game at ten thirty or so, and then Grady Wilson would say, "Bus leaves
at midnight, y'all." Then you would spend the next five or six hours
or so on the bus to El Paso or Hobbs, or to Alpine, Texas. You'd try to
grab some sleep when you arrived and then be at the ball yard at four
o'clock, to get ready for that night's game.

I learned right away that I could compete as a professional. Grady
put me in my first game—at home. There was a lot of publicity, a UNM
player signing with the Athletics and going to play ball in Albuquerque. Tingley Field, where we played, was packed that night. I had never
played there; at UNM we played at Lobo Field, which sat at Girard and
Central. My adrenaline was flowing, my nerves jangling. But I did OK.
I pitched seven innings, I recall, and had some strikeouts. There were
no high fives or fist bumps or rump bumps. You got a handshake and
maybe a pat on the back or the butt.

Some of the Latins, like Aurelio Monteagudo from Mexico, could not
speak a word of English. Winston Llenas, a Domincan, served as the
translator. For a lot of the Latins, a bus like the Dukes' had seemed like

first-class transportation. Some of the Latins would climb up on the overhead luggage racks to sleep. That was fine with them.

I learned not to make a big deal of my education. I think less than 30 percent of the players on the Dukes had college degrees. There was some rubbing it in—"You college boys have everything going for you." That sort of thing.

Being away from home so much you had to find ways to stay busy. To fill those hours before games, I walked around and tried to familiarize myself with a town. Playing golf or going swimming were no-nos. Some of us would go to the town's public library. A library was always air-conditioned. I remember I started reading the *Wall Street Journal* in those libraries.

I left Albuquerque fairly certain I would make it to the major leagues. I had a six and four record and an ERA of 3.45. Down in the minor leagues you could sometimes be misled by a won-lost record, but not by an ERA. It was more important.

I spent two more seasons in the minors. In 1963, I was at spring training in Daytona Beach, Florida, when my shoulder started getting sore. I kept pitching. There was no physical therapy back then. If your arm hurt, you would take a big wad of tobacco, or in my case sticks of bubblegum, and go on pitching. I opened the season with the Burlington, Iowa, Bees and got seventeen strikeouts, a league record. My arm continued to bother me. Burlington sent me to a guy who may have been a chiropractor. He sure wasn't an MD. "You got to take these supplements," he told me, handing me a bottle. He was well intentioned, I suppose, but the supplements were like vitamins. They wouldn't help me. He said, "Make sure you go get some analgesic balm and rub that in, too." There was no lifting weights back then, no one doing stretching or other types of rehab. You were expected to work your way out of an injury.

I went from Burlington to Lewiston, Oregon, but I could tell the end was near. My shoulder still hurt—when I got out of baseball it was diagnosed as bursitis—and I wanted to go back to graduate school, which I had started the fall before. I didn't want to be one of those guys who kicked around the minor leagues for a long time. I wanted to get on with my life, to get married to Jeanne, which I did.

I never regretted those three years. They taught me a lot. I entered the brokerage business, motivated perhaps subconsciously by reading the *Wall Street Journal* in those libraries on the road. I worked my way up to be manager of several securities offices across New Mexico. When I interviewed prospective employees, I found myself always looking for competitive people. Some I hired were athletes, but all liked to compete, even at bridge. Grady Wilson was also an influence. He was only in his mid-thirties, and this was his first managing job. But he knew how to deal with people. He never tried to be buddy-buddy with his players. He was gracious, but in the end he expected you to be a man.

. . . .

VOICES: CARLTON HANTA

1955: shortstop, Amarillo Gold Sox
1957: shortstop, pitcher, El Paso Texans

It was just after seven in the morning when I heard the bombs. I was playing marbles in the dirt and it was December 7, 1941. I had no idea what the noise meant. Our little farm was on the windward side of Oahu, Hawaii, in the town of Kaaawa, sixteen miles from Pearl Harbor.

Soon my oldest sister came running out and saying that a war with Japan was happening. We looked up in the sky to see a dogfight taking place right above our farm. Bullets were flying all over. We ran behind a coconut tree to watch. One plane caught fire and crashed. I don't know who the plane belonged to. It was all like a movie.

Our family had a truck farm, and we took what produce we harvested downtown for the army and the navy. So the military left us alone. We were very fortunate. We heard later so many were taken away from their homes and relocated.

I was born in Kaaawa and had started to play baseball when I was six or eight years old. My father would come in for lunch at the farm and we would play pepper with him. My parents were Nisei; they had emigrated from Japan. My dad, Masuichi Hanta, loved all sports, especially baseball.

I played baseball in high school. After the war, there were no jobs available. I begged my mother to let me go to the mainland. Once there, I bummed around. I picked lettuce at first in California. Then I went to Chicago and washed dishes in a nightclub. Then back to California I went, where I picked strawberries and grapes.

For some crazy reason I decided I wanted to play football. I was five foot five and weighed 130 pounds and had never played football before. I just liked the idea.

I went to the library and started looking up colleges. I sent a letter to the University of Houston. I thought I might have a chance to play football there, since it was then smaller than some other colleges. They accepted me.

I made the freshman team in football and played both ways, halfback and defensive halfback. The next year I played jayvee football. They hit much harder, I found out right away. I got hit so hard I didn't think I would walk again. I knew when I was beat, so I quit. I decided that I would try baseball.

I told the coach of the baseball team I was a pitcher. "You're too small," he said. OK, I made up my mind I was going to be a shortstop. I had never played there. A friend hit me fungoes at shortstop every day for weeks. In those days, nobody taught you how to pick up ground balls. You learned on your own—the hard way. I got hit in the face, the head, the chest, the legs.

I played varsity baseball for three years. My proudest moment was earning a varsity letter.

The Korean War had started, and the coaches at Houston advised athletes to join ROTC and that way you would get a deferment. My eligibility ended at Houston in 1954, so I received a commission and my degree in education that same year.

In the summer of '54 I signed with Beaumont, Texas, a farm team of the Chicago White Sox. What I remember most is that I hit a home run with Beaumont. When I tell my kids about this, I don't think they believe me. We were playing the Houston Buffaloes and the pitcher was Willard Schmidt, who later pitched for the Cardinals. There was an overflow crowd that night. It was a benefit night and the fans in the outfield stood in a roped-off area. If the ball goes into the crowd there, it was a ground-rule double. I hit a deep fly ball. When I reached second base, the umpire is circling his hand in the air. I looked at him not quite understanding what it means. He is saying, "Go! Go!" Then it dawned on me: my fly ball went out of the park. Oh, my God, the good Lord must have given me this opportunity. It gives me chicken skin just thinking about it now.

Max Lanier was my roommate at Beaumont. I was put in a room with these veteran players to maybe learn something. Max had already played a long time as a pitcher for the Cardinals. He was an All-Star.

We had black players on the Beaumont team, and when we went to play Shreveport, I remember, they couldn't get on the field with white players because of Jim Crow laws. I never saw much discrimination until I got to Houston. Then I saw bathrooms marked "Whites" and "Coloreds." I had never seen that. Everywhere I went people thought I was Hawaiian. Nobody asked me about my ethnic background. I am an American of Japanese ancestry. One summer in Houston during college, I had a job loading cases of beer on freight trains. Another worker, who I'm pretty sure was a veteran who saw action in the Pacific, came over to me and said, "I used to kill people like you." I didn't say anything.

At spring training in 1955, I went back to Beaumont. They wanted to option me out to Amarillo; I loved that town. It was so easy to play ball there. The wind was blowing out and I hit three home runs in Amarillo. We traveled in a Continental Trailways bus, which was nice. Chico Heron was a good third baseman, I remember, and Eddie Locke, a good hitter.

In 1956, I went into the army to finish my military obligation. For more than a year I never touched a baseball. When I returned to the game, in 1957, it was at Austin of the Texas League. I had a tough time there; I had been away for so long. Austin optioned me to the El Paso Texans of the Southwestern League. This time we traveled in old station wagons. We would go on long trips to Midland, Odessa, and San Angelo, and when we came back, your own car would be filled with sand. Those sandstorms were all over. I even pitched in one game in El Paso.

Austin, a Milwaukee Braves team, knew how I was doing with El Paso. I was hitting over .300 for the first time in pro ball. Austin was AA, and they asked me to join them in Tulsa. Being stupid, I asked for more money than they offered. "We can't do that," they said. "Thank you," I said. "I quit." I knew I would never make it into the big tent, as they called the major leagues. I wasn't kidding anybody; I was a little guy. Guys my size were not getting into the big tent. Maybe I could have stayed in minor league baseball a little longer, but I didn't want that. I used to see Max Lanier sitting around, drinking and talking with guys about what it was like in the major leagues. I didn't want to be like that.

I got a job teaching in Yuba City, California. A man there introduced himself and said he negotiated for a professional baseball team in Japan. So I went to Japan and played for the Nankai Hawks. I played with them for three and a half years until I got traded to the Chunichi

Dragons. I had finally made the big time—the major leagues of Japan. I played one year for Chunichi, and then I quit before the opening day of the second year. I was tired. They killed me in spring training. Japan spring training lasts for hours and hours every day. I got worn down. Larry Doby was on that team, and so was Don Newcombe. He was playing first base; he could no longer pitch. It was a thrill for me being on the same team as those guys I had read about.

I stayed on in Japan for ten years as a coach, for Nankai, Chunichi, and a defunct team, the Toei Flyers. Those were year-round jobs. You belonged to the company that owned the team and you trained all year long.

After Japan, I came back to Hawaii and worked for a commercial luau business in Honolulu for twenty years. Then I retired.

Sometimes I think about when I was a boy on the farm, listening to those bombs very close by. My journey has been long since then. I tell my children and grandchildren, "Follow your dreams." I say to them, "Don't ever look back and wonder why you had done this or done that."

I never did.

CHAPTER SEVEN

The Worst Fear

Lamesa Rally Beats Dukes 6–3, as
Dawson and Okrie Are Hospitalized.

It's likely that banner headline at the top of the *Albuquerque Journal*'s sports page for August 11, 1949, made many readers take pause. Perhaps it made some of them pour a second cup of Chase & Sanborn as they sat in their breakfast nooks. It's a certainty the story accompanying the headline that Thursday morning made many of those same readers light with jittery hands another Old Gold cigarette.

The night before, the Albuquerque Dukes had begun a two-game matchup in Texas with the Lamesa Lobos. Those games, held in the small cattle-ranching and cotton-growing community south of Lubbock, would kick off a lengthy road swing. At the time, the Dukes were in first place in the West Texas–New Mexico League. Generally, a report on one more ball game, even with Albuquerque doing well, would not create much of a stir in those dog days of summer. This particular story, however, created an explosion of equal parts panic and pandemonium.

The Dukes' left fielder, Richard Dawson, had been standing in the team's dugout when a foul ball hit by Albuquerque's player-manager Hershel Martin conked Dawson behind the left ear. A skull fracture was suspected, and teammates carried Dawson off the field on a stretcher. Dick Dawson collected trauma the way barn swallows stockpile twigs. Back in May, a pitched ball had smacked him in the face with such force his cheek bones collapsed.

For the many fans of Frank Okrie, the Dukes' able shortstop, the news was far more alarming. Okrie had not played that first road game. When he boarded the bus in Albuquerque with his teammates late on Tuesday, August 9, Okrie complained of a headache. Throughout the 375-mile journey to Lamesa, Okrie slept fitfully. Upon arrival, the team checked into the Dal Paso Hotel, once the largest hotel between Dallas and El Paso, thus its name, and set upon Lamesa's town square. In the early morning, Okrie went to Hersh Martin's room and said he needed to see a doctor. Martin, a talented outfielder who had spent six years in the major leagues, two of them with the New York Yankees, sensed urgency in his shortstop's voice. He quickly arranged for Okrie to be taken to Lamesa General Hospital. There a spinal test confirmed a preliminary diagnosis—Frank Okrie had polio.

A few hours later, Martin gathered the team together in the lobby of the Dal Paso. A pitcher for the Dukes, Don Ferrarese, now living in Apple Valley, California, remembered how shaken up he felt. "I didn't know Frank well," Ferrarese said. "He was a veteran and I was in my second year of pro ball. Twenty years old is all. Frank had a real high fever, I do know that. All of us were really frightened. Polio was so contagious."

· · ·

In 1949, the word "polio" carried with it the deepest fears. Paralytic poliomyelitis—the formal name—was easily the most terrifying public health problem of the postwar era. Polio then was an acute, infectious disease, a hideous virus that, if it didn't kill you, could leave you crippled. In 1949, 42,173 cases were reported, as were 2,720 deaths. Twenty cases had turned up in Albuquerque thus far that year, and many more, it was believed, went unreported.

At that time no cure for polio existed, nor did any identifiable causes. Though other diseases of the period, such as influenza, had much higher mortality rates, none had the permanent ramifications that polio did. Polio could paralyze you for life or leave you with a withered limb or two. Or it could stick you in an iron lung. Even with an iron lung, the fatality rate for patients with bulbar polio, which attacks the brainstem and which doctors said Okrie had, exceeded 90 percent. Children were especially susceptible to polio, but adults suffered from it as well. Even healthy adults could get polio. Adults like professional baseball player Frank Okrie, who was twenty-nine years old.

Okrie was batting .276 at the time, which for him was subpar. His fielding, however, kept him in the lineup. Early in his career, which began in

1942, he was prone to errors. He worked on that shortcoming and became adept at putting a glove on the most blazing ground balls. He coupled that skill with a strong throwing arm. Albuquerque felt lucky to get Okrie in a trade from Amarillo, in 1947. Well liked, he was a quiet leader and popular with fans at Tingley Field, then the home of the Dukes and located near the city's zoo.

That polio had struck a pro ballplayer—even a ballplayer who toiled in the low minors in the sparingly populated Southwest—was national news. The Associated Press and United Press filed numerous stories about Okrie. Such reports reminded Americans that anyone can be on the receiving end of the nightmarish disease. That a president of the United States could get polio did not mean much in 1949. Franklin Roosevelt had been dead for four years, and more important, he had been diagnosed back in 1929, the Dark Ages of the disease.

· · ·

Frank Okrie may have been a bush leaguer, but he came from a baseball family, and that fact brought still more attention to his story. The Okries were Detroit people. Frank's father, Frank Anthony Okrie, had pitched for the Tigers. His time there had been brief, and almost thirty years earlier, but that did not matter to fans. Once a man has worn a major league uniform, even for a short spell, he will always receive from baseball followers a high measure of respect.

Leonard Okrie, the eldest of Frank Anthony's three sons, was already in the major leagues, performing periodically in 1949 as a catcher for the Washington Senators. Bob Okrie, the middle son, was playing Double A ball for San Antonio, a club under the aegis of the St. Louis Browns. Meanwhile, the youngest boy, Frank Raymond Okrie, was fighting for his life inside an iron lung in a dusty town whose name is pronounced "Luh-*mee-*suh" and that coincidentally has a street named Detroit.

· · ·

On Friday, August 12, 1949, the *Albuquerque Journal* reported Frank Okrie to be "desperately ill." There were for a while plans to take him to Plainview, Texas, for treatment. That soon changed as citizens everywhere rallied around the ailing ballplayer. New Mexico National Guard officers made plans to fly Okrie's wife, Mary, from Albuquerque to Texas. Though

Lamesa sits on the flat Llano Estacado, its airport was too small. That forced the plane to land in Lubbock. Waiting on the tarmac was the wife of the Lubbock Hubbers' manager, Jackie Sullivan. A Lubbock pitcher, John Myers, took Mary Okrie to the Lamesa hospital. The couple's two small children would stay with family friends in Albuquerque.

Bill Black, the Bernalillo County, New Mexico, chairman of the National Foundation for Infantile Paralysis, once the name for polio, announced that Frank Okrie would get the best care possible in Texas—and soon enough, in a hospital in Albuquerque.

The media jumped in with its own support. Radio station KOAT, which broadcast the Albuquerque Dukes games, along with the *Health City Sun* newspaper, started the Frank Okrie Fund, which fast grew to more than $3,000 in donations. Milton Price, president of the West Texas–New Mexico League, wired $100 on behalf of the league.

Almost hourly, it appeared, physicians updated Okrie's medical condition, sparing few details. Okrie, though paralyzed in his upper abdominal and lower chest muscles, had a good chance of escaping further paralysis. He wouldn't go to Plainview as planned. He was being treated with hot packs on his muscles and was given penicillin and aureomycin to prevent a lung infection. He was taking food by mouth, mainly fruits and light vegetables. He was smiling. His fever was going down. He was asking how the Dukes were doing. He would rejoin the team very soon, he said.

The Texas Health Department had to clear Okrie's departure from Lamesa, and the New Mexico Health Department had to OK his entrance. He would travel by ambulance to Lubbock and then by a U.S. Army airplane to Albuquerque's Kirtland Field. Plans called for Okrie to come home from Texas on Saturday, August 13.

Dick Dawson by now had recovered and had rejoined the team. X-rays showed Dawson did not have a skull fracture. Okrie's spot on the team was taken by a young shortstop brought over from the Oakland Oaks, a Triple A franchise in California. The request to reach out and help had grown so strong that a Frank Okrie Night was scheduled for August 17.

• • •

Stories about polio now showed up daily in most American newspapers. The March of Dimes campaign, in place since 1938, increased its volunteer force, which sought funds for research. Quarantining had grown rampant. In Albuquerque that same week in August, twelve-year-old Jimmy Chacon was diagnosed with polio after swimming at the Albuquerque Country Club. Club officials immediately closed the swimming pool. It would be reopened, the club's secretary said, "if there are no further developments."

Fifteen friends had been there with Jimmy shortly after he became ill. They too were quarantined at their homes. Across the country, swimming pools, beaches, and ponds were suspected to be breeding grounds of the polio virus and thus declared off limits. Bathing suits were locked away, cafés and theaters were shut down, and screens were placed on windows. The Dal Paso Hotel remained quarantined and sat empty. The Dukes had moved to a Lamesa boardinghouse before continuing on their road trip. When the Amarillo Gold Sox arrived to play a series with Lamesa, the team was forced to look around for other quarters in the Texas town.

The Carrie Tingley Hospital, then located in what is now Truth or Consequences, New Mexico, reported fifteen cases of polio in August 1949. Many more cases, particularly in rural parts of New Mexico, a hospital official said, might be occurring. A health officer warned people not to be alarmed, for having polio did not necessarily mean being paralyzed. But very little could calm the public's jitters. Indeed, paralysis was dreaded more by some than death.

· · ·

On August 15, news stories said the severe headaches that had plagued Okrie on the trip to Lamesa and afterward had ceased. His high fever had dropped back close to normal. He was removed from the iron lung, but it remained nearby in case of a setback. Okrie's attending physician in Lamesa said Okrie would be playing baseball again the next year, even though some paralysis remained.

As Okrie's return to Albuquerque approached, *Journal* sports editor Wilbur Bentley led the cheers. "The Dukes had a wonderful opportunity to curl up and quit last week when Frank Okrie was stricken with polio," Bentley wrote. "Well, the boys kept their chins up and business as usual was the order."

Bentley's observations were accurate. Though Albuquerque had lost its two games in Lamesa, neither contest had resembled a rout. The Dukes went on to Abilene, where they split a series with the always tough Blue Sox, and then Albuquerque beat the Hubbers in Lubbock three times in a row. "And so they ended on a high note a trip that had begun under a heavy cloud," Bentley wrote in Angle Shots, his column in the *Journal*.

A photograph of Okrie on August 17 shows him grinning as he arrived at Albuquerque's Kirtland Field. In the photo, he is lying on a portable bed and is holding his wife's hand. Mary Okrie and a nurse had flown with him from Texas. "I am glad to be home," Okrie told reporters.

More than two thousand fans came to Tingley Field for Frank Okrie Night, a game in which the Dukes hosted the Pampa Oilers. Still ailing, Frank Okrie was not able to be there.

At the end of the sixth inning, a check for "well over" $5,000 was presented to Mary Okrie. Addressing the crowd through a microphone, Mary expressed her gratitude. Fans then heard Frank's brittle voice in a greeting that had been recorded at his bedside. His was hardly Lou Gehrig's famed luckiest-man-on-Earth speech, but it brought a hefty round of applause. The two Okrie children, Tommy, three and a half, and Gail, thirteen months, were on hand to watch the proceedings, though neither seemed to understand what the fuss was all about. Knowing the significance of the game, the Dukes crushed the Oilers, fifteen to six.

The Okrie tributes continued. Almost $400 more was added to the Okrie Fund, just from Frank Okrie Night. That included 10 percent of the gate receipts, donated by the team, and money deposited by fans in barrels set up just inside the gates of Tingley Field.

Fans in Amarillo had not forgotten Okrie and soon held a night for the stricken ballplayer that brought in $850. Like all proprietors in the leagues, Gold Sox owners Bob Seeds and Buck Fausett were careful with their money. Nonetheless, they chipped in $50 each. Abilene fans sent $389, Lamesa, $325, and Pampa, $301. When the Dukes traveled to Clovis on August 22 for a doubleheader, that city designated the night be in honor of Okrie, and fans came up with $124.25. The Dukes responded rather unkindly by taking both games from the Pioneers.

Frank Okrie was getting better. "Splendid progress," the *Albuquerque Journal* reported on August 23. Okrie was moved from the Community Health Center on North Broadway to an apartment on Rio Grande Boulevard. He was permitted to get out of bed and walk a few steps each day. Okrie returned to the family home in Detroit in mid-September. "His chances of playing baseball next year appear brighter daily," an Albuquerque medical official announced.

The Dukes won the West Texas–New Mexico League pennant that year and finished ten games ahead of Abilene. Frank Okrie, however, was finished with baseball. He did not play in another game as a professional.

• • •

In a tragic coincidence, four months after Okrie was struck down by polio, an Albuquerque Dukes teammate, pitcher Frank Shone, thirty-two, was killed when the vehicle he was driving left a road just west of Fort Sumner, New Mexico, and crashed into a creek bank. Shone died on impact, and a friend, a passenger, was badly injured.

Shone had pitched well that season and the preceding one for the Dukes. Two months before Albuquerque had sold him to Hartford in the Eastern League, a Boston Braves farm team. He had played Triple A baseball and clearly wanted another chance to do so and perhaps springboard to the majors. Shone was on his way that night to buy some kitchen equipment for a sandwich shop he planned to open in Albuquerque. He left a wife and two small children.

• • •

Bad luck seemed to follow the Okries on the diamond and off, going all the way back to Frank Anthony. A slender lefthander, the elder Frank Okrie wound up pitching in only twenty-one games for the Tigers. He ended with a one and two lifetime record in that single season of 1920. The highlight of his short stay was truly a lowlight. During his brief span in the majors, the elder Frank Okrie gave up two home runs in Detroit's Navin Field—one, a towering wallop far into the right field stands from the bat of Babe Ruth, newly acquired by the New York Yankees, and the other to the Washington Senators' Sam Rice, who in twenty years in the big leagues averaged fewer than two home runs a season.

Frank Anthony Okrie died of stomach cancer in 1959. He was sixty-three. His grandson, Thomas Okrie, has but two memories of the old hurler. He liked to take out his false teeth and scare his grandkids and he liked to chew tobacco.

Bob Okrie, the middle Okrie boy, played in six minor league seasons, from 1944 to 1949, mostly for Double A teams. He was showing the makings of a future major leaguer when suddenly his health began to fail. By 1949, he came to bat only twenty-five times. Doctors were puzzled until tests showed he had something wrong with his blood. He was advised to quit baseball. Robert John Okrie died of leukemia in Detroit on April 16, 1950. He was only twenty-five. He is buried in a Detroit cemetery, alongside his father.

Leonard Okrie, the oldest boy in the family, began his baseball career in the minors in 1942. Tall and strapping, he had the physique of a backstop as well as good acumen for the game. In 1948, the Washington Senators drafted him. Would an Okrie finally succeed in the major leagues? For this Okrie, not so much, as it turned out. He played three years with the Senators and one with the Boston Red Sox, always inserted as a backup catcher, sometimes the third-string backup. He came to the plate during those four years just seventy-eight times. His career batting average was .218.

Len Okrie did, however, become a minor league manager—with modest results—for fifteen seasons in the Red Sox and Tigers organizations. Twice in the 1960s he served two-year stints as a coach for the Red Sox. And one year, 1968, he served as the Tigers bullpen coach. Len Okrie today lives in North Carolina. He does not remember much about his brother Frank's struggle with polio, he said in a telephone interview. "I really didn't pay attention. I was working on my own baseball career."

• • •

The Okrie family has never been close knit. According to Frank Raymond's son Thomas, his father's marriage did not last long. "Tumultuous," Thomas, who lives just outside Detroit, called the union of his parents. "After the polio, they did not have an amicable relationship." Mary Okrie, he said, kept him and his sister Gail away from everyone on the Okrie side of the family. "You will never see your father again," she reportedly told her children.

Speculation exists that the younger Frank Okrie battled depression when forced to stop playing. It's possible, Thomas said, that the depression led to the divorce. Without baseball, Frank Okrie had to earn a living. That vocation came in factory jobs, mostly operating boilers. He eventually remarried, and three more children came along. Thomas Okrie did not get to know them because his mother, he said, forbade it. Frank Okrie married a third time, also to a woman named Mary. The couple met in a pharmaceutical plant in Detroit, his wife Mary said. "My girlfriend was dating a guy who worked in the boiler room and that was Frank." They wed in 1964 and eventually moved to Florida.

• • •

If a cat has nine lives, Frank Okrie had a dozen. Before he came down with polio, he was wounded at Saint-Lô, France, a week after D-day, in 1944.

A shell fragment lodged near his spine, and he couldn't walk for several months. Doctors told him he would not play baseball again. But somehow he did. In fact, he played in more than a hundred games in each season, from 1946 to his last in 1949. Later, while working at a pharmaceutical plant in Michigan, a boiler exploded and Okrie suffered severe burns to his face and arms.

Thomas Okrie did see his father again, but only twice. When Thomas was a teenager, his father took him to see a Detroit Tigers game. Uncle Len Okrie was there, and he got Tigers great Charlie Gehringer to sign a baseball for his nephew. Thomas Okrie was thirty-four when he saw his father a final time. Thomas then was going through a divorce and wanted to talk to his father about why marriages break up, a subject on which Frank Raymond surely knew something. Thomas sought advice or at the least some comforting words. All he received from his father, he said, was a single word: "Eh."

Thomas Okrie is a retired educator who taught in high schools and colleges. He holds a doctorate in health sciences from Brigham Young University. Early on, he realized, he had to take care of himself. He could not depend on his parents, he said. Some years ago he traveled to the Southwest in a motor home and stopped in Albuquerque. He had hoped to find some trace of his father there. Perhaps he might rekindle a memory of when his parents and their two young children lived in the city and were treated like royalty. Albuquerque had, of course, grown since August 1949, and Thomas Okrie did not recognize anything and found nothing. Even Tingley Field, where he had once stood as a small boy and heard applause for his father, was gone, the land now a city park. "I didn't know my father when I was growing up," he said. "I didn't really know him as an adult."

• • •

Unsuccessful cures for polio came and went. Give the patient vitamin C. Do not give any patient vitamin C. Put the patient in a cast. Do not put polio sufferers in a cast. Let patients exercise. Do not let them exercise.

During the early 1950s, polio epidemics rose faster than the population, and this was the height of the baby boom. Thirty-three thousand cases of paralytic polio were diagnosed in 1950. In 1952, more than 59,000 cases and 3,000 deaths were recorded.

On August 25, 1955, six years after doctors diagnosed Frank Okrie with polio, Vic Wertz, a slugging first baseman for the Cleveland Indians, received a similar diagnosis. Wertz's polio, however, was nonparalytic. The news about Wertz received much greater attention than the Okrie case simply because Wertz was a prominent major leaguer. A home-run hitter, he had already been named an All-Star three times.

The year before, in the first game of the World Series, Wertz achieved lasting fame by hitting a ball that that seemed destined to be lost in the deep confines of the Polo Grounds in New York City. But the New York Giants' Willie Mays, playing center field, chased after the speeding high fly and grabbed it in a sensational over-the-shoulder basket catch. Mays then whirled and threw the ball to home plate to keep the Indians from scoring.

Wertz sat out the remainder of the 1955 season but came back in 1956 to hit 32 home runs and knock in 106 runs. Coincidentally, Wertz, like the Okrie family, had strong Detroit ties. The Tigers signed him and he played his first major league game in Detroit.

Twenty days in the hospital. That's all Wertz's polio cost him. He never talked about it much, perhaps because he felt he had been lucky. His luck ran out on July 7, 1983. He was fifty-eight when he died during coronary bypass surgery in Detroit.

By the time Vic Wertz made the news, researchers were already at work on an almost frantic, nonstop search for a cure. Jonas Salk's vaccine had been field-tested in 1954 and then dispensed nationwide for real in 1955. Polio cases began to decrease rapidly. Trials for an oral vaccine, conceived by Albert Sabin, began in 1957. That vaccine was licensed in 1962 and was followed by a huge decline in polio outbreaks. By 1961, only 161 cases of polio were reported in the United States.

Frank Okrie battled and won a lot of wars. He could not, however, defeat Alzheimer's. He died of complications from the disease on November 3, 2013. He was ninety-two years old.

· ·

VOICES: ROY WOLDT

1946: center fielder, Clovis Pioneers
1950: second baseman, Pampa Oilers
1951: center fielder, Pampa Oilers
1952: center fielder, Pampa Oilers
1953: center fielder, Pampa Oilers

1954: center fielder, Pampa Oilers, Amarillo Gold Sox
1955: center fielder, Pampa Oilers

I knew of Frank Okrie and I played against Frank Shone. To learn what happened to each of them was definitely a jolt. But baseball people out this way were probably even more shocked when they heard that Grover died. Everybody knew Grover. Even if you didn't much like Grover, you probably had a soft spot for him.

Grover Seitz for a long time was familiar to fans who followed the West Texas–New Mexico League. He was one of those baseball men, like Stubby Greer, Art Bowland, Hersh Martin, Joe Fortin, and Jackie Sullivan. He was around forever. Then suddenly he was gone—and just fifty years old.

Grover telephoned me that afternoon, but I wasn't home. My son told him I was still on the practice field with the Pampa High School team, which I coached. Later, I figured out what Grover probably was calling about. He had been let go by Pampa after the 1956 season and was going to take the managing job at Plainview. I really think he wanted me to go there and play for him again. But I'll never know.

I grew up in Wisconsin, north of Green Bay. I bounced around Cleveland's farm system, back east and then in Oklahoma. The Indians wanted me to return to the Eastern League. Nothing doing, I said. I went to college instead and got Cleveland to sell my contract. Eventually I got a job teaching in Pampa. I coached baseball and golf and taught classes there. I would play baseball for the Oilers when school let out. I spent thirty-one years in the Pampa schools. I married a local gal.

I think I knew Grover as well as anyone. He was a good friend all that time, which seems long ago since I'm ninety-five years old. Like everyone, Grover called me "Deck." As a kid, I got a Decker model catcher's mitt for a birthday present. I strapped that mitt to the belt of my pants and went everywhere with it. My friends in Wisconsin started calling me "Decker," then they shortened it.

Grover had been a great athlete as a young man. He grew up not far from Pampa, in White Deer, Texas. He started playing professionally in 1929. Later, he became a manager. One thing he did was keep his players out of bars. We had a very good pitcher at Pampa, Red Dial. Red drank a lot. Not in the dugout, but he definitely was a night owl. Pampa was a wet town, so there were places to go. Grover owned a pool hall, upstairs on Kingsmill Street, and they served beer. The Pampa Athletic

Club, it was called. Grover wouldn't allow his players in there or in the Bluebonnet, a Pampa nightclub.

Was Grover a drinker? On road trips, he usually disappeared by himself at night. He might drink, but he would never do it so people could see him. People thought Grover might have been drunk the night he died. Not a chance. He was driving with Lettie, his wife, a lovely, lovely gal. Also with them was a cousin and the cousin's wife and a friend. They were all on their way that night to see a Golden Gloves boxing tournament in Amarillo. Grover loved boxing.

Here's the thing. Grover had a lead foot. He liked to drive fast. He didn't want his teams to travel in buses. We always went in cars, and the reason was, Grover wanted to drive one of the cars. He'd get stopped a lot by police, but I don't think he ever got a ticket. All the cops, they knew Grover and they liked him. I was usually in the front seat with Grover on road trips, and I'd tell him, "Now watch it up ahead," and he'd get mad at say, "Let me drive, Deck." I sat in front with Joe Fortin, a terrific player who should have gone to the big leagues. He hit more than two hundred home runs in the minors. Joltin' Joe is gone now too.

Grover was an umpire baiter. He'd bump an ump or kick dirt on an ump. He'd stand there off third base, remove his cap, and scratch his bald head. Then he would take the cap and smack it on the white chalk line to show the ump where a ground ball hit. Sure, sometimes those spats were for the fans. He played to the fans lots of times. Grover was a showman. He would argue and dance around. The crowds loved it. Nights when we were getting our socks beat off, Grover really liked to stir things up.

Grover wasn't a big guy. Maybe five feet ten is all. He was portly but not afraid to use his fists. He could be a raging bull. He never dodged a fight. At Clovis, a rookie for the other team had been riding Grover from the dugout. Grover, who was coaching at third, told a pitcher on our bench to take his place. He was going to coach first base. "I'm going over there and have a little chat with that kid who's been heckling me," he said. The problem was Grover didn't know how big this kid was until the kid came out of the dugout. The kid was huge. Grover didn't back down. The kid hit Grover with a haymaker and down he went. Grover put up his hand. "Enough," he called. "Enough."

Grover could get on you if you made a stupid error. In all the years together, he never got on me. People wondered why his teams did so well. Here's why: Grover would always look for veterans. He didn't teach fundamentals. When you came to play for Grover, you had to know how to play. He wanted to be solid down the middle. Good catcher, pitcher, second base, center field. If he had that, his teams would do well. He won a lot of league titles.

The first of February 1957, Grover was at the wheel of his car. To get into Amarillo from the east you had to cross two railroad tracks. Both tracks were unlighted and unguarded. They didn't have signals on them. It was about seven thirty at night. Dark out. Grover passed over the first set of tracks. At the second set of tracks, he hit square the front of an engine pulling a freight train. Remember, Grover never eased off the accelerator. The train was only going about thirty miles per hour. Still, there had to be plenty of force in the collision. No seatbelts in those days, so all five people were ejected. On impact, even the car's motor was thrown a good ways. Those five, Grover and Lettie and the three others, they never had a chance.

The accident was big news not just because of the number killed but because Grover was driving. Baseball people all over knew him and they knew how tough he was. Buck Francis, the sports editor of the *Pampa News*, said he was surprised Grover didn't survive the crash.

They held the Seitzes' funeral in Pampa, at the First Baptist Church. Not a seat was empty. Grover and Lettie were alongside each other in one open casket. Their two sons, young men, stood there and cried out loud and even screamed for a long time. Both boys played baseball for me at the high school. Oh, it was a sad, sad day.

Grover and Lettie are buried in Fairview Cemetery in Pampa. I can look out my window and see the cemetery from home. The tracks in Amarillo where the accident happened isn't used by trains anymore. You can still drive over those tracks. Every time I do, I can't help but think of Grover. What a loss.

· ·

VOICES: ESTEBAN NÚÑEZ

1954: pitcher, Wichita Falls Spudders, Sweetwater Spudders, Roswell Rockets

1955: pitcher, Amarillo Gold Sox, Roswell Rockets, Carlsbad Potashers

1956: pitcher, Carlsbad Potashers
1957: pitcher, Hobbs Sports

I wouldn't be anything in this world if it wasn't for a young woman I met in Roswell, New Mexico. She changed my life in so many ways. Every day I wish I could thank her.

Mr. Pat Stasey, he saw me playing baseball in Cuba. I grew up in Palma Soriano, near Santiago, Cuba, where baseball is big. All good Cuban ballplayers came from around Santiago. Orestes Miñoso, Minnie Miñoso, was there, and he was a hero of mine. I started pitching in Cuba when I was fifteen. Camilo Pascual was my same age. He was the best. He pitched for Big Spring, Texas, before I came to the States. Nobody had a better curveball than Camilo Pascual.

When I played in the States, I always asked to wear number seventeen. That was the number Camilo wore for most of his time in the major leagues. He pitched up there almost twenty years. No Cuban ever pitched better than Camilo. Not even Fidel Castro.

When I came to Roswell in 1954, where Mr. Pat Stasey was managing, I didn't know one word of English. Nothing. There were a lot of Spanish-speaking players on that Roswell team. Four Cubans, I think. Nobody was speaking English to us, so we didn't speak English. Mr. Pat Stasey, he didn't know any Spanish.

I went to the Valdez Café in Roswell all the time. I ordered a hamburger every time. It was the only food I knew how to say in English. *Hamburger.* I got five dollars a day meal money and all of it goes to hamburgers. A waitress at the café, she was friendly. She felt sorry me. Frances Valdez was her name, she said. Her parents owned the Valdez Café.

Frances was eighteen, I was twenty. She helped me with my English. She would point to my hat and say *capuchón* and then say "hat." After a while she only talked to me in English. She refused to speak Spanish with me. She said it would be better for me if she didn't. It was really, really hard for me to learn. I had a ninth-grade education. But I was determined to learn English. I wanted to do it for Frances.

I finally did learn English, but it took a long, long time. I became a citizen in 1963, thanks to Frances. I can recite the Preamble. I don't think many Americans can say the Preamble to the Constitution without reading it. I can say the Pledge of Allegiance. I can sing the national anthem. I read English books all the time. I like to read James Patterson novels.

I broke my arm pitching. That's what I remember most about baseball. I was playing for Roswell, in my first year in the States, 1954. I had seen a pitcher on TV throwing a screwball. Maybe Warren Spahn of the Milwaukee Braves or Mel Parnell of the Red Sox. They threw screwballs and they were both very good. I wanted to be a better pitcher. I thought a screwball would get me to the major leagues. And that was my dream. To pitch in the major leagues.

A screwball is different from a curveball. A screwball breaks in the opposite direction of a curveball. I practiced throwing it on my own for a while. I didn't know it, but I was throwing it the wrong way. Instead of twisting my wrist and hand, I was twisting my whole arm. The first time I threw a screwball in practice, the ball went way over my catcher's head and into the stands. But I wanted to use it. I waited until one of the last games of the season. Roswell was playing Sweetwater. On my first pitch in the second inning, I threw a screwball as hard as I could. Really hard. As soon as I did, I felt something. My pitch flies into the grandstand and I fly to the ground. I got up and pulled gently on my right arm at the wrist. That's when I heard this sound. It was a rattle sound.

I turned to our shortstop, Ossie Alvarez. He was also from Cuba. I called him over. "I think I broke my arm," I told him. Ossie watched as I pulled at my wrist for him. He frowned and said it sounded bad. Then Mr. Pat Stasey, the manager, he came out to the mound to see what was wrong. He looked at my arm. He listened when I pulled at my wrist. "Yes, it's broke," he said. He had never heard of a pitcher breaking his arm throwing a baseball. But it happened to me.

I went to St. Joseph Hospital in Roswell and they x-rayed me. They operated on my arm and put a plate in there and two screws, and I got this long scar on my arm. Sixteen stitches I got. Then they put a cast on my arm. I went home to Cuba that winter, and they took the cast off and x-rayed me and the doctor told me not to be afraid to use my arm.

My arm felt better than before, but I never threw a screwball again. I went back to my fastball and changeup, which were pretty good.

Frances and I got married in 1957. We have five children. All of them were born in Roswell, and all went to college. Three are teachers, one is an attorney, one a handyman. Not one of them can speak Spanish.

I remember the long bus rides to Texas, to Big Spring and San Angelo and Abilene. I was young and I slept in the back and it didn't bother me.

When you are twenty years old, you can put up with a lot. In Roswell, they called me "Steve." Some called me "Noonie."

I hit my first home run that first year with Roswell. People stuck fifty-seven dollars into the fence—*for me!* I had never seen that before. Back in Cuba, nobody did that. Nobody had any money, especially after the revolution. I had a job in a sawmill as a boy. I earned three dollars a day. Now that job pays one dollar a day.

At first Frances would cook rice and kidney beans for me. Then she introduced me to Mexican food. I love enchiladas and tacos now and prefer them over Cuban food. In a way, I am more American than Cuban. I visited Little Cuba in Miami and I didn't like it. "You can have it," I told my friends there. When my parents left Cuba after the revolution, they settled in Miami. They were happy there. My father lived to be ninety-eight. My mother loved to play bingo in Miami and she lived to be one hundred. She never needed eyeglasses to sew or to thread a needle. I think I got good eyesight from her.

I was really disappointed that I didn't make the major leagues. They knew about my broken arm and I think they always held that against me. I am not bitter anymore. Frances wouldn't let me be that way. When I retired from baseball, Frances said, "You need to find a job." I went to work for the Mayes Lumber Company and I made forty-seven dollars a week. After thirteen years there, I was still making forty-seven dollars. I asked for a raise. The boss said no, so I quit.

I got a job with Southwest Distributors, delivering beer. I used to see Joe Bauman now and then. He was with Schlitz beer, doing sales work. I got a job as a school janitor until I had to retire because I had a neck injury. I used to be five feet nine inches. Now I am five feet six.

Roswell has been my home all this time. I built my own house on Kansas Street. I would not have met Frances if I didn't come to Roswell. When Frances got the cancer, she went for treatments. To take my mind off it, I started reading James Patterson novels. Then the cancer came back. Frances died the week after we celebrated our fiftieth wedding anniversary. That was 2007. I have her ashes in my house. With my James Patterson novels.

CHAPTER EIGHT

Diamond Ritual

"Do you take this left fielder to be your lawfully wedded husband?"

Oh, to seal the bonds of holy matrimony on a scruffy grass-and-packed-dirt playground before a thousand strangers wolfing red-dyed frankfurters and slugging down Dr Pepper.

Can't visualize it? Well, such scenes, like mosquitoes, used to cause a buzz every summer.

Because instructions for these events were not set down on paper, variations occurred. Typically, however, the groom, usually in uniform, would walk from first base to home plate, the bride from third base. They would be joined at home by an attendant, though not always.

After vows were exchanged, the couple customarily turned toward the pitcher's mound. Standing on both sides of a path leading to the mound were the groom's teammates and, often, players from the opposing team. Instead of raising swords, as seen in military services, each player would hold aloft a baseball bat to form an archway. And under this canopy of treated wood, the smiling newlyweds would stroll arm in arm.

If the ballpark were so equipped, Mendelssohn's familiar "Wedding March" would be piped in from the press box. A large floral wreath from the ball club usually completed the picture.

• • •

In days gone by, understaffed minor league teams organized only a few special nights each season. Merchants' Night, Ladies' Night, Children's Night, and Family Night just about covered it. Minor league teams today have busy marketing forces that prepare different nights nearly all season long. Most of these evenings—Desk Blotter Night, Rearview Mirror Dice Night, Nite Lite Night—involve free knickknacks to the first thousand patrons. Because a Wedding Night did not happen all the time, the occasion became special. When a wedding was about to occur, a ballclub did whatever it took to publicize it. Marriages always brought more people to a ballpark, and that meant more money for a team's owner to keep a club solvent. It helped that fans loved such ceremonies. Spectators generally knew the ballplayer, and no one was required to bring a gift, though such offerings or cash were always welcome.

If an engaged couple agreed to go public with their vows, the hype by a ball club would soon begin. For example, when Dean Franks, a pitcher for the Roswell Rockets, was about to be married, the *Roswell Daily Record* on August 17, 1949, placed two large photographs on the front page, above the fold. One photograph showed Franks in a windup on the pitcher's mound. The second photo, just as large, was a head-and-shoulders shot of his fiancée. That two pictures and an accompanying article appeared the day before the ceremony at Roswell's Fair Park Stadium was not happenstance. Nor was the sellout crowd on August 18.

Roswell's other newspaper, the *Morning Dispatch*, announced to readers that members of the Lions Club would leave their meeting early that week so they might attend the nuptials. The newspaper explained the premature exit this way: "This was done in accordance with the policy of the Lions Club to co-operate in every way with the local Rocket promotion program. The Lions Club earlier in the month held a special meeting to honor the Rockets during 'Get Acquainted' week."

To announce the intentions of Albuquerque Dukes' pitcher Jesse Priest and his bride-to-be, the *Albuquerque Tribune*, on July 11, 1952, placed this headline in large bold type across the top of the sports page: "Priest Wedding Precedes Dukes-Oiler Tilt Tonight." It is fairly safe to assume that the Dukes management convinced the newspaper of the "importance" of this story. After all, it's not often that a starting pitcher's betrothal on game day is the lead story. To further entice Priest, Albuquerque owner Cy Fausett promised to give the pitcher and his bride-to-be, Barbara Wages, 10 percent of the gate receipts on the night they married. Fausett knew how valuable Priest was to the Dukes. The year before, Priest won a record seventeen consecutive games. Moreover, Barbara Wages was from Lubbock, and there was no way Fausett was going to let them get married at Lubbock's Hubber Park.

When another Roswell pitcher, Gary Young, was hitched in that city in 1952, the photo of him reciting vows also appeared on page one of the *Roswell Daily Record*. However, the picture of the wedding party showed up two days after the ceremony, which was held on a Friday in June. The *Daily Record* did not publish on Saturdays. Even without that advance publicity, the word had spread and approximately twenty-five hundred fans turned out at Fair Park Stadium.

• • •

Many Americans were introduced to minor league ballpark weddings in 1988, via the movie *Bull Durham*. In that film, Jimmy, a devoutly Christian player for the Durham Bulls, marries Millie, a relentlessly desirous groupie to whom the term "around the horn" has nothing to do with baseball. The stands are filled for the ceremony and everyone appears delighted.

These days it is mostly fans who take part in ballpark weddings, if such an event happens at all. Engagements of fans can also be seen on million-dollar electronic scoreboards, complete with a greeting that expresses best wishes to the couple. Weddings on minor league fields for ballplayers are looked upon now as corny and archaic. However, once upon a time they were considered near-extravaganzas to a young couple, to a team, and to a town.

Most of the time, the fiancé had more interest in getting married this way than his intended. Bob Lemmel, an infielder, had been best man for his Roswell teammate Gary Young when Young married Ima Jean Long on June 20, 1952. When Lemmel's contract was sold to the Albuquerque Dukes the following year, his bride-to-be said *Not on your life* to a ballpark wedding when the topic came up. "She put her foot down," Lemmel re-called. "She wanted a church wedding." They were married at Albuquer-que's Episcopal Cathedral of St. John—without fanfare or fans.

• • •

Not every parent was overjoyed when they learned their daughter was to be married on a baseball field. "My parents didn't know what to think about that kind of wedding," said Emma Doe, who married Big Spring, Texas, catcher Bob Doe on June 23, 1955. "Daddy was stubborn-hard. He wasn't all that happy that we were getting married in the first place."

Emma Stephens, then nineteen, had first spotted Bob Doe in March

1955, at a professional wrestling match held in a barn on the Big Spring rodeo grounds. She liked what she saw. "He was sitting up at the top of the stands," she recalled. "He was real cute and he kept flirting with me." Then she noticed that he was sitting with a young woman and a baby. Married for sure, Emma thought. The wrestling over, Emma approached Bill Battle, a Big Spring barber who had announced that night's matches. She asked him about the young man in the stands. "Single," Battle said.

The next morning when the doorbell rang at her home, Emma Stephens found Battle and the young man she had seen at the wrestling match standing on the front step. If Emma wore a look of disbelief, it was likely because the two men had driven twenty-seven miles to see her. Battle introduced the fellow beside him as Bob Doe. He was twenty-five, Emma soon learned, and was called "Huck" by everyone. He had acquired the nickname from his sister, who read *The Adventures of Huckleberry Finn* when they were kids. Oh, one other thing. He was the starting catcher for the Big Spring Cosden Cops. (Coincidentally, during the 1954 Big Spring season, Huck Doe several times faced a Roswell Rockets pitcher named Tom Sawyer.)

From the day the Longhorn League began, in 1947, the Big Spring ballclub had been known by its nickname, the Broncs. In 1955, the team received a new mascot, a Cosden Cop. That name belonged to a chapter in the history of Howard County, Texas. In 1929, Native Americans were forcibly evicted from land purchased by James Cosden in the oil-rich Permian Basin. Those who did the ousting became known as Cosden Cops. Today, the Cosden Refinery in Big Spring is one of the largest refineries in the Southwest.

Bill and Retta Stephens, Emma's parents, remained tight-lipped when they met their daughter's suitor. "Huck had been in the army already," Emma recalled. "What's more, he was older and had lived for a time in San Antone." The inference being that San Antonio was a big city and big cities were sinful places. "Daddy had heard all these things about ballplayers." Before the two went on a date, Bill Stephens insisted that Emma's younger sister, also named Retta, tag along. "We mostly went to the ballpark to watch games," Emma said.

Emma had been raised in Garden City, Texas, south of Big Spring. A crossroads of 250 people, Garden City then had one red light. That light now blinks. Emma's parents ran the Garden City Café, a mom-and-pop place where Emma grew up waiting tables. She had never seen a baseball game until she started going out with her future husband.

Pepper Martin, who was no relation to the old St. Louis Cardinals ballplayer, was the Big Spring manager in 1955. He heard the couple was going to get married, and he encouraged them to do it at the team's home field, Steer Park. The announcement was soon made in the *Big Spring Daily Herald*—on the sports page.

That the marriage was to take place just three months after his daughter met Bob Doe only increased Bill Stephens's doubts. However, as the big day drew closer, he gave his blessing and accompanied his daughter on her walk from third base to home plate. It should be noted that the father of the bride wore a wide grin. Big Spring pitcher Mike Rainey served as Huck's best man.

Most of Garden City turned out for the ceremony. "All the seats were filled," Emma said, still amazed. "People were even looking over the fence." The actual attendance number was 1,166 paid, the largest figure since opening day that season. Emma Doe laughed. "Fans paid to get into our wedding," she said. Some of those same fans stuffed more than thirty dollars into the screen behind home plate.

The newlyweds were supposed to spend that night at the fifteen-story Hotel Settles, where the ballplayers stayed. One of Huck's pals advised they not go there. Hijinks might await them if they did. Instead, the couple went to Huck's mother's house in Big Spring. They stayed up all night talking with friends. The next night they went to the Settles—where they had the bridal suite. Emma laughed again. "We didn't get a honeymoon because Huck was playing ball."

• • •

As more black players entered the leagues of the Southwest, baseball teams reached out to attract black fans to the ballparks. When the Pampa Oilers' front office personnel heard that second baseman Benny Felder was engaged to Irene Boyd, a local schoolteacher, the Oilers decided to capitalize on a growing need to get more African Americans to watch baseball games. The team promised gifts to the couple and 10 percent of that night's ticket revenue—if Felder wed at Oiler Park. On August 19, 1953, an hour before a game with the Amarillo Gold Sox, a crowd of 3,202 spectators, many of them black, paid to see the wedding and the game that followed. The attendance was the second largest that season. The Oilers had coaxed the *Pampa News* and the *Amarillo Daily News* newspapers to build up the game. The teams' two aces were picked to start on the mound: "Sad Sam" Williams would win twenty-five games that year for Pampa, and Amarillo's Eddie

Locke would finish with twenty-one victories. It was no coincidence that both men who were chosen to pitch the game were black.

The all-black ceremony in Pampa was not the only one in the history of the leagues. A year later, Cy Fausett of the Dukes got wind that outfielder Herb Simpson was engaged. Fausett confronted Simpson during the 1954 season and asked about the player's wedding plans. At that point, Simpson had none, so Fausett presented the idea of a wedding at Albuquerque's Tingley Field. Simpson told Fausett he wasn't sure because his fiancée, Sophie Harris, lived in New Orleans. No problem, Fausett said. The team would pay to have Simpson's wife and mother travel to Albuquerque. The wedding was on.

• • •

On occasion, newspaper stories about ballpark weddings gave information on what a bride wore, an unusual detail for a sports page. Such uncredited information probably was written by the editor of the paper's society's page. For instance, when the Dukes' Jesse Priest married Barbara Wages, it's unlikely that the *Albuquerque Journal* sportswriter came up with this paragraph on his own:

> The bride wore a light gray shantung dress of ballerina length, with a matching bolero with rhinestones. She wore a white starched hat, also rimmed with rhinestones, navy accessories and a white orchid corsage.

Sportswriters often strained to be clever if they wrote about a wedding. An unsigned report in the *Roswell Daily Record* had this to say about the Dean Franks–Alma Belle Messick vows:

> One balk was called against the pitcher, as he reached for his bride to seal their marriage bargain with a kiss before Dr. Thompson finished the ceremony.

Because a baseball game immediately followed a ballpark wedding, some pressure for a groom to do well might be expected. The Dukes' Jesse Priest apparently was not bothered by such expectations. On the night of his wedding, Priest scattered eight hits and struck out eight as Albuquerque routed Pampa 16–1. It was Priest's eleventh win in a row. Priest's best man at the wedding, catcher Art Cuitti, got his battery mate off to a good start by hitting a two-run triple in the first inning.

In the game that followed the marriage of Albuquerque's Herb Simpson to Sophie Harris, Simpson went hitless against Amarillo but scored a run and made a sensational leaping catch in left field as the Dukes edged the Gold Sox, 3–1.

Pampa's Ben Felder went one for four at the plate the night he was married. His Oilers, however, fell to Amarillo, 11–2. And Huck Doe on his wedding night went zero for three at the plate, with a walk. Alas, Big Spring lost to the Midland Indians, 3–1.

Early in his baseball career, Doe had slid into home plate and turned his ankle. It continued to give him trouble until he finally retired from professional baseball after that 1955 season. He worked for a while in the oil fields with his father, then took a civilian job at Webb Air Force Base in Big Spring, maintaining heating and air-conditioning units. He was laboring in a boiler room at the base when a boiler blew up and burned him badly. The government gave him a medical retirement and he and Emma moved to Garden City. Doe continued to play fast-pitch softball for much of his life. He played a game on a Wednesday in 1988, and on the Saturday following he suffered a massive heart attack at home. He was fifty-eight. His father-in-law, who had become his biggest champion, outlived Huck by a year.

Emma Doe has a grandson named Brett Doe, who plays baseball for Baylor University. "He's a catcher, like his granddaddy," Emma said. More laughter. "He wants to get married at home plate."

• • •

Roswell pitcher Gary Young was only eighteen and his high school sweetheart the same age when the two got married at Fair Park Stadium's home plate. A photograph of the couple reciting their vows appeared on the front page of the *Roswell Daily Record*. "Odds were against us because we were so young," Young recalled. "But I wanted to do it and I guess it worked. We've been married more than sixty years."

Sertoma of Roswell, a national service club, stepped in to help the young couple with their big night, arranging for a pickup truck to enter the ballpark carrying an organ upright in its bed. While an organist played "Here Comes the Bride," Young, at first base, began walking to home plate, as did Ima Jean Long from third base. Standing with Young and Bob Lemmel in the wedding party were Rockets manager' Alex Monchak and his wife, who was Ima Jean's attendant. After the ceremony, the Rockets' management passed a hat among the crowd, and $168, much of it in quarters and dimes, was collected. Local merchants kicked in gifts for the couple, including a floor lamp.

Roswell gave Young the remainder of the night off. The team left the following day on a road trip, but Young didn't go along. For a wedding present, the ball club gave him that entire week off. With a 5–1 record, Young's future seemed bright indeed. In fact, three days after the wedding an article in the *Roswell Daily Record* bore this headline:

Rocket Southpaw Gary Young Is Tops in Longhorn League Hurling

Good things don't always last. Young had grown up in Alameda, California. "There was no Little League for us back then. We just learned to play in a city park," he said. On his own, at about age twelve, he started throwing curveballs. "That's what got me signed. I had a very good curveball. But I paid the price for throwing it too much when I was a kid." Did Roswell management wonder if perhaps his left arm was not right and because of that give him extra time off? Young did not know. However, by midsummer of 1952, Young's arm began to hurt so much that he could only pitch every five days or so, which was a luxury no Longhorn League team could afford. When he did get in a game, he was either walking batters or giving up hits. With a month to go in the season, the Rockets released Young. He finished with a record of seven and five and a 5.13 ERA. In his one season in the minor leagues, he pitched in only fourteen games. He would never pitch a baseball again.

"I have no regrets," Young said of his brief career. He and Ima Jean have raised three daughters, and as a couple they're as happy as that night they were married in Roswell. "Quaint," Young called the ballpark wedding. "Even so, we both thought it was pretty romantic."

• • •

The marriage ceremony in Roswell of Dean Franks, twenty-one, and Alma Belle Messick, a nineteen-year-old schoolteacher, was not the first time the couple wed, according to their son, Joe Franks, who lives in Batesville, Arkansas. The pair actually got married on August 13, 1949, at Alma Belle's home near Mountain Home, Arkansas. Why two ceremonies? "My grandfather wouldn't let them travel back to New Mexico unless they were married," Joe Franks said. It seems that Alma Belle's father, Herbert

Messick, was a Baptist preacher who did not think such a journey together would be proper.

Thus Mr. and Mrs. Lois Dean Franks motored west from northern Arkansas. They stopped the first day in Green Forest, Arkansas, and that's where they celebrated their wedding night, in one of the tourist cottages at Shady Court. The newlyweds did not dally. The couple likely arrived in Roswell on August 15, and the very next night Franks took the mound. The Rockets lost that game to the Sweetwater Spudders, 9–8. If the long automobile trip had made Dean Franks weary, he did not have time to be tired, because two nights later he was pitching once more, minutes after his ballpark wedding. With teams in the leagues having only six pitchers maximum, it was not unusual for someone to throw on two days' rest. Roswell fell again that night, to the league-leading Big Spring Broncs by a 13–11 score. Franks gave up sixteen hits in that game before being relieved in the tenth inning.

Dean Franks was born in Oakland, Arkansas, and moved to Ada, Oklahoma, when he was six years old. He and Alma Belle were kin to the same people in rural Baxter County, Arkansas. Franks returned there one summer to visit those relatives, and it was on that trip that he first laid eyes on the woman he would marry two times. They met at a pie supper held at the Monkey Run School. "Daddy bought Momma's pie—I think it was apple—because he thought my mother was so cute," Joe Franks said.

Dean Franks's given name was Lois, but he seldom used it. His mother intended him to be named Louis, but when someone went to fill out a birth certificate and asked for his name, a family member responded in an Arkansas drawl, swallowing the "u" in "Louis." All his Okie cousins knew him as "Lois Dean."

To New Mexico and Texas newspapermen, Franks was always "Big Dean." Sportswriters then tended to place the modifier "Big" in front of a lot of first names, even when that athlete was not noticeably large. Dean Franks deserved his description, however. He stood six feet four inches and weighed 220 pounds. He could bring it, especially his slider, known then as a "slurve."

Franks played ten years in the minors, most of that time in the Longhorn League, where he was a certified star. He put in four terms with the Roswell Rockets, then split two seasons with the Plainview Ponies and the Midland Indians of the Southwestern League. He finished up in 1956 with Wichita Falls, then part of the Big State League.

Based on his statistics, Franks clearly showed the makings of a future

major leaguer. In 1951, he went thirty and nine with Roswell. On that pitching staff with him was Jesse Grimes, who won fifteen games and shared
with Franks roots in the South. Grimes, who had grown up in backwoods
Alabama during the Depression, went barefoot as a boy, his family unable
to afford shoes. As an adult, Grimes felt more comfortable without socks—
even when he played baseball.

Franks followed his superb 1951 season with twenty or more wins
the next two years. He posted those records for Class C teams, but they
were impressive nonetheless. Why didn't he go up? "Those clubs were
independently owned and he couldn't go anywhere unless the club sold
Daddy's contract," Joe Franks said. "Even when scouts wanted him, he
couldn't leave." By the time Franks did have a chance to advance up
baseball's staircase, his arm was shot. Twice he had pitched more than
300 innings in a season for Roswell. On two other occasions he threw 288
and 274 innings. Franks accepted the ironman role, but such figures can
easily take a toll on any pitcher's arm.

Big Dean didn't mind all the throwing, at least at first. Joe Franks remembered his father telling him Roswell's hot, dry climate made his fastball jump. Alma Belle liked Roswell too. She found the people friendly and
kind. She enjoyed sitting with her two small sons in Roswell's Fair Park
Stadium on game nights. Toward the end, however, it was hard on her,
especially when Big Dean's arm began to ache. "A lot of time Daddy would
relieve between starts," said Joe. "He never had time to recover." Later in
life, he had surgery on his pitching elbow.

His playing days over, Big Dean returned to Arkansas, did construction
work on the White River, and hired on with the U.S. Army Corps of Engi-
neers, from which he retired.

His baseball life may have been gone, but not the careers of his sons.
He coached sons Joe and Jim Franks in American Legion ball. Both boys
wound up pitchers for the University of Central Arkansas, and Jim made
All-American at UCA. Jim later coached baseball at Arkansas Tech and Joe
at North Arkansas College at Harrison, Arkansas.

"Oh, Lord, yes, Daddy threw the ball with us all the time," Joe said.
"But he never could really pitch again, even for local town teams."

Big Dean Franks died February 2, 1994, at the age of sixty-seven. He is
buried in Pilgrims Rest Cemetery in Baxter County. Alma Belle, who died
October 8, 2013, from complications of dementia at the age of eighty-four,
joined him there.

"Daddy was a private man." Joe Franks said. "He never talked about

himself very much. He just focused on our lives, mine and Jim's and Momma's I do know Daddy was proud about how he got married out West."
For the second time.

• •

VOICES: HANK PASKIEWICZ

1951: third baseman, Clovis Pioneers
1954: third baseman, Clovis Pioneers
1955: third baseman, shortstop, pitcher, Clovis Pioneers
1956: third baseman, right fielder, pitcher, Clovis Pioneers

The team wanted me to get married in the Clovis ballpark, but I told them no. My wife was a Baptist and I was a lousy Catholic. I think it took me ten years to finish catechism. We went to talk to Sacred Heart Church in Clovis. They wouldn't let us get married in the sanctuary. We had to get married in the church office or maybe it was the vestibule. This was September 4, 1954. We got married in the morning and I played a twilight doubleheader that day. No, I don't remember how I did. [He went hitless against Amarillo but had an RBI in the first game.]

When I first got to Clovis, I rented a room. Few of the players had cars, so a buddy and I would hitchhike to the ballpark. One day, two women stopped to pick us up. They were fans on their way to the ballpark, too. Dolores Petty, one of the girls, was the daughter of a barber. She told me her father thought I was God. I started calling her Dodie. She was the woman I married.

I was raised in Chicago and was a White Sox fan. When the Cubs offered me a $500 bonus to sign, I became a Cubs fan. I never had $500 in my life. After a year in Carthage, Missouri, the Cubs shipped me to Clovis, New Mexico. I never heard of Clovis.

They could pronounce my last name in Clovis fine. "*Pas*-kuh-witz. It's Polish. They just had trouble spelling it. On a scorecard they'd write, "PASK-Z."

The Clovis Pioneers had been around since 1938. They were never tip-top. Paul Dean managed the team for a while and co-owned it with his brother Dizzy. Dizzy supposedly got up to bat one time in Clovis. This was before I got there. The Deans sold the team to a group of Clovis businessmen, including a bootlegger.

Grover Seitz managed a couple of times in Clovis and lots of years at Pampa. Grover was like a bull. Most guys were afraid of him. He was a strong guy, barrel-chested, and had a deep voice. One time Grover thought an umpire was taking too much time talking to a pitcher. Grover went to the mound and said to the ump, "Let me see that watch." The ump took off his wristwatch and Grover threw it into the stands. Guess he wanted to see time fly.

There were a lot of big hitters, not just Joe Bauman and Bob Crues. There was Frosty Kennedy for Plainview, in 1956. Also, Isaac Palmer for Lubbock. And Plainview's Don Stokes. They made more down there with home-run money than they could in the major leagues. They knew they weren't going anywhere. Don Stokes made more home-run money than he did with his salary. He could make two hundred bucks right out of the screen.

Most of the time there were no scouts at our games. I batted third. I didn't have a gun for an arm, like you see infielders today. [The Seattle Mariners'] Robinson Cano going to his right in the outfield, catching a ball and then throwing it on the line to double up the guy on first. You never saw that in my time. We used to leave our gloves on the outfield grass between innings. It's a wonder nobody ever tripped over a glove. Nobody had batting gloves, nobody had pine tar or helmets.

We got five dollars a day meal money. I was born in the Depression, I knew how to save my money. Five dollars was good if you ate only two meals a day. We'd sleep in late, to noon maybe, then eat a good meal for seventy-five cents and eat a lighter meal before the game. As a young guy, I had a cast-iron stomach. You needed it at some of those places we ate.

Clovis management was thrifty, like a lot of clubs. We'd get six bats per person. They had to last you all season. We knew how to make them last; we hit the ball on the fat part of the bat. Ballparks didn't drag their fields like they do now. Today, they drag the infield every couple of innings. A lot of fields we played on were rock piles. The ball would hit a rock, bounce up and bang you in the neck. "Get in front of it, get in front of it," all the managers would yell. Who wants to get in front of a ball that might carom into your face? In Clovis, they would flood the field to soften it up. Two days later it would be hard as the top of a table.

I was a kid, though. I was playing baseball and I was earning money. I liked it. They called me "Hammerin' Hank" in Clovis.

Nobody did pitch counts back then. Nobody knew what a pitch count was or what it meant. Red Dial, he pitched for us. One year he pitched more than 300 innings. Just think, Washington was so worried about that young kid Strasburg they cut him off at 160 innings. There were no pitching coaches back then. Pitchers could shake off signs. They were just starting to throw the slider. If you threw a hanging slider belt high, it was goodbye.

No team trainer, either. One time I told Grover I wanted to see a doctor. He said, "Aw, he'll tell you have a broken bone and you'll be out six to eight weeks." Old Grover was old school.

Grover didn't have signs. He'd sit in the dugout, and if you wondered whether you should take a pitch or hit away, he'd open and close his fist. Meaning, do what you want. The base coaches were there to send you on your way or hold you. Grover would let them know by opening and closing his fist. Do what you want.

When I came out of the service, the Cubs assigned me to Winnipeg. I didn't want to go there; it was too damn cold. So I went back to Clovis for three years. In 1956, I could see the finish line. The Cubs had teams in ten minor leagues. All ten of those teams had shortstops, where I liked to play. I knew I wasn't going to beat out ten other guys for a spot. I was already going to college and I wanted to be a coach, which I did do, in high school in Albuquerque.

I finished in the minor leagues with a .303 batting average. Not too bad, when I think about it now. Dodie and me? We're coming up on sixty years together.

. . . .

VOICES: GEORGIE LUTZ

1951: concession stand, Brainard Park, Artesia
1952: concession stand, Brainard Park, Artesia
1953: concession stand, Brainard Park, Artesia

Those ballpark weddings, they never happened in my time in Artesia, and I'm sure I would have remembered if there was one. If there was one, I probably would have let the couple eat at the ballpark for free. What I do remember is that everybody in town knew who the ballplayers were. Artesia was small enough for that to happen.

My grandmother was born on George Washington's birthday. Her name was Georgie and so is mine. She wasn't a Georgian and neither am I.

My grandparents settled on a ranch at Mayhill, New Mexico, in 1903. That's about an hour west of Artesia. I grew up around baseball. Not as a player; girls were only playing softball then. Mother and Daddy ran the concession stand where the Artesia Drillers played. I was at the ballpark every summer night and Sunday afternoon for three years. My job was selling popcorn. Seems to me it was twenty-five cents a bag. Maybe less, I don't know.

Daddy ran the concession stand for the extra income, I think. He was James Mulcock, but everyone called him "Buster." His regular job was with Guy Chevrolet in Artesia. Daddy was a baseball fan. He was also was a glad-hander. He loved to stand out in front of the concession stand and greet people and talk with them.

Mother was a hard worker. She did all the preparing and the selling of the hot dogs, the ice cream, and soft drinks. The stand was right behind home base. We never sold beer, not ever. Getting a liquor license cost so much, and a license was hard to obtain. Anyway, Artesia wasn't that kind of place. It's always been a churchgoing town. My parents were very active in the First Presbyterian Church. They were deacons and elders for years.

We had a popcorn popper, one of those old-fashioned kinds that rises up from a cart with wheels. I liked working there because it was the only money I had. I don't even remember my parents paying me a salary. They just gave me some money now and then to go to the movies.

Joe Bauman and all the other players on the Drillers, they were a part of the city. It wasn't like today in baseball, where you come in when the season starts and take off as soon as the season is over. Some of those players stayed on. Floyd Economides, you know, they call him "Greek," he played one year here, in 1954. He liked Artesia so much he found work at the big refinery and stayed on in the town. He served on the city council and retired in Artesia.

Some people think Joe Bauman played his whole career in Roswell. He didn't. He spent two years in Artesia before he hit all those home runs while at Roswell. I remember him as a very large man. He was large for those days but probably not that big for these days. Players like Joe came and went into the ballpark on their own. They didn't come in buses. They lived here. So it was no big deal when Joe or any of them were around.

The concession stand faced the field so you knew what was going on. You always knew when Joe hit a home run. First, there would be this noise, the sound of a ball being hit. A *thunking* kind of noise. Then there would be another noise, the crowd. Everybody here loved Joe. Even when he left here for Roswell.

Brainard Park was always a pretty ballpark. Oh, not a major league ballpark, but it was special. When it was built, on Thirteenth Street, it seemed far out of town. But it's a lot closer in today because Artesia has grown. We lived on Eighth and Texas.

When I worked those nights at the ballpark, I didn't see my friends from school. Baseball is an older person's game, at least it was back then. We had a lot of men from town who went to every game. More men than women. I don't ever remember a bunch of kids coming. Now and then there would be a young couple with small children. My brother Bud, he worked as the Artesia batboy for a summer. He was probably one of the youngest kids there.

I stopped working before my senior year in high school. I graduated in 1955. I was getting too old to sell popcorn. After three years with the concession stand, Mother and Daddy gave it up too. They moved to a farm at Richey Street and Freeman, sort of at the edge of town. They had a milk cow and they ran some cows. Mostly they gardened. They had a large vegetable garden. They sold chili peppers and tomatoes at a stand behind their house for years.

My parents stayed baseball fans all their lives. I had moved to the Bay Area of San Francisco and they came out to visit. We saw the Giants play a couple of times. They also came out to watch one year when the A's were in the World Series.

Daddy died when he was eighty-six. Mother died four years ago, when she was ninety-three. She kept up with Joe Bauman all that time. When she died, I found several baseballs from the Drillers that she had kept in a drawer. Some of the balls were autographed. I took a few to Central Valley Electric, across from the stadium. They have a glass display case there in the office. They were going to put the baseballs in there. The other baseballs I gave to the Artesia Historical Museum.

I don't know if those baseballs mean that much to the people who live in Artesia now. But seeing those baseballs again, after both my parents were gone, that meant a lot to me.

CHAPTER NINE

Beaning

Baseball and the Fourth of July go together like a lemonade with extra ice and a hot dog with the works. In July 1947, fans of the Sportsmen, the proper name for the professional baseball team in Sweetwater, Texas, more familiarly known as the Sports, could already taste the mustard. Up ahead for the Sports was a three-game home series with their chief Class D rival, the Ballinger, Texas, Bearcats, or Cats for short.

The first game of that matchup originally was planned for Independence Day, until the town fathers, after huddling with the managers of the two teams, agreed to push back the contest to July 3. The Sports and the Cats would then play a doubleheader on the holiday, preceded by a soap box derby and a picnic out at Lake Sweetwater. All were welcome to come, according to the weekly *Sweetwater Reporter.*

Ballinger sits an hour south of Sweetwater. The two communities share a history of ranching and railroading, supplanted today by booming oil and gas industries. Ballinger has always been smaller in size and less prosperous than Sweetwater, insecurities that perhaps led proud residents to call the community the "Greatest Little Town in Texas." Sweetwater acquired its name from the Anglos who came there in the 1870s to kill off all the buffalo. When they weren't shooting, the hunters were gulping the extremely palatable water. Even today, many citizens like to say Sweetwater's clear bubbly can make an old grouch smile in a second.

The midway point of that 1947 season found the towns' two professional baseball teams in close competition. Ballinger stood at third place in the Longhorn League, Sweetwater in fourth. Doing well in the upcoming encounters would give either the Cats or the Sports a chance to move up in the standings, perhaps gain ground on league-leading Big Spring, Texas.

Homer Garner in early July 1947 had just turned eighteen. He was listed on the roster as a pitcher for Sweetwater but thus far had not played in many games. His principal task on the team was to do dirty work for the manager, an old-school crusty named Joe Dotlich.

"Joe made me load and unload the station wagons we traveled in," Garner remembered. "He'd stand there and dribble tobacco juice and bark, 'Rook, get my bags.'"

Garner had another job, unrelated to baseball and slightly more complicated. When the Sweetwater Sports were at home, all but the team's married players stayed in the Macie Hotel, a seen-better-days hostelry near the Santa Fe Railroad tracks. Bud Wimberly resided one floor up from the players. Wimberly, known by townspeople as Ol' Bud, was a bent-over cowboy decades past his last cattle drive. In his golden years he had become a permanent guest at the Macie.

Nolan County, Texas, was then a dry county, so there would be no public sale of alcohol that Fourth of July holiday, or any day. Residents, however, had long figured out different ways to bring in the devil's brew. Every time the Sports were about to leave on a road trip, Wimberly would pull aside young Garner, the greenhorn hurler. "Homer, you bring me back some Hill and Hill, you hear?" With that Ol' Bud would stick a wad of cash in the young ballplayer's hand. Never having touched a trickle of spirits, Garner had to ask around in order to find out that Hill and Hill was a Kentucky bourbon. It was also, Garner learned, the aged cowpoke's most favored companion.

Upon the delivery of said bottles, Wimberly would disappear into his room at the Macie and not be seen for several days. Once each week or so, the same scenario took place. The owner of the Macie would say, "Homer, better go check on Ol' Bud." In other words, how about going up to see if that drunken cowpuncher had met his Maker from too much Hill and Hill?

Garner would then go up to Wimberly's room and knock loudly. Typically, no sound arose from within. In fact, the only thing coming from the room was a smell strong enough to nearly knock backward the kid pitcher. Only then would Garner get up his nerve and enter. Ol' Bud was breathing, but as always he needed a shower something fierce.

"Every time, I fought to get him into the bathroom," Garner said. "Boy, did he cuss me out."

• • •

When the Ballinger Cats arrived in Sweetwater on July 3, a bluebird afternoon, their best player was a twenty-year-old outfielder named Jimmy Hugh Davis, called "Stormy" by all. Stormy Davis was in his first year of minor league baseball. He had started the season with the Tyler, Texas, Trojans of the Class C Lone Star League. He went from there to Ballinger. It's not clear why Davis dropped down a level, for he had performed perfectly well at Tyler. In any case, in the short time he had been with the Cats, Stormy had gone great guns. By July 3, Davis, a first baseman, was displaying a .333 batting average. The Sunday before, playing at Ballinger, he had cracked a grand slam, his twenty-first home run of the season. In that home stand, he hit six home runs altogether. "Davis smacked the apple," a *Ballinger News* account reported.

Davis roomed on the Cats with Roy McMillan, a gifted shortstop out of Bonham, Texas. Though two years younger than Davis, McMillan was a steady hand, a quality that let him play sixteen years in the big leagues, mostly for Cincinnati, where twice he was an All-Star and three times a Gold Glove winner. Later, he served as a coach and manager in the majors.

McMillan's youthful maturity helped Davis. As did the genes of his own father, Cecil Davis, also nicknamed "Stormy." The senior Davis, who was born in rural Kentucky and lived in Chickasaw, Alabama, was a minor leaguer all his playing days. He spent thirteen seasons with such outfits as the Okmulgee Drillers and the Pine Bluff Judges. Cecil Davis was a better than average batsman who collected 270 home runs all told. In the field, he was an accomplished trickster. Before every game he would hide baseballs in the grass in right field, where he roamed. With bad lighting the norm in many bush league ballparks of the 1920s and 1930s, few fans or umpires could follow closely anything hit in Davis's neighborhood. From out of nowhere Davis would pounce on an unseen ball and fire it in to catch a base runner napping. Cecil Davis had the fastest jump on a baseball anyone had ever seen.

The younger Stormy did no such fooling around on the field. He was determined to reach the major leagues, which his father had not done. Guided by McMillan, Davis played the game the right way and he played it hard, more reasons why everybody liked him. A tall youth with a biscuit-and-sausage voice and a kind face, Stormy was soon running with a Ballinger girl, Pat Richards. They make a good couple, folks there said.

"Stormy had a way about him," Wilburn Sooter, who pitched for Ball-inger that year, recalled. "He was a lot of fun to be around. You just knew he was going to succeed."

The Thursday night game seemed to be going Sweetwater's way as the Sports cruised from the get-go to take a snug lead. Trouble came in the eighth inning as the Sports ran through three pitchers trying to get a single out. An exasperated Joe Dotlich called in a fourth, hoping Magnus Wilson could close the door on the Cats.

Wilson's middle name was Stanley, and most people called him "Stan." He also went by the nickname "Spec" for the horn-rimmed eyeglasses he wore. A slender southpaw, Wilson had not thrown much that season, his first year in the minor leagues. Wildness stood at the root. How wild was he? As Marty Robbins liked to sing, "Wild as the West Texas wind." Joe Dotlich sent Wilson into so few games for Sweetwater that Homer Garner had no memory of Wilson at all. In fact, at the mention of Wilson's name, Garner was certain Wilson had not even been a member of the team. But Stan Wilson definitely was with the Sports for part of that year, as news-paper reports bear out. And he was on the mound that summer night in Sweetwater.

Homer Garner did not pitch the July 3 game. For a while that evening he threw in the Sportsman Park bullpen, a metal hut that clanged loudly when struck by a baseball. But Dotlich trusted rookies about as far as he could spit a mouthful of Red Man, and thus he used Garner sparingly. "Every eighth or ninth game, I think," Garner, mostly a reliever, said. By the eighth inning, Garner had moved to the bench in the dugout, which offered a much better view of the game.

Wilburn Sooter was twenty-one that year. He played several positions for Ballinger, though mostly he pitched. Sooter said that when Stormy Davis joined the Cats, the team started to do much better. "He was so good he hit balls over light towers," Sooter recalled. "One time in Ballinger he hit a home run and I pulled the money out of the screen for him. It came to $110."

Sooter remembered something else about Davis, something that might now have some relevance. "Stormy seemed to have something wrong with him. A severe headache, maybe. He was constantly swallowing aspirin. He was taking these pills all the time. Maybe seven per game."

In the eighth inning, an errant pitch by Stan Wilson caught Davis be-hind the left ear. "Stormy should have gotten out of the way of that one," Sooter said. "It wasn't a fastball. It was a high curve that floated in there."

"He didn't move his head," Garner said. "He didn't duck. He just froze right there where he stood. I can still see him standing there."

To both men it was almost as if Stormy Davis wanted to get hit by the pitch. Sooter thought that all the aspirin may have sedated Davis and slowed his reactions. Perhaps it slackened his response to a baseball that was traveling directly toward his cranium. The impact caused Davis to crumple to the ground. Meanwhile, a Ballinger substitute was sent in to run for him. After some discussion, it was decided that Davis needed to go to the hospital.

To the next batter, Stan Wilson threw another wild pitch and then, according to the *Sweetwater Reporter*, asked on his own to be relieved. Sweetwater went on to win, 10–6. Stan Wilson received credit for the victory.

・ ・ ・

Beanings have taken on many names: "plunkings," "brush backs," "knock downs," and "chin music." Technically, a beanball means a pitched ball that hits the noggin, though a struck ball can also produce a beaning. In 1952, Alex Monchak, the player-manager of the Roswell Rockets, was beaned as he pitched batting practice and was unable to finish the season. At last report, Monchak, at age ninety-six, was one of the oldest living former major league ballplayers.

Beanings have been part of baseball since Colonel Doubleday drew in the dirt his idea for base paths. Some beanings are the result of the ball being released too early or too late by a pitcher; some are used as means of intimidation, getting a batter to worry about a head-high pitch rather than letting him stand in the batter's box and swing away naturally. Regrettably, some beanings are intentional. A pitcher might feel he's been shown up by a team and decides payback is needed. Not necessarily to the head directly, but close enough. Many a batter has dropped down or moved out of the way to avoid being hit. Many have charged the mound in anger, certain the brush back or the beaning was deliberate.

Beanings can ruin a batter's career. Boston Red Sox star outfielder Tony Conigliaro returned to the lineup a year after being seriously beaned in the face in 1967. A comeback failed. He was never the player he was before getting struck.

On rare occasions, a beaning can cause a fatality. The most famous beaning in baseball history took place at New York City's Polo Grounds on August 16, 1920, when the New York Yankees' Carl Mays, who pitched with an exaggerated sidearm motion, reared back and threw to batter Ray Chapman, the shortstop of the Cleveland Indians. Chapman was known to inch up on the plate. Mays was known to give batters a close shave—not with a razor but with a baseball.

With his submarine-like delivery, Mays made it difficult for batters to read his pitches. Chapman apparently did not get a good look at Mays' pitch that day. The fastball crashed into his left temple. The sound of horsehide meeting cranial bone could be heard in the better seats of the Polo Grounds. Believing Chapman had made contact with his bat and not with his head, Mays hustled off the mound to field the slow roller and then threw to first base. There was, of course, no base runner.

Sprawled in the batter's box, Chapman did not move. Helped up finally, he appeared dazed and had trouble walking. Even so, he seemed to be all right. As a precautionary measure, he was taken to a New York hospital. A skull fracture was diagnosed and emergency surgery ordered. He appeared to be better following the surgery, but two days later he died. He was twenty-nine years old.

Mays claimed the ball he had pitched did not feel right in his hand as he unleashed it. Maybe the ball had a bump or something on it, he said. In any event, Mays swore up and down that he did not throw purposely at Ray Chapman. Besides, he said, Chapman seemed be a statue up at the plate; he barely moved out of the way. Mays pleaded his case and Major League Baseball accepted it, calling the incident an accident. Mays, however, seldom received more than a cool reception thereafter. In particular, players and fans in Cleveland routinely booed him.

• • •

Stormy Davis, like Ray Chapman, did not wear a batting helmet. That headgear would not become mandatory in the minor or major leagues until more than two decades later.

"Most of us wore just plain old cotton caps," Wilburn Sooter said.

Homer Garner always believed that his teammate, Chester Zara, a southpaw fastballer from Staten Island, New York, let go the pitch that struck down Stormy Davis. "I remember Chet was really shook up about it," Garner said. Chet Zara died in 2010. His son, Chester Jr., said, "If my father had done that, he definitely would have talked about it." It took a newspaper clipping from 1947 to prove to Garner that Stan Wilson, not Chet Zara, was on the mound when Stormy Davis was hit.

Three hours after the beaning, Davis, now a patient at Sweetwater Hospital, appeared "irrational," according to the *Sweetwater Reporter*. An attending physician at the hospital couldn't understand that, for there was no skull fracture or brain hemorrhage. Nonetheless, the hospital contacted Davis's family members in Alabama, who left immediately for Texas.

The Sweetwater Sports, meanwhile, went on to sweep the scheduled doubleheader with Ballinger on Friday, the Fourth of July.

On Sunday night, a doctor and a special nurse from Ballinger assessed the situation and determined the need for a specialist. On Wednesday afternoon, July 9, Davis underwent surgery so doctors could examine the extent of the injury. A Dallas surgeon performed the operation, assisted by another brain specialist.

The surgery did not reveal a blood clot, as had been suspected. It did, however, show swollen brain tissue. To the hospital staff's astonishment, on Thursday afternoon, July 10, a week after the beaning, Davis rebounded and began chatting with his nurse, asking after the Cats and inquiring about his teammates. Then, just as suddenly, Davis ceased talking. He closed his eyes as if to sleep and never woke up. The time of death was 1:30 p.m. Though there was no clot or noticeable bleeding in his brain, the cause of death was given as "brain hemorrhage."

• • •

Soon after Davis died, the Stormy Davis Fund was established and contributions quickly reached $400, which was used to pay Davis's hospital expenses. Howard Green, president of the Longhorn League, asked each club to set aside one game in its schedule as Stormy Davis Night, with all proceeds going to the fund. Davis's body was shipped to Mobile, Alabama, close by Chickasaw. A funeral was held in Mobile, and burial there soon followed.

Cecil Davis, who had played baseball for a long time and had always drawn pleasure from it, was not prepared to have the game he loved turn on him. Reportedly, he never got over the tragedy that took his son. The senior Stormy died May 26, 1957. He was only fifty-six. Roy McMillan is said to have also taken hard the death of his teammate. McMillan died in 1997.

Wilburn Sooter does not remember visiting Davis in Sweetwater Hospital before he died. Nor does Sooter recall a grieving period, other than Ballinger canceling its next game with Big Spring out of respect. There was no counseling and not much reflection. Even then baseball was a business. You played it and then it was over until another game the next day.

Homer Garner spent part of the following season at Sweetwater and finished the year at Alexandria, Louisiana. He played three more seasons in the minors, rising to Class A, before putting away his glove and spikes. "I was never more than a mediocre pitcher," he said. "I met a wonderful woman who encouraged me to go back to school." Garner completed college and went on to graduate school as well, obtaining two degrees. He taught history and physical education for thirty years, mostly in the Dallas area. He lives in Paris, Texas, now and is eighty-five years old.

"I quit baseball because I felt I was not getting anywhere," Sooter said. "It was fun, but I knew I could never make a living at it." Sooter spent four seasons in the minors, including a final one with the Amarillo Gold Sox in 1948. His overall performance indicates that his decision to leave the game was probably the right choice. He departed with a ten and twenty-seven pitching mark and a .188 batting average.

After his last year in baseball, Sooter went back to Ballinger to visit people he had met there. Someone offered him a job driving a cottonseed truck and he took it. After working there for a few months, he eased the truck over to the side of a road one day and stopped. What in the world am I doing here? he asked himself.

Soon as he could, Sooter returned to his home state of Washington, where, as Homer Garner had done, he finished college and became a schoolteacher, mostly at the elementary level. He taught for thirty-two years. He also coached—freshman baseball in high school and to grade schoolers. Now eighty-eight years old, he lives in Bothell, Washington.

His final year in Sweetwater was the last time Garner saw the town. "Never had a reason to go back," he said. Twenty-five years ago, while motoring across the country, Sooter decided to see Ballinger, Texas, once more. He could not find anyone there he once knew. The Ballinger Ballpark and Rodeo Arena, where the Cats had played in 1947, was long gone, he learned. "It was never a very good field," Sooter said. Today, a cement plant sits on the site.

• • •

Everett "Ebb" Grindstaff, Ballinger's city attorney since 1957 and a teenager when Stormy Davis played for the Cats, remembered Davis's romance with Ballinger's Pat Richards. Grindstaff said Robert Wright, who manages Higginbotham Brothers, a hardware chain, likely had additional information.

To everyone in Ballinger, Wright is "Bob-O." He acquired the nickname, he said, in grade school after he took a test and did poorly: at the top of his test paper the teacher wrote "Bob" followed by a dash and then a zero. Bob-O was not born until long after Stormy Davis died, but he is something of a history buff and keeps under a bed at home a lot of old newspapers and such. After some digging around, he apologized when he could not come up with much about Stormy Davis's brief time in Ballinger. He did learn that Pat Richards later married and worked in the Soil Conservation Service office in Ballinger until she retired. Her office, he said, gave her a plaque. Richards died about eight or ten years ago, according to Bob-O. She had a son who died young and a daughter whose whereabouts Bob-O did not know.

Bob-O recommended talking to Pete Bryan, whose real name is not Pete but Alan. It seems Pete has a younger brother, and when they were small they looked alike to people in Ballinger, so Alan became "Pete" and his kid brother, whose given name is Clarence, became "Repeat." Pete reckoned that, yes, it might appear to some that everyone in Ballinger has a nickname.

Pete Bryan, who is retired from both the army and teaching school, was nine years old the summer of 1947. He worked the scoreboard at the Ballinger ballpark for all home games. He remembered Stormy Davis, at least by name, and said he would ask his brother—not Repeat, but another, older brother—if he knew anything. That brother, who is Robert but called "Bobby," had been the batboy for the Ballinger Cats in 1947.

Pete and Bobby apparently racked their brains for a few days but came up empty on the subject of Stormy Davis. "We couldn't even remember how we got to the ballpark that summer," Pete said. "We couldn't decide if Momma took us or if we rode our bikes."

• • •

Carl Mays remained in the game after beaning Ray Chapman. In the ninth inning, Mays was removed, though he too wound up the winning pitcher. Mays went on to play nine more years in the major leagues. He won 207 games and lost 126 before retiring. Never well liked before the Chapman beaning, he was much less so afterward. Though he had put up creditable numbers, he came up short in Hall of Fame voting. His demeanor, so often irascible, and Chapman's death, so terrible, apparently kept Mays out of Cooperstown.

On July 14, 1947, one day after Stormy Davis died, Stan Wilson departed the Sports and hooked up quickly with a new team, the Clovis Pioneers, in a new league, the West Texas–New Mexico League. It's not known why Wilson left Sweetwater, though one might surmise he no longer felt comfortable there and sought new surroundings. He knew of Clovis from an earlier stay and knew Clovis needed help—from anyone. The Pioneers were in the midst of a horrid season. During one stretch that summer, the team lost twenty-three consecutive games. Clovis finished fifty-seven games out of first place that year. Wilson, inconsistent at best, did not help much. In fact, he was still periodically wild. On July 15, an errant pitch he threw struck Pampa Oilers shortstop Tom O'Connell, though exactly where the ball hit O'Connell is unclear. O'Connell did continue to play the rest of that game as well as seven more seasons in the minor leagues.

Why Stan Wilson ended up playing baseball far from his hometown of Red Wing, Minnesota, is also a mystery. This much is known: In 1946 and early 1947, he had unsuccessful tryouts with the Amarillo Gold Sox. In 1947, he played some with Clovis, and when that team's manager, Joe Dotlich, left to go off to Sweetwater early in the season, Wilson apparently went with him.

During one season and a little more he spent in the minors, Wilson never overcame his inability to get the ball over the plate. He walked sixty-four batters in eighty-eight innings. He left professional baseball with a three and nine record and an ERA of 9.00. He did not fare much better as a batter, managing just one hit in forty-five trips to the plate.

Robert Pirack, a teammate at Clovis, remembered Wilson's name but nothing else about the fellow pitcher. The Society of American Baseball Research, or SABR, has a file on Wilson, but the file is empty.

It's believed Wilson tried his hand in a semipro league in the Duluth area after returning to Minnesota. Leaving baseball behind, he studied physiotherapy in Wisconsin and worked much of his life as an athletic trainer. He spent half a dozen years as an assistant trainer at the University of Minnesota then went to the Canadian Football League and worked for two teams. Back in Minnesota, he served for more than two decades as the trainer at St. Paul Academy, a private school.

It is possible that Wilson went into athletic training because of what took place in Texas in 1947, but that too cannot be confirmed. He is remembered as an unusual trainer who had a bit of a temper. He used pressure points to treat some athletes and home remedies to assist others, and when people questioned his methods, he would grow angry. Though he could be chatty as he taped ankles and massaged shoulders, he apparently did not volunteer to any athlete, coach, or friend information about the summer he had spent playing baseball in the Southwest. It's not known if he told family members or relatives about his connection to Stormy Davis.

The death of Stormy Davis was reported in the media, but accounts were never in-depth and they seldom mentioned who threw the fatal pitch. Decades later, revelations that Stan Wilson had accidentally beaned and killed a batter came as a shock to those who knew him. "I didn't even know Stan had been a pitcher," Clyde Nelson, who pitched for the University of Minnesota in the 1950s and 1960s, said. "You'd think he would have told me. I guess I can understand why he never talked about it. That was probably something he never got over."

John Mastel, the owner of a health-food store in St. Paul, Minnesota, and a good friend of Wilson for forty years, was stunned when told that a wild pitch by Wilson had unintentionally taken the life of a batter. "In all the time I knew Stan, he never even alluded to such an incident. Never once. Knowing Stan as I did, I think it would bother him that someone died on his watch. I think Stan probably didn't want it known because he worked with a lot of kids and young men and he didn't want them to know."

Magnus Stanley Wilson died May 25, 2000, in a New Brighton, Minnesota, nursing home of complications from diabetes. Earlier, doctors had amputated one of his legs. He was seventy-eight years old.

. . . .

VOICES: JIM WALDRIP

1955: pitcher, Roswell Rockets
1956: pitcher, Roswell Rockets
1957: pitcher, Hobbs Sports

It's true pitchers tried to hit guys sometimes, but not in the head. Back then a player only wore a plastic liner in his cap. That stopped nothing. If a batter crowded the plate, you did what some called "loosening him up": come in close with a pitch. The unspoken rule was if you were going to hit somebody, aim for their feet, never their head.

Old ballplayers like to say they had a cup of coffee in the big leagues.

In the minor leagues, I never had a *sweetener* for my cup of coffee. Sure, I won eighteen games one year at Hobbs, my best season. But I wasn't fooling anybody. They called the Southwestern League Class B, but it was more like C and probably tending toward D.

I didn't mind the travel, except one time. We were crossing West Texas and we came across the Clovis team on the highway coming back to New Mexico. Their old bus had gone off the road and into a bar ditch near Midland. Know what a bar ditch is? That's a roadside channel dug for drainage in these parts. Bats and gloves and equipment were scattered all over the highway. I don't think anybody was hurt, but it gave all of us a scare.

There were always places to go in all the towns, especially in Texas. Ballinger, Texas, home then of the Ballinger Westerners, was a dry town. Outside Ballinger was a little crossroads called Lowake that wasn't dry. The Ballinger players would buy beer there for twenty-five cents and then come and sell it to our players for fifty cents. Everybody liked to eat at Lowake. They had kind of a meat market there where you picked out your own steak and they would cook it and you would get a big glass of beer with it for a dollar or so. Nobody liked to play in the Ballinger ballpark, though. We called it "Fort Apache." It was a real broken-down old place. There was always a water leak behind second base, and in the middle of center field was a big depression.

Everywhere we played it was always hot, it seemed. Dizzy Dean, you may know, was part owner of the Clovis Pioneers back then. Remember what he used to say? "I don't know why it's so hot, with all these fans." In the early spring it was often so cold fans huddled under blankets.

Tom Brookshier pitched one summer for the Roswell Rockets and went seven and one. He was just out of Roswell High, where he was All State in three sports. At the University of Colorado, Tom was a three-year letterman in football and also played some baseball. He went on from there to be a star defensive back for the NFL's Philadelphia Eagles. Made All-Pro a couple of times at least, and his number is retired. Tom later was a longtime NFL broadcaster. Why he is not in the Albuquerque, New Mexico, Sports Hall of Fame is a mystery to me.

I'm fairly certain Vallie Eaves will never be considered for any hall of fame. Vallie must have been in his mid-forties when he pitched for us at Hobbs. He was called "Chief." I think he may have had some Cherokee blood in him, I don't know. He was with Sweetwater, Texas, for a while, poor guy. Sweetwater lost 109 games that season. Vallie pitched twenty-four innings and gave up forty-two hits. I looked it up; his ERA was through the roof.

Sweetwater couldn't keep old Vallie sober, nor could we in Hobbs. To make a living, Vallie roughnecked in the oil fields during the week. On Sundays he'd pitch for twenty bucks. Vallie would do OK so as long he wasn't too hung over.

For much of the time I played we used a McGregor and Goldsmith 97 baseball. Fans wanted home runs and that ball was hot. Hit on the ground, that ball would come at you like a bullet from a gun. With that ball you would hear, "Get the married guys off the infield." Teams could get a cheaper ball made by Worth, but that was a dead ball and pitchers hated it.

Some teammates started calling me "Seagull." When I asked why, they said, "You're either shitting or squawking." Lots of guys had nicknames. Carlos Pascual played in the Longhorn League when I did and he was "Big Potato." His younger brother, Camilo, the great pitcher, was "Little Potato." One guy you didn't want to knock down was Big Potato. He was wide and short, but he would come right after you on the mound.

Thurman Tucker, my manager at Hobbs, was called "Joe E. Brown." Thurman was an absolute dead ringer for the comedian. The owner of the Hobbs team was "Tootie" Schnaubert, who owned Tootie's Cashway Food Market. In Roswell, we had a batboy named "Fumes." Between innings, Fumes would go out in the parking lot, undo a car's gas cap, put in his nose in there, and sniff away. When done, he'd wobble back to the field.

In Bender Park at Hobbs, we had a lot of what was called "spring and fall" fans. They'd sneak into games by springing over the fence and falling on their ass.

Bench jockeying was a part of life then. If the other team had a manager who was fat or had a big belly, we'd yell, "Move over, Bob, you're causing the field to tilt." One night at Hobbs our pitcher, Will Ernst, started hollering at the home plate umpire. The umpire finally came over to the dugout and said, "One more word out of you Ernst and you're out of here." As he was walking away, I said, "Put your mask back on, Ump. You're scaring the kids." The umpire turned and I was out of there.

Hotel Clovis had the best chiles rellenos in their restaurant. Theirs was fried with cornmeal instead of flour. Usually hotel food was more expensive, but back in the fifties there were no fast food places anywhere.

Everybody liked to go to El Paso. You could get cheap meals and cheap cerveza there. I liked the food, but I was married and didn't go to some of the places the guys did. Such as Irma's Club, where the prostitutes came at you in twos, I heard. The Kentucky Club served cheap drinks and had a standup comic and mariachi music. You could get tequila and a Coke for ten cents. The Cave had music and sideshows. The Central Café, near the bridge, had the best carne adovada. You could get anything you wanted in Juárez, including a dog track. If you played a Sunday afternoon game, you went to the dog track that night.

The leagues had what was called a five-day look and a ten-day look. In other words, a team could look you over during the season for five days or ten days and then make a decision whether to keep you. Teams were allowed only sixteen players, and the leagues were real strict on that. After either a five-day look or ten-day look, you stayed or you looked for the door.

· ·

VOICES: JOSEPH GIEL

1955: second baseman, Odessa Eagles
1956: second baseman, Ballinger Westerners
1957: second baseman, pitcher, Ballinger Westerners

When I was playing baseball, it's a wonder more people weren't killed. I got beaned once. I was about fifteen and playing sandlot ball in Maspeth, New York, which was part of the Borough of Queens. This was in PAL, the Police Athletic League. There was no Little League in those days of the 1940s. A friend of mine, Gene Kirley, pitched the ball. He got me good. Caught me right between the eyes. I was dazed and had to sit down. Like a smart ass, I said, "If that's the best you have, I got nothing to worry about."

I came out to Texas to play for Odessa. The team had been known as the Oilers for a long time, I heard. I don't know why that year they were now the Eagles, but they were in a new league, the Southwestern League, and teams did that a lot back then—had their names changed.

I didn't play more than half a season for Odessa. I got spiked on a double play. The runner didn't do it on purpose; he made a good, clean slide. I just didn't get out of the way. His spikes ripped my foot apart. My big toe just about got torn off.

The thing that I remember best about Odessa was one Sunday game I hit a home run. It went right over a sign for this company that sold mattresses. So I won a free mattress. I was living in a private house there in Odessa, so I didn't have need for it. I sent the mattress to my dad in Queens, New York, where I grew up.

Tony York was my manager at Odessa and then at Ballinger both seasons. Matter of fact, Tony was my manager at Crowley, Louisiana, when I played in the Evangeline League. I got to like Tony; he was a good guy. He had played with the Chicago Cubs during the war years. He was the only person I ever saw who smoked a cigar in the shower. Not chewed on a cigar but smoked a lighted cigar. He would lather up and rinse himself off, all the while puffing away. Dale Scales, our first baseman at Ballinger, called me when Tony died. This was 1970, I think. Tony was only fifty-seven.

When I was a teenager back in New York City and playing sandlot ball, the major league teams would invite you for tryouts and workout days. These were held at the ballparks, like Yankee Stadium, Ebbets Field, and the Polo Grounds, when the teams that played there were out of town, on the road. I remember I would run around those fields and the grass would feel like a thick carpet. I would think, How the hell can they make an error here? Some of the fields I played on in Texas were rock quarries. You could turn your ankle just walking around.

My roomie in Ballinger was Jim Moore. He was a big guy, six feet five or so. He weighed only 180 pounds. A string bean. Jim was an outfielder and he could run like a deer. He was from Rebecca, Georgia, I remember. He was kind of a wacko.

When we went to El Paso to play, Tony was always warning us about Mexico. "Don't land your ass in jail there," he'd say. "They throw away the key." We used to walk across the bridge to Juárez. One night Jim Moore and me were in a bar at Juárez. Jim told this musician he wanted to hear the Harry James number, "The Brave Bulls." It was about 1:30 a.m. The trumpet player goes and asks the boss and the boss says no. Jim got pissed off and emptied a bottle of beer on the floor. We took off out the door. The owner is running after us and shouting, "Policía! Policía!" Next thing I know, the paddy wagon pulls up and we're pushed into it. The jail, it's like a dungeon. All I could think of was Tony's warning. I put all my money in my socks. I was afraid they were going to strip us. About 3:30 that morning the judge comes in. We tried to explain things to him. All we got back was "Yo no comprendo, yo no comprendo."

The judge fined us five bucks each for disorderly conduct. I remember I got a receipt for the fine. I kept that receipt for many years, along with all my other baseball souvenirs. Then everything got lost in a move.

In Ballinger, Jim and I lived in a garage apartment. Jim was always bringing women to the apartment. I liked the local girls, but I didn't want a marriage ticket. Ballinger was in the boonies, and the girls there, a lot of them, were looking for a way to get out.

Ballplayers in Ballinger were treated like gods. People were always inviting you to eat at their house. We would have a dinner at four thirty at somebody's house, and then you'd get to the ballpark by six o'clock for batting practice. A married couple would often invite you out for a meal at a restaurant after the game. They didn't expect anything in return. It was amazing.

We traveled in Dodge station wagons. There were three of them, all 1955 models. I was given one of the station wagons to drive. I had access to it all the time. I used to drive it to Mass on Sundays. I was friendly with Father Ryan there. I drove the station wagon to the ballpark every night. I even drove it on dates with local girls.

Ballinger held its spring training in McAllen, Texas. This was a short distance from Reynosa, Mexico. You could get any kind of sex you wanted in Reynosa for two dollars. I stayed clear of that because I didn't want a dose of something. Instead, I spent my money on gifts to send home. They had these beautiful alligator purses at Reynosa. Five dollars for a leather purse. I'd buy several and send them to New York for Christmas presents. They were gorgeous, those purses. You couldn't touch them in the U.S. for a hundred bucks or more.

The teams in the Southwestern League were not drawing many fans. Even on giveaway nights the stands were empty. Tony was good friends with Dizzy Dean, and one night Tony had Dizzy come down to make an appearance in Ballinger. Tony was trying to get more people into the ballpark. There were a few more people that night, but the next night hardly anyone showed. Maybe a hundred or so fans.

Now and then the president of the Southwestern League, W. J. Green, an oilman from San Angelo, would drop by for a game. He would be driving a new '57 Chrysler, the one with the big tail fins. After the game,

Mr. Green would buy dinner for the entire Ballinger team. I think he kept that league going all by himself.

At the end of the 1957 season, Tony said the team would be in touch. Next thing I knew I had a letter from Tony and one from Mr. Green. The team wouldn't be back and the league was going under. For me, that was it for baseball.

I played six summers in the minor leagues. In the off season, I worked at Wollman Skating Rink, a public rink in New York's Central Park. When baseball ended, I went back to Wollman to work year-round. I was working at the rink one night in 1958 when I got a telephone call. It was Father Ryan on the phone, calling from Ballinger. Father Ryan said this young woman in Ballinger was telling people that she was pregnant and that I was the father of her baby and that I was coming back to marry her. What the hell? I thought.

I admitted to Father Ryan that I had sex with the woman. I told him when the last time was, right before we were going to take a nine-game road trip. Father Ryan looked up when that trip was and calculated how long that had been and said it was more than nine months. No way that baby could be mine.

The case was going to court, Father Ryan said. I found out soon enough that the woman said she had a miscarriage, but I didn't believe that story either. Thanks to Father Ryan I got out of what could have been a real mess. That woman was trouble with a capital T.

One night this pretty young woman came by to skate at Wollman Rink. She collided with somebody on the ice and got this big cut above her eye. I gave her my handkerchief to hold against the cut and then I took her to the hospital and then to her home. I was a Good Samaritan; I didn't see her again. About a month later, she comes back to the rink. She came there to give me back my handkerchief. Not long after that we got married.

Vivienne was the most beautiful woman in the world. We had thirty-six wonderful years together, until she died in 1992. Then she was gone, like all those old baseball memories that I lost.

CHAPTER TEN

Strike Three

On the evening of August 29, 1961, a temperate night in southeastern New Mexico, the Hobbs Pirates, the defending Sophomore League champions, defeated the Albuquerque Dukes 7–1 to sweep the season-ending playoffs. The next day, Bob Guidry, the sports editor of the *Hobbs News-Sun*, began his story on the game with this sentence: "The Sophomore League Championship pennant will continue to fly at Bender Park."

That pennant never flapped in the breeze at all, for the game marked the end of the Sophomore League, the last of four minor leagues that once flourished in the American Southwest during the mid-twentieth century. In fact, the only celebrating that night came when members of the Pirates, formerly the Hobbs Cardinals, threw their manager, the hooked-nose Al Kubski, into the showers. The next day, the *News-Sun* did not put the pennant-clinching game on the front page. There was no parade, no picnic, no city hall proclamation, no banquet at Furr's Cafeteria.

Few people were truly surprised when the Sophomore League and the other three leagues died, for almost everyone could see the demises coming. As clear as that picture was, no one—not Joe Bauman, not Bob Crues, not the many players, owners, managers, or fans—could prevent the leagues from going under.

Immediately after World War II, owning a baseball team was a profitable profession. America badly missed its national pastime, which had been drastically reduced during wartime. Following the war, fans gladdened at the sight of baseball resuming, especially baseball at the easily accessed minor league level. Simply, leagues popped up everywhere. By 1947, America had fifty-two minor leagues and a paid attendance of $40.5 million. Two years later, the United States reached an all-time high with fifty-nine minor leagues. Crowds packed ballparks, and minor leagues seemed here to stay.

Then, almost as swiftly as it had risen, minor league baseball began to wither. By 1960, only twenty-two minor leagues endured. Semipro ball, once a reasonable fallback, was now nearly extinct. The remaining minor league teams were bound tightly to major league clubs. The small, unaffiliated teams of previous decades no longer existed. Attendance decreased noticeably and steadily.

The West Texas–New Mexico League, which had its beginnings in 1921, shut down after the 1954 season. The Longhorn League, where Joe Bauman gained lasting fame, found itself beset by numerous headaches and called it quits in 1955. The Southwestern League, which can be traced to 1904, replaced the Longhorn League, only to expire after two years. The Sophomore League, created in 1958 with much huzzahs, went belly up three years later.

A consuming problem during the lives of the leagues was a scarcity of fans. The Del Rio, Texas, Cowboys, which joined the Longhorn League in 1948, drew only 13,000 that season. The great distances Del Rio had to travel forced it to flee the league after a year. In San Angelo, Texas, the postwar Colts were attracting 1,500 fans per game. By the early 1950s, however, no more than 500 or so showed up each night at Guinn Field. In 1948, the Ballinger, Texas, team drew 44,000 fans. In 1957, only 16,000 spectators came out to see the Cats perform. That 1961 championship playoff game in Hobbs drew a meager 818 onlookers.

Few players or managers stayed with a team long. By the middle of the 1950s, baseball followers in New Mexico and West Texas towns did not know from one year to the next whether their team would be back in business. The Borger Gassers ran out of gas—and money—in 1954, with a few weeks left on the schedule. Owners in dire straits sold their teams outright, often for minimal sums. Lubbock, for instance, which in 1947 had one of the finest teams in minor league annals, went on the block in 1949 for $225,000. Even with inflation figured in, such a deal was akin to giving away the once-illustrious Hubbers. Fortunately, the sale didn't go through and Lubbock remained a member of the West Texas–New Mexico confederation until 1955, when the league packed it in.

Teams in the leagues began changing their nicknames as a means of generating interest, but that backfired. In 1947, Sweetwater's team was known as the Sports. A year later, the team became the Spudders. The Sweetwater Swatters existed from 1949 to 1952. The 1953 season brought forth the Sweetwater Braves, and in the team's final year, 1954, the Spud-ders, named for the workers who rig up oil wells for drilling, took the field once more. For a fan, such changes made it difficult to keep track and loyalty waned.

The disbanding of franchises began in the early 1950s. The Lamesa Lo-bos, the pride of Lamesa, Texas, since 1939, had in June 1953 a miserable record and crowds that averaged in the high two figures. In desperation, the owner jammed equipment into duffel bags, jumped the team from the West Texas–New Mexico League to the Longhorn League, and decamped to Winters/Ballinger, Texas, where the Lobos became the Eagles. Four days later, the Eagles crash-landed. The surviving players and manager were left to catch on elsewhere—if they could.

Such an impetuous relocation strategy today would be as if the New York Yankees had suddenly decided to resettle in Poughkeepsie/New-burgh, New York. Sharing one team with two smaller towns was never a good idea, though owners of flagging minor league clubs grew desperate enough to attempt it.

With the Lobos out of the baseball business, the Lamesa ballpark's light poles and grandstand were sold to Plainview, so a new team, the Ponies, could attempt a go of it. The El Paso Texans of the Southwestern League called it quits in the middle of the 1957 season and gave little notice. The owners declined to relocate or acquire a new name. The team simply died. Two teams listed on the Southwestern League's original schedule—the Pueblo, Colorado, Braves and the Pecos, Texas, Cowboys—never played a single game.

In the face of falling revenues, owners pinched pennies. On the road, groups of players were forced to stay in a single room. Bats were rationed. Shares of stock were issued by teams only to wind up being worthless. Nothing seemed to work.

The initial culprit in the erosion of the fan base came in two letters: TV. Americans in growing numbers preferred to recline in comfort on a couch in front of the family television than sit on unforgiving seats in the often-windy outdoors. Almost four million households had a television set in 1950, and that figure rose quickly in succeeding years. Ten million in 1951, fifteen million in 1952, and, by 1960, forty-five million households, or 87 percent of American homes, revealed a glowing screen almost every night. And nights, of course, were when the minor league teams played almost all their games.

Baseball, meanwhile, was at odds with itself. Though ballplayers such as Joe Bauman detested baseball's reserve clause and believed it was killing the minor leagues, George Trautman, president of the National Association of Professional Baseball Leagues, told Congress in 1953 that smaller and weaker minor league ball clubs faced extinction without the protection of the clause.

Starting in the early 1950s, *The Game of the Week*, which featured major league teams, was broadcast nationwide on television, while minor leagues struggled. The power of television was obvious. Who wanted to go to a minor league ball game when you could see the Brooklyn Dodgers or the Cleveland Indians in your living room? Or watch an episode of *Dragnet* or *Our Miss Brooks* or tune in to *The George Burns and Gracie Allen Show*? If a husband and wife had three young kids and wanted to catch a ball game and make purchases at the concession stand, that could be a bank-breaking night out. Staying at home meant catching *The Milton Berle Show*, which reached its zenith in 1956 with a guest appearance by Elvis Presley. For a TV viewer, that cost absolutely nothing.

Teens also were becoming a hard sell for the minor leagues during that era. Rock 'n' roll was sweeping the country. This was especially true in the Southwest, where in Lubbock, Texas, Buddy Holly and the Crickets had their roots and in Clovis, New Mexico, the group did much of its recording. Dancing to a 45-rpm record of "That'll Be the Day" was a lot more fun than rooting for a team that might not be around the next year.

Old or young, if you considered stepping out at night in the 1950s, drive-in movie theaters offered a mighty pull. Drive-ins were new, they were entertaining, they were different. You could head for the local Stardust or Twilight drive-in and see a double feature of *Creature from the Black Lagoon* and *The Beast from 20,000 Fathoms* for fifty cents a carload. In 1954, New Mexico had 45 drive-in theaters. In 1958, Texas had 382 drive-ins. Most drive-ins offered playgrounds where kids could hang out until it was time to sleep in the car. Ballparks didn't add such diversions until years later.

Teams also missed out on the sale of souvenirs. Today's minor league clubs peddle all number of items, from bobblehead dolls to lunch boxes, every one emblazoned with a franchise logo. A search of the eBay website turns up virtually no mementoes of the teams that played in West Texas and eastern New Mexico.

Quick fixes came into vogue. Team owners began inflating attendance figures in box scores or did not give out that information at all. Snow cones, the shaved-ice-and-syrup snack served in a paper cup, were so popular in the mid-1950s they briefly offset teams' financial woes. For a while the leagues held "Queen of the Minors" beauty contests, believing that would help fill the seats. In June 1955, the Longhorn League ordered teams to reduce their rosters to fifteen players in an attempt to stem the payroll bleeding. The El Paso Sun Kings, desperate for an attendance spike, held a One-Cent Night on August 5, 1961. Happy to put out a penny to see a ball game, 3,468 fans filled the adobe-brick grandstand of ancient Dudley Field to watch the Sun Kings go against the Artesia Dodgers, formerly the Artesia Giants. Spectators were rewarded with a twelve-inning, four-and-a-half-hour game that featured thirty-four hits and six home runs. The exceptional batting display went for naught. A little more than three weeks later, the Sophomore League was history.

The Sun Kings found a spot in the AA Texas League, while Artesia ended up teamless. The Albuquerque Dukes' owners were already maneuvering a move to the Texas League before that championship playoff series with Hobbs in 1961. Hobbs, like Artesia, like so many of the smaller communities in eastern New Mexico and West Texas before them, would never again field a professional baseball team.

As soon as one quick fix wore off for teams, another difficulty developed. With the beginning of the interstate highway system in the 1950s, there was no holding back vacationing families on the faster roadways. "See the USA in your Chevrolet," Dinah Shore sang in praise of the sponsor of her popular 1950s–early 1960s television show. And households did just that, climbing in their Chevy Nomad wagons, the back windows plastered with tourist-site decals. Who wanted to see a new hitter acquired by the Amarillo Gold Sox when you could glimpse Old Faithful at Yellowstone National Park? When Disneyland Park opened in 1955, the stream of station wagons heading west resembled the wooden-wheel Conestoga adventurers of a century before. Who wanted to watch the Clovis Pioneers play on Wednesday night when you could spend a good part of a day at Frontierland?

Television, drive-in movies, and summertime auto trips together put the leagues on wobbly legs until the real deathblow arrived—the home air conditioner. In the 1920s, movie theaters had offered air conditioning to bring in customers on hot summer nights. The Depression and World War II hampered the spread of air conditioning, but by 1947, some 50,000 homes in the United States had air conditioners. The devices took off in the 1950s, particularly for those living on the east side of New Mexico and in West Texas, where summer heat can be relentless, and by 1955, there were about

430,000 homes with window air conditioners. That number skyrocketed to 3 million over the next ten years. Suddenly, you could not only stay home and watch TV but also cool off doing so.

Even as they disappeared, the four minor leagues furnished a legacy on which to build. That more than anything is why the teams in the leagues and their players should not be forgotten. For instance, when the Potashers departed Carlsbad, New Mexico, in 1961, they left behind a strong baseball presence—one that had not been there previously. Games played at Carlsbad's Montgomery Field over time helped bring about the installation of a Little League, a Babe Ruth League, a Connie Mack League, and a fine high school program. Several outstanding players, including Cody Ross, a bona fide star for the San Francisco Giants during that team's National League playoff run in 2010, honed their skills in Carlsbad. Charlie Montgomery, who brought professional baseball to Carlsbad in 1953, would be proud. Minor league baseball there may no longer exist, but other forms of the game will keep going and going and going.

Acknowledgments

In addition to the many people named in this book, numerous others provided valuable information, leads, amplification, or simply friendly advice and encouragement:

Danny Andrews, Jon Mark Beilue, Ray Birmingham, Ron Briley, Larry Crues, Ronnie Crues, Bill Currier, Jim Davidson, Nancy Dunn, Elvis Fleming, Steve Gehrke, Bob Gorman, Karen Gunn, Roy Hall Jr., Dana Harrington, Gary Herron, Mike Higgins, Jim Hulsman, Charlie Jurva, Pat Kailer, Kevin Keller, Richard Kemp, Doug McDonough, Ben Moffett, Jay Moore, Kent Perry, Dan Pinto, Steve Pinto, Julian E. Pressley, Mitch Ramsey, Bob Rivas, Dennis Roberts, Evans Rutledge, Wayne Smith, Garet von Netzer, and Jerry Williams.

Also, the staffs of the following:

Albuquerque Public Library, Albuquerque, New Mexico
Amarillo Public Library, Amarillo, Texas
Artesia Historical Museum & Art Center, Artesia, New Mexico
Bryan Wildenthal Memorial Library, Sul Ross State University,
     Alpine, Texas
Carlsbad Family History Center, Carlsbad, New Mexico
Carlsbad Public Library, Carlsbad, New Mexico
Carnegie Library of Ballinger, Ballinger, Texas
Dawson County Public Library, Lamesa, Texas
Historical Center for Southeast New Mexico, Roswell, New Mexico
Howard County Library, Big Spring, Texas

Hutchinson County Historical Museum, Borger, Texas
Lovett Memorial Library, Pampa, Texas
Mahon Public Library, Lubbock, Texas
Midland County Public Library, Midland, Texas
Mobile Public Library, Mobile, Alabama
New Mexico State Library, Santa Fe, New Mexico
Roswell Public Library, Roswell, New Mexico
Society for American Baseball Research, Phoenix, Arizona
Southwest Research Center, Zimmerman Library, University of
      New Mexico, Albuquerque, New Mexico
Sweetwater County-City Library, Sweetwater, Texas
Texas Tech University Libraries, Lubbock, Texas

Further Reading

Books

Adelson, Bruce. *Brushing Back Jim Crow: The Integration of Minor-League Baseball in the American South*. Charlottesville: University Press of Virginia, 1999.

Burke, Bob, Kenny A. Franks, and Royce Parr. *Glory Days of Summer: The History of Baseball in Oklahoma*. Oklahoma City: Oklahoma Heritage Association, 1999.

Deford, Frank. *Over Time: My Life as a Sportswriter*. New York: Atlantic Monthly Press, 2012.

Gorman, Robert M., and David Weeks. *Death at the Ballpark: A Comprehensive Study of Game-Related Fatalities of Players, Other Personnel and Spectators in Amateur and Professional Baseball, 1862–2007*. Jefferson, NC: McFarland, 2009.

Hemphill, Paul. *Lost in the Lights: Sports, Dreams, and Life*. Tuscaloosa: University of Alabama Press, 2003.

James, Bill. *The Bill James Historical Baseball Abstract*. New York: Villard Books, 1988.

Johnson, Lloyd, and Miles Wolff, eds. *The Encyclopedia of Minor League Baseball*. 3rd ed. Durham, NC: Baseball America, 2007.

Leavy, Jane. *The Last Boy: Mickey Mantle and the End of America's Childhood*. New York: HarperCollins, 2010.

Mote, James. *Everything Baseball*. New York: Prentice Hall, 1989.

Obojski, Robert. *Bush League: A History of Minor League Baseball*. New York: Macmillan, 1978.

Stargell, Willie, and Tom Bird. *Willie Stargell: An Autobiography*. New York: Harper & Row, 1984.

Sutter, L. M. *New Mexico Baseball: Miners, Outlaws, Indians and Isotopes, 1880 to the Present*. Jefferson, NC: McFarland, 2010.

Newspapers

Abilene Reporter-News

Albuquerque Journal

Albuquerque Tribune

Amarillo Daily News

Amarillo Globe-News

Amarillo Globe-Times

Artesia Advocate

Artesia Daily Press

Ballinger News

Big Spring Daily Herald

Carlsbad Current-Argus

Clovis News-Journal

Hobbs News-Sun

Lubbock Avalanche-Journal

Pampa News

Plainview Herald

Roswell Daily Record

San Angelo Evening Standard

San Angelo Standard-Times

Sporting News

Sweetwater Reporter

Index